The Effect of Information on Consumer and Market Behavior

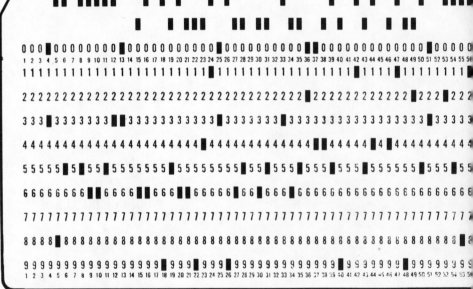

Edited by:

Andrew A. Mitchell
Carnegie-Mellon University

A/MERICAN **M/ARKETING** A/SOCIATION

222 South Riverside Plaza — Chicago, Illinois 60606 — (312) 648-0536

American Marketing Association

© 1978

Printed un the U.S.A.

Cover Design by Mary Jo Krysinski

Library of Congress Cataloging in Publication Data
Main entry under title:

Effect of information on consumer and market behavior.

   Proceedings of a workshop sponsored by Carnegie-Mellon University and
the American Marketing Association, which was held at the university May
20–21, 1977.
   1. Consumers—Congresses.   2. Motivation research (Marketing)—Congresses.   I. Mitchell, Andrew A., 1939–   II. Carnegie-Mellon University.   III. American Marketing Association.
HF5415.3.E45   658.8'34   77-15505
ISBN 0-87757-103-1

This Proceedings was prepared from camera-ready copy supplied by the editor
and/or authors.

TABLE OF CONTENTS

v

ACKNOWLEDGEMENTS

There are a number of individuals whose contribution to the conference and these proceedings deserve recognition. First, I would like to thank Arnold Weber, then Dean of the Graduate School of Industrial Administration, for providing both the encouragement and the financial support for the conference. Without this support the quality of the conference would have been greatly diminished.

Second, I would like to thank all the individuals who helped plan and coordinate the conference. Those deserving special recognition are Richard Staelin, J. Edward Russo and Ed Prescott who provided valuable advice on organizing the conference and Eleanor Riess who made all the arrangements and donated many extra hours of her time to ensure that the conference ran according to plan.

Third, I would like to thank all those attending the conference for their cooperation and contribution to the discussions. A special thanks is extended to those presenting papers at the conference. Most of the papers were written especially for the conference and required considerable time and effort.

Finally, I would like to thank all the individuals who helped put together these proceedings. A special thanks is extended to Janice Koerth, who typed many of the papers.

Andrew A. Mitchell

INTRODUCTION

There has been a general concern recently that the market system is not providing enough information to buyers and much of the information that is provided is biased and misleading. These problems, it is believed, create inefficient markets and give sellers undue power over buyers. Government agencies have attempted to correct these problems by regulating both the quantity and quality of the information that is provided. This effort, however, has not always been successful. Identifying markets with imperfect and/or deceptive information has proven to be a difficult task. In addition, simply providing more information to buyers has not always corrected the alleged imbalance between buyers and sellers.

The understanding and analysis of these problems must come from the general areas of economics and consumer psychology. Recently, economists have begun to examine information as a commodity and the effect of asymmetric information sets on the behavior and structure of markets. In this analysis economists have, by necessity, made assumptions as to how buyers search for and use information. At the same time, consumer psychologists have recently directed their attention at examining how consumers acquire, encode, store and integrate information for decision making. Consequently, both economists and consumer psychologists are examining the same phenomena, however, they use different perspectives, levels of analysis and paradigms.

The purpose of the conference, which was held at Carnegie-Mellon University on May 20-21, 1977, was to bring together leading researchers from the areas of economics, consumer psychology and public policy who are concerned with understanding the effect of information on consumer and market behavior. By making researchers in each area aware of the perspectives, paradigms and recent developments in other areas, it was hoped that a better understanding of the issues would be obtained, research in all three areas would be strengthened and important new research directions would be identified.

All of the papers in this proceedings are revised versions of the papers presented at the conference. The proceedings follows the same structure as the conference with seperate sections on The Effect of Information on Market Behavior, The Effect of Information on Consumer Behavior and Information and Public Policy.

The section entitled the Effect of Information on Market Behavior contains papers by economists. The first paper, by Salop (chapter 1) discusses the economic paradigm for understanding information imperfections in markets and presents some of the main results in the area. Butters (chapter 2), then, examines alternative economic views of advertising and the problems involved in examining advertising effects within the economic paradigm. Avery and Mitchell (chapter 3) present a model which views advertising as information and investigate how the transmission of different types of information may affect the behavior of firms. Next, George Haines (chapter 4), discusses alternative definitions of information and their implications. He also presents empirical findings concerning the effect of intransitivity of preferences on information search.

Papers by consumer psychologists are in the second section which is entitled The Effect of Information on Consumer Behavior. Bettmen (chapter 5) provides a critical review of the behavioral literature on consumer information search and economic models of information search. The second paper, by Olson (chapter 6), examines current theories of information encoding and storage and their implications for consumer research. Next, Wright (chapter 7) discusses alternative approaches for evaluating advertising effects and why our current understanding of these effects are limited. Russo (chapter 8), then, compares the economic paradigm to the behavioral science paradigm and suggests reasons why normative models of human behavior may be inappropriate.

The third section, Information and Public Policy, contains papers on related public policy issues. The paper by Scott Maynes (chapter 9) presents a procedure for identifying markets with information imperfections. The use of consumer research by the Federal Trade Commission for identifying deceptive advertisements is discussed in the second paper by John Eighmey (chapter 10). Ray and Dunn (chapter 11), then, examine problems in designing consumer information systems. Next Wilkie (chapter 12) elaborates on the issues raised in the previous papers.

A summary and discussion of the issues raised during the conference is presented in the final section (chapter 13).

PART I: THE EFFECT OF INFORMATION ON MARKET BEHAVIOR

PARABLES OF INFORMATION TRANSMISSION IN MARKETS

Steven Salop*, Civil Aeronautics Board, Washington, D.C.

INTRODUCTION

Accurate information is a scarce and valuable resource to the economy and society. Like other commodities, it is produced by economic agents for personal use, free distribution to friends and trading partners, and sale for profit through markets for information. As with other commodities, economists study the processes by which information is produced and distributed in a market economy in an attempt to measure the efficiency of the process and the distribution of its gains to the various agents in the economy. The purpose of any economic analysis is an attempt to discover aspects of the production and distribution process that might indicate an inefficiency.

Information as a commodity and markets for information contain the kind of peculiarities that frequently signal inefficiencies and market breakdowns. First, it is difficult for information-sellers to fully capture the returns on the services they provide, if purchasers are able to resell the information to others; in economists' jargon, this is a problem in the viobility of property rights.[1] As a result, information is often transmitted by "interested parties" who "tie-in" the provision of information with the purchase of some other commodity. For example, the surgeon who provides information regarding the health of ones appendix will generally offer to remove it as well. The value of a piece of information is generally not known until after it is purchased. In the case of stomach pains, if they were caused by a dinner at a mediocre restaurant that will never be patronized again, that information has trivial value, whereas the information has high value if the pains were caused by (curable) appendicitis. The value of some piece of information may not be known until some other knowledge has been learned; should one go to a psychiatrist or surgeon for the stomach pains, to a divorce lawyer or a doctor? Moreover, the actual value of information may never be known at all, but rather must be purchased solely on the credibility of the seller. The patient who undergoes an appendectomy may never discover whether his appendix was diseased or whether the surgeon simply removed it for profit.[2]

The patient might offset somewhat the doctor's informational advantage and potential for deception by obtaining additional diagnoses before undergoing surgery, requiring a guarantee by making payment contingent on a positive post-surgical biopsy, patronizing a surgeon with a high reputation for credibility, or using some screening device to discover an honest, competent physician. These sorts of solutions to the buyer's informational disadvantage can improve the efficiency in some cases, but not others. Gathering additional information is costly and may even be impossible. Guarantees force an honest surgeon to bear risk he prefers to avoid and for which he will extract an addi-

tional charge. Reputations may endow the seller with monoply power and may perhaps be profitably run down. Use of screening devices gives sellers an incentive to respond to the screening device rather than to the variables being screened. In this paper, these potential solutions and the dynamic responses they create are studied. We begin by outlining the general framework of analysis.

The dynamic process relating expectation formation, information gathering and information transmission in a market may be viewed in the following stylized Bayesian framework:

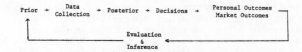

Individuals enter any market period with some initial information and expectations about the relevant variables. This _prior_ derives from general knowledge and past experience; it may be truthful though limited in scope and detail, or it may be biased as a result of previous experience, false or deceptive claims by information transmitters, or simply general ignorance of the relevant information.

Armed with his prior, an agent gathers _data_ to improve the performance of his decisions. This information-gathering consists of search activities such as talking to acquaintences, experts and salesmen, sampling prices at various stores, and purchasing data from information-sellers such as _Consumer Reports_, _Road and Track_, or _The Morning Telegraph_. This new data is then used to update the prior expectations (according to Bayes' Law) to form _posterior_ expectations.

The quantity of data gathered is governed by the individual's expectations of the improvement in his prior relative to the cost of gathering the information. Individuals may differ in these expected costs and benefits due to differences in income, analytic ability, and opportunity cost of time, as well as preferences over the learning process itself. Some individuals are bargain-hunters, who derive special satisfaction from gathering information and obtaining the best buy available; others are impulsive shoppers.

Decisions are made on the basis of these posterior expectations. The decisions yield the individual some actual level of satisfaction or _Personal Outcome_. This outcome is utilized in the _Evaluation_ of his information-gathering performance and in the formation of a new prior for the next period. At this stage, an individual may be able to make indirect _Inferences_ of the expectations and data collected by other individuals by observing their market decisions and associated outcomes. This information is transmitted by the marginal effect each individual's decisions have on market variables such as prices and quantities. For example, an individual who discovers that the expensive, bitter-tasting coffee he purchased earned only a small share of market, might infer that his unsatisfactory experience was no accident, but instead that other individuals had previously been dissatisfied with that brand. If he observes that his inside-tip on Exxon's earnings turned out to be correct, but its stock price fell, then he might infer that other individuals had expected earnings to be even higher than in fact they were. The potential for market outcomes to indirectly transmit useful information from individual to individual is the main focus of the economics of information.

*The views expressed herein are solely those of the author and do not necessarily represent the views of the Civil Aeronautics Board. I am grateful to Mary Flaherty for excellent typing and to Curtis Bristol, Ronald Bush, and Andrew Mitchell for helpful conversations.

[1]This is the rationale for the patent system. See Arrow [3].

[2]See Arrow [4] and Darby-Karni [7] for expositions of these aspects of the economics of information.

This paper presents a series of examples of the possible dynamic paths a market may follow during this information-gathering and transmission process. The examples differ in individuals' initial endowments of information, their potentials for gathering information, and their responses to possible inferences made from market and personal outcomes. Each presents a stylized picture of the particular market being studied. The analysis is not intended to be complete. Instead each example should be viewed as a parable in the theory of information.[3] Although the examples trace out the dynamic adjustments of a market to the gathering and transmission of information, their main emphasis lies in the description of the market after all the dynamic adjustments have taken place and the dynamic information flows have all equilibrated.

In terms of the Bayesian framework, an _Equilibrium_ is a state in which all information has been gathered and no further inferences may be made from market outcomes. The initial prior, posterior, and subsequent prior all agree. In equilibrium, expectations, outcomes, and inferences have the property that expectations are "self-fulfilled" or "self-confirmed" by the outcomes generated in the market. No further adjustments occur, since there is no new data being generated or responses to new data being made that entail adjustments.

This does not imply that the starting point of the process has no importance to the equilibrium state. In at least one of the examples, that of self-fulfilling prophecies, the equilibrium is determined solely by the initial expectations. In other examples, however, initial expectations and their responses do disappear in the equilibrium state. The power of the equilibrium approach rests on its ability to both present a coherent picture of a very complicated process and, at the same time, force the analyst to examine the nature of the process logically and precisely. Since some insight is certainly lost by this approach, it should be treated merely as a first step towards a complete analysis of the dynamic process. The possibility that this is a case of economists looking for a key under the light of a distant streetlamp rather than in the nearby darkness where it was dropped, is left for the reader to decide.

The reader should also note that economic theory generally studies what others might consider or might hope are "normal" human beings.[4] Instead, economists generally focus attention on an ideal (?) called The Rational Economic Man, or "Rat." Rats have complete transitive preferences for commodities or characteristics of commodities. They are generally risk-averters and are always compulsive with regard to planning and consistency. They are not criminally dishonest, that is, they do not have a "taste" for dishonesty; but neither do they obtain any explicit self-satisfaction from revealing the truth. Instead, they choose to tell the truth or misrepresent according to the relative profits of the two strategies, unencumbered by any moral bounds. They are skeptical of others' claims, believing only those claims that are confirmable or in others' self-interest to truthfully reveal. A Rat maintains a high reputation if it is profitable and becomes a fly-by-night gypsy, if it is not.

In general Rats fully understand Bayes' Law of updating prior probabilities with data to form rational posteriors; they never respond to cognitive dissonance by discrediting the information transmitter or otherwise ignoring relevant data. They are perfect, though possibly, limited calculators; they do not irrationally anchor decisions to meaningless priors. They do not believe in the "law of small numbers" or fall victim to the gambler's fallacy" that a

run of _red_ on a roulette wheel makes _black_ more likely on the next spin.[5]

I might add that, in spite of the glee with which we discuss Rat behavior, economists do not necessarily condone its less ethical implications. Moreover, economists do not even necessarily believe in pure Rats, but rather, in a way similar to the emphasis on equilibria, utilize the Rat construct as a first step towards understanding the basic logic of the underlying economic process.

In the next section, we will study a series of examples of the dynamics of information-gathering and inference in Rat economies. In each example, the emphasis is placed less on the process of direct data collection and more on the process of indirect inference from market outcomes. Moreover, we focus on that transfer of information from informed to uninformed individuals in the equilibrium state of the process. At the same time, we will at least implicitly deal with the possible nonexistence of any equilibrium state. In the final sections, the difficulties in analyzing non-rational behavior are briefly discussed.

MARKET EQUILIBRIA

The first example presents the ideal, an efficient market in which all private information is transmitted freely through market prices.

An Efficient Market for Medical Services[6]

Suppose physicians differ in the quality of medical services provided and that these differences may be quantified in dollar terms. For example, suppose the best doctors provide $4000 worth of services per year, the worst provide $2000, and the rest provide services in the $2000-4000 range. An efficient market would be one in which the relative prices of medical services of the various physicians are proportional to their relative values; that is, the $2000 doctors ought to earn one-half the price of the $4000 doctors.

If the quality of medical services provided are easily observable by well-informed patients, then the market prices will reflect relative values in equilibrium. Otherwise, if some physicians offer a better buy than others, then they will gain patients at the expense of other doctors. As they gain patients and others lose patients, there will be an incentive to charge a price that reflects value more closely. This dynamic process of customer movements and price changes will continue until an equilibrium is reached in which prices do reflect values.

What doctor should a new uninformed patient choose, one who has no notion of the relative values of the physicians in the market? Since prices perfectly reflect the relative values placed on the physicians by the informed patients, an uninformed patient may randomly select a physician providing services concomitant with the patient's income and preferences: the weight of the search by the informed patients transmits value information through the equilibrium prices.

It is for this reason that economists recommend that uninformed investors choose common stocks by dart throws, and, with a leap of generalization, that uninformed consumers with "average" tastes select the product brand with largest market share or advertising expenditure and infer quality by price. If the proportion of informed buyers is large enough, then the weight of their informed decisions will

---

[3]Schelling [36] presents a somewhat parallel set of interesting examples.

[4]cf. Simon [37].

[5]Tversky [44], Grether-Plott [12], Kagel-Battalio [17] survey experimental evidence on the existence of Rats.

[6]See Fama-Laffer [8] and Hirshliefer [14].

force market prices to correctly reflect the values they place on the commodities. At the opposite extreme from the efficient market equilibrium are markets in which buyers have little or no information, but sellers are well-informed; we examine such a market now.

Informational Breakdown: The Market for 'Lemons'[7]

Consider the interrelated markets for new and used automobiles. Suppose there are two groups of drivers who purchase automobiles: The Chromes desire both transportation and a shiny new car in their driveway. They are each willing to pay a price, say $100, over and above the value of an automobile in providing transportation services, to own a new rather than a used car. The Rusts desire an automobile solely for its transportation services. Suppose new cars cost $4000.

If every car provided exactly 8 years of identical transportation services, Rusts would be willing to pay $3500 for a one year old used car as opposed to a new $4000 automobile. Chromes would be willing to accept a price of $3400 for a used car ($3500 less $100 value). Thus we could envision an equilibrium in which Chromes purchase new cars, keep them for a year, and then sell them to Rusts for a price somewhere between $3400 and $3500.

To provide a role for information, suppose automobiles do not depreciate identically. Some ("exceptions") last for 20 years and hence depreciate by only $200 per year, some ("lemons") last only 2 years and hence depreciate $2000 per year, and the rest ("in-betweens") differ continuously in their depreciation between the two extremes. Thus, Rusts would be willing to pay from $2000 for a Lemon up to $3800 for an Exception, depending on the exact depreciation rate of the particular automobile under consideration. Suppose this depreciation rate is known to the new car owner after one year.

If this depreciation rate were known upon a pre-purchase inspection to a potential purchaser (or his hired mechanic), then the market price of a used car would lie somewhere between its depreciated value and that value less $100. This is the Efficient Market Equilibrium.

On the other hand, suppose the value is not apparent or inspection to the prospective purchaser. Now the price of a used car cannot depend on its exact value, since the purchaser cannot ascertain that value. Every seller can claim his car is an exception.

This asymmetry in information creates a problem for the market. At any single price, say $3500, only cars worth less than $3600 will be offered for sale by Chromes; no owner of a more valuable car will offer it for sale. The average value of a randomly selected car will lie somewhere between $2000 and $3600. If in-betweens' values were uniform between these two extremes, the average value would be $2800. But, no Rust will be willing to pay $3500 for a car worth on average only $2800. The price of $3500 does provide the uninformed buyer with reliable information. He is able to infer that through "self-selection" no car on the market is worth more than $3600, and the average value is only $2800. Thus, from an understanding of this self-selection process, the Rust is able to infer that a randomly selected automobile is worth less than its $3500 price.

We can envision the following dynamic self-selection process: The price falls to $2800. But now all the cars worth more than $2900 are removed from the market, lowering

the average value to $2450. As the price falls to $2450, the cars worth more than $2550 are withdrawn, and the average value falls to $2775. The process continues until the price falls to $2100. Now all cars worth less than $2200 are offered for sale and the average value of $2100 just equals the price. Only Lemons are bought and sold. This is the market equilibrium.

There is a serious market failure here. At the equilibrium price of $2100 there are more valuable cars that Chromes would be willing to sell at $100 under value and Rusts would be willing to purchase. Yet the shortage of buyer information, in conjunction with the self-selection of sellers to their informed price-value comparisons, prevents other mutually advantageous trades from taking place. Only if the process of information transmission can be improved will the performance of the market improve.

Faced with this destructive information asymmetry, one would expect buyers to attempt to gather some value information prior to purchase and owners of high quality automobiles to attempt to transmit that information to buyers. There are a number of possible information transmission devices such as guarantees, reputations, and screening devices which will be taken up after a few general conclusions are drawn.

Lemons and Efficient Markets are the polar cases of the transmission of direct information through the price system. The pure Lemons equilibrium has uninformed buyers obtaining correct but quite limited information from market prices, while the pure Efficient Market equilibrium has informed buyers effectively transmitting complete information to uninformed buyers through market prices. In terms of the Bayesian prior-data-posterior-decision-market outcome-prior framework, the Lemons market equilibrates at a low information-inefficient outcome while the Efficient Market equilibrates at the efficient-perfect information outcome.

The polar cases differ with respect to the proportion of agents endowed with perfect information. Intermediate cases will lie closer to one or the other extreme according to the proportion of informed and uninformed agents. The analysis becomes more complex, however, if agents are not costlessly endowed with information, but rather must become informed through their own costly private data-gathering efforts. An agent's data-gathering decision will depend on his cost of information relative to the gain from becoming informed. This gain depends in turn on the efficiency with which prices themselves costlessly transmit information, which in turn depends on the proportion of informed agents. This circular argument leads to the following central conundrum of the economics of information: If prices perfectly transmit information (Efficient Market) then no agent will gather costly information. Yet, if no agent gathers information, then prices will not transmit information.

Recognition of this statement might lead information sellers such as Consumer Reports to limit the effectiveness of their data, for if they are too successful in spreading information, then prices will adjust and thus eliminate the need for their service.[8] Instead, the seller should limit the dissemination of his data so that some imperfections in information, some "noise," remains in the system.[9]

---

[7] Akerlof [1] is the original statement of this model. Rothschild [28] surveys the following set of models in a slightly more technical way. We remain faithful to the original by casting the problem in terms of automobiles rather than physicians.

[8] This inability to charge consumers who indirectly benefit from the information provided is in addition to the usual problem mentioned in the introduction that information-sellers are often unable to prevent resale of their information by purchasers. These two problems act to limit the efficient allocation of information through free markets.

[9] See Salop [34].

Having some noise remain the system is also the solution to the conundrum just posed.[10] If only partial information is transmitted through prices, then there remains some gain to becoming informed and, hence, an incentive for agents with lower information-gathering costs to become informed. Those agents with higher search costs do not directly gather data, but do gain indirectly from others' information-gathering activities and associated effect on market prices. Only if information is prohibitively expensive will the Lemons equilibrium obtain, and only if enough agents can gather perfect information costlessly will the Efficient equilibrium obtain. However, before analyzing the intermediate cases, and as a way of introduction to them, a few indirect information-gathering and transmission techniques are briefly discussed.

Guarantees

Since the seller has information on the actual value, he may be willing to eliminate the buyer's risk by guaranteeing the car's performance value. This will clearly solve the problem, if the seller is willing. However, there are serious limits to the efficacy of guarantees. First, the seller may not honor the guarantee; in a sense, the buyer requires a guarantee on the guarantee. If the car does perform badly, the parties must somehow ascertain whether the guarantee covers that particular contingency or whether the performance is due to a problem with the car or rather lack of care and maintenance by the buyer. This problem of "due-care" is in itself a serious information problem.[11]

Reputations

The institution of the reputable used car dealer, who buys from Chromes and sells to Rusts at fair value with honest guarantees, could conceivably arise to solve the problem. However, as with guarantees, the buyer requires a guarantee of the dealer's reputation. Unsubstantiated claims of high reputation are worth no more than the unsubstantiated claims of high value by the original sellers. In fact even reputations substantiated from past experience may have limited value. Consider the case of the Fly-by-Night Tout: Suppose an individual freely distributed a diverse set of "tout-sheets," each recommending a different horse in each race for every racing day in the month. One of these tout-sheets would have a perfect record and many others would have provided large winnings if followed faithfully. Thus, the tout could build up a positive reputation for at least some of his tout sheets for sale of future worthless information. Ultimately (next month?) he would lose his reputation, but the strategy might still be profitable.[12]

More pertinently, reputations may be subject to a dynamic exploitation process, if the dealers are Rats. Consider a dealer who has built up a truthful reputation by providing good value and service for some period of time. Since reputation is based on past performance, it may be in the dealer's self-interest to earn extra short-run profits by shading performance below the level consistent with his current reputation. This policy is surely at the expense of his future reputation, but it may still be a profitable strategy for him to persistently keep his performance one step below his reputation. Volkswagons, Paul McCartney records, and tenured professors are possible examples of this process.[13]

---

[10]See Grossman-Stiglitz [13] and Salop [33].

[11]See Arrow [4].

[12]Apparently, such frauds occasionally arise with respect to stock market tout sheets.

[13]See Phelps-Winter [25].

Screening Devices

Uninformed buyers will also attempt to infer the actual quality of prospective purchases by making an informed guess on the basis of available observable data. For example, buyers may infer that low mileage cars owned by religious old ladies have not depreciated significantly. Red sportscars, former taxi-cabs and dealers named Nixon will be avoided. Average repair data from Consumer Reports may be consulted. Screening devices are surely imperfect solutions to the Lemons problem, since they rely on use of an average statistic; however, they can improve performance somewhat. In fact, if they are accurate enough to predict value within the $100 buyer-seller price differential, they completely solve the information problem, and create an Efficient Market.[14]

Two types of screening devices may be distinguished. Indices are rules of thumb that sort on the basis of observable variables that directly bear on value. On average, former taxi-cabs have high depreciation rates; dealers named Nixon are thought to be unethical Rats. On the other hand, Self-Selection Devices sort on the basis of evidence revealed by the seller's own decision. King Solomon's threat to cut the baby in half caused each mother-claimant to reveal her true identity. A red sportscar is avoided not because red sportscars are inherently of lower value; rather the personality-type who prefers a red sportscar is thought to be the type who engages in reckless driving and performs insufficient maintenance: The decision to purchase a red sportscar reveals information regarding the owner and, hence, the quality of the car.

For either type, if sellers are aware of buyers' use of these rules-of-thumb, they have an incentive to exploit the screening device to misrepresent the value of their product. At a cost, a red sportscar can be painted blue, the identity of a former taxi may be camouflaged, and a dealer can change his name from Nixon to Carter. In this way, both indices and self-selection devices have similar implications for market behavior. If these responses are made, over time a dynamic lemons process might ensue to decrease or even destroy the value of the screening device. This occurs if the cost of misrepresentation is low relative to the increase in predicted valuation. Moreover, in a more general context, this incentive to respond to the screening device rather than to the valuation variable may introduce a bias into firms' decisions away from the production of high quality goods and towards the production of high "predicted" quality. For instance, even reckless drivers will purchase blue sportscars. Squeezing bread was once a useful method of ascertaining its freshness; now bakeries produce, not fresher bread, but rather more squeezable bread that never becomes stale, but is never really fresh either.[15] The dynamics, equilibria, and rational use of screening devices in inferring information have been studied in economics under the labels of Signalling and Self-Selection. One of the neatest examples is called the Rat Race.

---

[14]If a buyer offers $2700 for a car he correctly infers is worth between $2600 and $2800, chromes selling cars worth $2800 or less will accept that offer, and the average value of a $2700-priced auto will be $2700

[15]In terms of the decision rules discussed by Bettman [1977], firms have an incentive to produce products with high levels of easily observable attributes on which decisions are based. See Salop [34].

Signalling Equilibria: The Rat Race[16]

Consider a consumer faced with the decision of choosing a new physician. Physicians differ with respect to the quality of medical services provided. But suppose it is only possible to measure quality after one has patronized the doctor for some period, say one year. Thus the consumer's problem here is intermediate between that of the used car buyer in the Lemons markets, who never learns (until it is too late), and the consumer in the Efficient Medical Services market, who learns immediately.

Suppose a rational consumer examines his experience and observes that in the past those doctors who provided the highest quality care were the doctors who worked the longest hours. The consumer might infer that this correlation is a reasonable screening device, for if a physician is interested enough in his occupation to work long hours, then he is likely also to take the pride in his work to become highly competent. As a result of this inference, suppose the rational consumers begin to utilize working hours as a screening device for high quality medical care and choose their physicians accordingly.

In the short run, physicians who work longer hours will now gain at the expense of those who work shorter hours. If the actual statistical correlation between hours worked and competence is not perfect, then hardworking incompetents will gain new clients at the expense of lazy but competent doctors. The behavior of experienced clients will not change, since presumably they are able to make a well-founded prediction of their doctor's quality.

As the market evolves over time, rational (whether competent or incompetent) physicians ought to reckon consumers' use of the screening device into their calculations of optimal working hours. Every doctor will begin to work marginally longer hours in an attempt to exploit or offset the screening device. If each physician increases his hours proportionally, the relative hours chosen between competents and incompetents will remain the same, and the self-selection correlation that formed the basis of the screening device will not be destroyed. Instead, doctors will begin to pursue a "Rat Race" dynamics in which each physician works harder than he did before, discovers the other Rats catching up, and begins to work even harder. These dynamics may or may not settle down.

One possibility is simply that every doctor works harder than he would like (i.e. harder than he worked previously), with the relative hours basically unchanged. This occurs if the additional loss in satisfaction from working the extra hours is no greater for the more interested and competent doctors. It is noteworthy that in this case the least competent-shortest hours doctors will not join the rat race. Since their hours remain the shortest after everyone else increases his working day, they remain pegged as lowest quality and, thus, would gain nothing by working harder. All higher quality doctors do work harder, however, in an attempt to certify themselves as higher quality than the next lower competence group. None can lower his hours to his personal optimum, for fear of being sorted by the screening device as lower quality than he is in fact.

On the other hand, if the less competent physicians can lengthen their hours with less loss in satisfaction then the more competent, perhaps by simply paying even less attention to the patients they minister, then the correlation between hours and quality, and hence the sorting value of the screening device, will be destroyed. At this point, however, the market is not fully equilibrated; once the screen-

ing device is no longer used, then the disinterested incompetents will decrease their hours relatively more than the competents, and the screening device will become useful again. There is no equilibrium, but rather the market may cycle around and around with the same or a new screening device.[17]

Assuming that the Rat Race does settle down to a stable equilibrium in which the self-selection device of working hours does sort, it is important to note that it is not a completely efficient information transmission mechanism, relative to prior perfect information (or perfect information after only one visit). First, all but the least competent doctors work harder than desired. Second, highly competent but lazy physicians get screened as less qualified. Consumers' benefits also change. Presumably, once the information is transmitted, then the more qualified doctors will be able to raise their fees more in line with their competence. The informed patients who had luckily discovered and now patronize competent doctors find that their cost of medical services rising; they no longer obtain a bargain. Instead, the bargains become the lazy but qualified physicians, who are forced to charge lower fees in keeping with the screening device.

Taking a longer run view, consider an individual pondering a career in medicine. The use of working hours as a screening device serves to attract into medicine hard workers as well as competent future physicians. Even though competent doctors wish to work harder than less competent doctors, it is not necessarily true that hard workers become better doctors than others.

Other biases could also be introduced. Suppose that when the screening device of hours worked was adopted, all physicians were males. Now suppose women begin to consider entering medical school. Suppose women, competent or incompetent, wish to work fewer hours than men of comparable quality. Two biases are possible. First, unless patients apply a screening device that includes gender in making the hours-competence inference, then female doctors will be screened as lower quality. In addition, women may choose not to become physicians at all. The latter is a more serious bias because of its permanence. Presumably, the incorrect inference would eventually be corrected as Rat-consumers experiment with different screening devices. However, if no women become doctors, then no data ever becomes available to overturn the original screening device.

This raises the issue of whether misperceptions and irrational expectations will ever be disconfirmed or rather will create "self-fulfilling prophecies" that rationalize the original irrational expectations. On the one hand, there are potential gains from experimentation with screening devices and other preconceptions. However, the experimentation is risky and may be quite costly to both patients and doctors; the potential female doctor must undergo perhaps 10 years of training and practice before discovering whether the statistical discrimination will be overturned. Before exploring self-fulfilling prophecies, however, it is useful to discuss a few more aspects of the basic signalling model.

The signalling model has been used by economists to analyze educational certification and income inequality[18], the use

---

[16]See Akerlof [2], Spence [38,39,40], Rothschild-Stiglitz [30].

[17]Fashion may be viewed as a rat race in which individuals attempt to transmit through their dress the information that they are dynamic, sophisticated, sexy, rich, elegant, (fashionable?) people. Over time, other less fashionable individuals adopt similar dress, and the more fashionable respond by selecting a new style signal.

[18]See Jencks [16].

of guarantees as an imperfect signal of quality, and advertising expenditures and market shares as predictors of "best-buys" in commodity markets.[19] The advertising and market share version of the model notes that high quality brands are more likely to be purchased by "repeat" customers than are low quality brands. Thus, for an advertising expenditure that attracts an equal number of new customers, the higher quality brands will attract more repeat customers than the lower quality brands. Since a given level of advertising is more productive for a higher quality brand, it will have an incentive to engage in more advertising. Thus, using advertising as a screening device for higher quality (or more generally, for "best buys") is a rational self-selection device. A Rat Race dynamic will ensue, and if certain conditions are met, the dynamic process will settle down to an equilibrium in which every (except the lowest quality) brand advertises more in response to the signal, and advertising expenditure continues to serve as a screening device, albeit an imperfect one. A variant of this model notes that if some consumers are informed about relative qualities and purchase the higher quality brands, while other consumers purchase randomly, then the higher quality brands will have larger market shares. Thus, a consumer with average tastes and income might find market share to be a useful screening device.

The idea that only an "average" consumer should use this rule-of-thumb is crucial here, because market share depends not only on the objective quality of the brand, but also on its appeal to specific consumer preferences. Brands that appeal to large masses of consumers will find advertising more profitable than those which appeal to only a small market, quality held constant. (This fact was implicitly assumed away in the statement that the advertising expenditures attracted an equal number of new customers.) For example, MacDonald's advertises more heavily than La Trianon. Moreover, that advertising serves as a positive screening device rests on the rationality of purchasers. If one believes that most consumers in a particular market are irrational (Scientology?), then high advertising or market share should be used to avoid those brands. If advertising attracts customers who wish to consume the advertising itself rather than the commodity, then the rationality of the screening device also fails. For example, it has been suggested that arthritis sufferers purchase Bayer Aspirin over other brands because of the sympathy offered it its advertising, and that some women smoke Virginia Slims because of its support of women's rights.

THE RATIONALITY OF EQUILIBRIUM

The previous examples concerned markets in which some objectively truthful information was possessed by some agents, but not by others. The information problem faced by the individuals in those markets was to discover methods of transmitting (or preventing the transmission) of that information to the uninformed in the most efficient manner. The lesson of the Efficient Market example was that information can be inferred from market prices. The Rat Race example pursued the idea that screening devices may also be used, although imperfectly, in inferring useful information.

Very little attention has been paid so far to the question of whether useful information will in fact be collected, or whether, perhaps, the market could become mired at an inefficient non-informed equilibrium. Stated another way, will the private process of gathering data to update priors proceed effectively? This problem arises in situations in which the value of information might not be known until after it is collected, if ever. The following example shows that even a rationally chosen rule-of-thumb may lead to an unfortunate equilibrium state.

The Two-Armed Bandit[20]

Consider a gambler confronting the following two slot machines: Machine #1 costs 50¢ to play and repays $2 if "cherry" appears and $0 if "banana" appears. The probabilities of cherry and banana are each 1/2; thus machine #1 has an expected gain per play of $1. Machine #2 also costs 50¢ to play and repays $2 or $0 according to cherry or banana. Suppose machine #2 is in fact the better machine, as its probability of cherry is 3/4 for an expected gain per play of $1.50. However, suppose the gambler knows the probability of #1, but not #2, a priori. Under the principle of equal ignorance, the rational gambler will assign #2 a prior probability of 1/2 to cherry and begin to play it to gather further information. Suppose he unluckily obtains a losing run of 10 bananas. Now he forms a strong posterior that surely places a probability of less than 1/2 on cherry. As a result, he rationally chooses to play machine #1, since it appears superior from his sampling experience. Moreover, he will never return to machine #2 to gather further information, but rather will rationally play machine #1 forever.

In this example, sampling according to a Bayesian procedure leads the individual to make inferior decisions based on "incorrect" information, yet if he behaves rationally he will never gather the additional information that would disconfirm his irrational expectations. This example is posed in terms of a private direct data-gathering activity; however, the idea has similar implications for indirect inference from market outcomes as well. For example, the possibility that women never become physicians and, thus, never disconfirm the irrational (for women) hours-worked screening device is a two-armed bandit problem when the cost and risk of the experimentation necessary for women to generate enough data is uneconomical to bear. Thus, the data necessary to disconfirm patients' misperceptions is never forthcoming and those incorrect expectations are self-fulfilled in equilibrium.

This type of self-fulfilling prophecy may arise in signalling models whenever individuals rationally or irrationally limit the size or scope of their information-gathering. In the Bayesian framework, an agent with a "certain" prior will rationally choose to gather no additional information. Many potentially valuable screening devices might exist, yet they may never be discovered by the participants in the market. Only if some agents have priors weak enough and information costs low enough to make further data gathering economical will more information be generated and transmitted.

Prior expectations may play the decisive role in the determination of the equilibrium state, even if there are no explicit information-gathering costs or indirect screening devices. Rather the circularity of the basic process of expectations → decisions → outcomes → expectations allows multiple self-fulfilling prophecy equilibria to exist, each equilibrium resting solely, or at least crucially, on the expectations initially held.

Self-Fulfilling Prophecies: The Love Bubble

In this section a circular model of requited and unrequited love is analyzed. Individuals optimally choose whether to offer unconditional love to those they meet. This unconditional love is offered in the hope that it will be requited, which in turn depends on other individuals' expectations of the probability that love will be offered to them.

More specifically, consider a large society of Males and Females, who pair randomly, one Male-Female pairwise meeting per period. Before the rendezvous, each individual

---

[19]Nelson [23].

---

[20]Rothschild [29].

must choose whether to offer unconditional love to the person he/she meets. Only unconditional choices are possible; offering love conditional on having it requited is not permitted.

An individual's satisfaction depends on whether he/she offers love and whether that love is requited by the other. The possibilities of one Romantic Male are tabulated below. He obtains a satisfaction level of 101 from requited love (love-love), a satisfaction of 50 from his own indifference, and a "normalized" satisfaction of zero from unrequited love (love-indifference). Note that the satisfaction of 50 from his indifference does not depend on her offers of love or indifference. (Note also that satisfaction levels themselves do not measure his absolute levels of "happiness," only satisfactions relative to each other).

| | | Female's Offer | |
		Love	Indifference
Romantic Male's Offer	Love	101 (Requited)	0 (Unrequited)
	Indifference	50	50

Romantic Male's Satisfactions

A similar table may be drawn for every individual. Suppose half the males and females (the "Romantics") obtain the satisfactions above, and the rest (the "Cynics") similarly obtain 101 from requited love and zero from unrequited love, but a higher satisfaction -- 80 -- from their own indifference as illustrated below.

| | | Female's Offer | |
		Love	Indifference
Cynical Male's Offer	Love	101	0
	Indifference	80	80

Cynic's Satisfactions

Offering love is riskier than indifference, since it may not be required. If individuals choose on the basis of expected satisfaction, then for any common probability expectation, Romantics receive greater expected satisfaction from offering love than do Cynics. For example, if the expected probability is 1/2, Romantics will offer love (1/2 _times_ 101 is greater than 50) whereas Cynics will not (1/2 _times_ 101 is less than 80). For expected probabilities of at least 4/5, all will offer love; for expected probabilities somewhat less than 1/2, none will offer love.

We can envision the following dynamic process in this market. Given initial probability expectations, individuals rationally offer love or indifference. This leads to a realized proportion of individuals giving love, and hence, a realized proportion having their love requited or not. Based on this actual proportion, individuals rationally update their probability expectations and make new choices, which in turn, yield a new outcome proportion. The dynamic adjustment process of expectations → decisions → outcome → expectations continues until a probability expectation is self-confirmed by its implied outcome. At this point, since expectations are self-fulfilled, there are no forces for change; we call this an equilibrium.

There are multiple equilibria here. If every agent expects love (a probability of one), then all offer love, and the expectation is fulfilled. This Pure-Love equilibrium is clearly the best state, since all prefer certain requited love to unrequited love or indifference. On the other hand,

if no one expects love (probability of zero), then no one offers love, and expectations are also fulfilled. An interior equilibrium at a probability equal to 1/2 is also possible. At probability 1/2, only Romantics offer love; since half the population are Romantics, then half the population will be offered love in each period, and the expectation is fulfilled. If instead of only two groups, individuals' satisfactions of indifference vary _uniformly_ between zero and 101, then every probability expectation would be a self-fulfilling prophecy.[21] Beginning at a Low-Love equilibrium, experimentation by just a few individuals in a large society may not be enough to drive the equilibrium to the preferred Pure-Love equilibrium, although it is surely true that if every individual begins to offer love regardless of the probability, then the Pure-Love equilibrium will be attained.

The most important example of a self-fulfilling prophecy in economics is the use of money rather than barter; an individual will only accept essentially worthless pieces of paper, shells or whatever in trade for labor services or commodities in the expectation that someone else will accept that "money" when he offers it in subsequent trades. John Maynard Keynes similarly described the Stock Exchange as a Beauty Contest in which each speculator picks "not those faces which he himself finds the prettiest, but those which he thinks the likeliest to catch the fancy of the other competitors, all of whom are looking at the problem from the same point of view."[22]

Finally, the Love Bubble may be reinterpreted as a Self-Hate Bubble for a single individual: Suppose an individual has an initial level of self-hate (self-love). The attentiveness with which he carries out his tasks is lower for higher levels of self-hate. Moreover, the quality of his performance depends positively on his attentiveness. To complete the circle, suppose his level of self-hate rises with lower quality performance. Thus, we have a self-hate → performance → self-hate positive feedback loop in which a higher self-hate level causes lower performance, which in turn creates more self-hate. Depending on the exact magnitudes of the relationships, there may be one or more equilibrium states to this process.

Rationality, Irrationality and Consumer Research

The self-hate bubble raises the issue of the meaningfulness of the term "rationality." The individual's choice of performance is so constrained by his previous level of self-love that the performance level is rendered completely deterministic. However, it is not clear that this constraint or the resulting behavior ought to be labelled irrational, although it is surely self-destructive.

This difficulty in distinguishing rational from irrational behavior is inherent in studying decision-making under ignorance. An individual who appears to have biased expectations may simply be the unfortunate victim of a two-armed bandit. A consumer who does not exploit a potential screening device or other available information may be acting non-economically, or alternatively, may simply have high information costs or a preference for impulsive behavior. Consistency of choices may be observed, but consistency is not rationality. Consistency merely implies that there _exists_ some set of complete and transitive preferences that would imply the observed choices. However, consistent behavior can arise from a non-rational

---

[21] This assumes love is offered when the expected values of each strategy are equal.

[22] Keynes [18].

9

decision process; madmen may exhibit very logical and consistent behavior.[23] A particular dynamic demand curve could arise from either a foresighted or myopic consumer. Nor does inconsistency imply irrationality when the consumer is learning his preferences or gathering other information during the observed decision process. For example, consider the inconsistent choices of a diner who first chooses steak when presented by the waiter with a choice of steak or lobster, but then chooses lobster when the waiter adds that lamb is also available. In the context of imperfect information, this inconsistency is easily rationalized: Suppose the waiter's mention of lamb suddenly reminds the diner that he had chosen steak over lamb at the previous evening's dinner.

Economists have been criticized for ignoring experimental evidence of non-rational and inconsistent behavior. It may be true that the self-selection process in career choice has attracted into economics admirers, if not adherents, of rational choice. However, other explanations are possible. For instance, many psychology and even consumer research experiments may be too far removed from economic contexts to be directly applicable. Moreover, the methodology of assuming individuals rationally choose from a complete and transitive set of preferences, subject to informational and other constraints, has been a fruitful one. In light of the difficulties involved in identifying irrational behavior in market responses, economists have been unwilling to give up the rational framework until a suitable replacement is found.[24]

Even without explicitly defining rationality to fit the complications introduced by ignorance, it is still possible to analyze market behavior. After the individual and market implications of this behavior are derived, then judgments regarding the rationality or self-destructiveness of the behavior may be more reasonably drawn.

Economists have begun to approach this issue with an expanded model of consumer choice, due originally to Lancaster.[25] In psychological language, individuals attempt to satisfy their basic emotional needs and desires through the purchase of commodities and the allocation of time and energy in various personal and market activities. Individuals act out their emotional needs in their economic decisions and market interactions. The "conflicts" of psychologists are the "trade-offs" of economists.[26] Preferences and demands for commodities are not given exogenously, but rather are derived from the more basic emotional needs. The manner in which the individual combines commodities and time to produce emotional states define his personality traits. Ignoring ignorance for a moment, if basic needs can be translated into complete and transitive preferences over emotional states, and if the relationship of the commodities and the time allocation to these emotional states is well-behaved, then the individual's optimization problem is straightforward. We might call this ideal the perfect "self-actualizing" individual.

In the absence of perfect information, individuals engage in personal experimentation, social and market interactions, and other information-gathering activities to better discover their true needs and the means of satisfying them. In this way, two individuals with similar needs might behave differently according to their particular experiences and sensibilities. In this sense, personality traits act as rules-of-thumb for behavior, and personal development is a two-armed bandit problem.[27] For example, need for power can be expressed be recklessly driving a red sportscar of by becoming a factory foreman.

Implicitly at least, this orientation was used in the earlier discussion of screening devices. Physicians who desired greater satisfaction from their work expressed that need by developing high competence and working longer hours. The need expressed in the purchase of a red sportscar correlated with a need to drive recklessly and ignore maintenance. Similarly, if authoritarian personalities make good foremen, then firms would be wise to utilize personality tests to hire applicants with that trait.[28]

In the Lancasterian framework, a typical television commercial presents a consumer with some conflict or unfulfilled emotional need, finding relief or fulfillment in the use of the advertised brand. For example, a homemaker who fears the disrespect of her neighbors quiets her anxiety by making her kitchen clean-smelling. More generally, commercials attempt to provide information by associating the advertised brand with a particular emotional state. Pepsi-Cola advertisements show smiling people im a series of pleasant leisure activities drinking Pepsi. In this way, consuming the soft drink is associated with those enjoyable activities. Similarly, stockbrokers attempt to evoke expansive feelings of optimism and excitement while insurance salesmen encourage pessimism and insecurity. Trademarks are selected with an awareness of this association process; RealLemon evokes a connection with fresh lemon juices, Miller's Lite Beer with an unbloated feeling.

If appropriate trademarks and advertising slogans facilitate a consumer's association of a brand with the satisfaction it provides, then information and decision costs are reduced. On the other hand, if the association is inappropriate or deceptive in that the claim promises to satisfy a need though, in fact, fails to do so, then decision costs rise: The consumer must guard against making poor decisions based on the inappropriate association. This is analogous to the additional difficulty one faces in performing arithmetic if the room is noisy or if one is periodically being told that 2+2 = 5. In this sense, the household cleaner advertisement gives false information if it

---

[23] For example in Catch-22, was Yossarian irrational for believing that the German anti-aircraft gunners were trying to kill him, or was the psychiatrist irrational in believing they weren't? cf. footnote 27.

[24] c.f. Fromm [9], Grether-Plott [12], and Stigler-Becker [41].

[25] For recent expositions, see Michael-Becker [20], Stigler-Becker [41], and Gintis [10,11].

[26] It is noteworthy that psychologists often discuss the "economy" of the psyche. e.g. "The Economic Viewpoint in the Theory of Analytic Therapy," Riech [27].

---

[27] Apparently irrational resistances to persuasive but dissonant information, such as derogation of the source, distortion, displacement and rationalization of the message, may be viewed as quite logical responses by a consumer who wishes to protect his beliefs. The complexities in neurotic behavior are logical, once the individual's own assumptions and experience are considered. (Horney [15]). R. D. Laing [19] has suggested that schizophrenia is a rational, albeit self-destructive, response to an insane environment.

[28] Economists have analyzed a variety of personality traits: Myopia, conservatism (risk-aversion), expansiveness (risk-preference), racism, altruism, envy, conformity, snobbery (status-seeking), rigidity (adjustment costs), moodiness, dependence, optimism, pessimism, authoritarianism, and perfectionism. These traits could be combined together in the context of a particular psychological model to form personality types. For example, expansiveness, myopia, and (over-) optimism might appropriately be combined; authoritarian types might also be rigid, risk-averse, and extremely foresighted.

either fails to adequately clean the floor or, in addition, if it is incapable of relieving the anxiety.

There are surely pitfalls involved in making this conceptual approach quantitatively operational. One difficulty concerns rationalization and unconscious decisions. If the association and decision process are viewed as purely unconscious, then an advertisement or other information can lead to a decision without the consumer's explicit, conscious knowledge. This is particularly difficult to measure, for just as economists are able to infer some set of rational preferences from consistent market decisions, a consumer might offer a rationalization of his own decisions. Only inconsistencies and biases in these rationalizations may be easily discovered. Moreover, even if the actual decision process can be identified, some quantitative measure of decision-making costs must be formulated for theoretical and empirical modelling.

One possibility is to model the internal decision process as one of sampling memory _without_ replacement for relevant purchase information.[29] This assumption of sampling-without-replacement captures the notion that even worthless information must be processed at a cost. Formally, a small urn-population is preferred to a larger yet equivalent urn-population; for example, if a 3 ball urn has values $\{1,2,3\}$ then 2 draws are required to obtain a value of at least 2 with certainty;[30] an equivalent 6 ball urn with ball values $\{1,1,2,2,3,3\}$ requires 3 draws to ensure an outcome of at least 2. An alternative conceptualization might view decision costs as constraints on total "channel capacity" allocated to problem-solving. Under this assumption, irrelevant information utilizes the scarce channels, thus increasing decision time. In both these models, if advertising messages are unable to be costlessly ignored, then an individual who is satisfied with his current preferences must still bear psychic costs to defend those preferences from dissonant information, whether the data is truthful or false.

Such a model of costly decision-making could be useful in deriving optimal (or reasonable) rules-of-thumb and for understanding experimental evidence in consumer research. For example, experiments by Bettman [1977] in which consumers searched a brand-attribute information matrix found that some consumers compared brands whereas others compared attributes. Russo [1976] discovered that presenting brands' comparative unit-costs altered consumers' purchase behavior. These results suggest that optimal behavior will vary according to the level of prior information and the cost of gathering further data.[31]

Finally, whatever exact formal model is finally adopted, it is clear that the gap between normative economic modelling and more descriptive consumer research ought to be bridged. It appears to me that interesting intermediate models can be constructed; however, at this time, such a belief remains conjecture, not observed fact.

---

[29] c.f. J. Olson [24].

[30] Let the value of 1 represent an undesired brand, 2 a mediocre brand, and 3 the most preferred brand.

[31] The Bettman experiment might test the effect of cost by explicitly charging consumers a cost for each bit of data. By varying the cost, the resulting changes in search behavior could be examined.

REFERENCES

1. *Akerlof, G. "The Market for Lemons: Qualitative Uncertainty and the Market Mechanism," Quarterly Journal of Economics, 84 (August 1970), 488-500.

2. Akerlof, G. "The Economics of Caste and of the Rat Race and other Woeful Tales," Quarterly Journal of Economics, 90 (November 1976).

3. *Arrow, K. "Economic Welfare and the Allocation of Resources for Invention," in The Rate and Direction of Inventive Activity, NBER, Princeton, 1962.

4. *Arrow K. "Uncertainty and the Welfare Economics of Medical Care," American Economic Review, 53 (December 1963), 941-973.

5. Arrow K. "Higher Education as a Filter," Journal of Public Economics, 2 (July 1973), 193-216.

6. Bettman, J. "Consumer Information Acquisition and Search Strategies," this volume.

7. Darby, M. and Karni, E. "Free Competition and the Optimal Amount of Fraud," Journal of Law and Economics, 16 (April 1973), 67-88.

8. *Fama, E. and Laffer, A. "Information and Capital Markets," Journal of Business, 44 (July 1971), 289-298.

9. *Fromm, E. The Sane Society, New York, 1955.

10. *Gintis, H. "Welfare Criteria with Endogenous Preferences: The Economics of Education," International Economic Review, 15 (June 1974), 415-430.

11. *Gintis, H. "On Commodity Fetishism and Irrational Production," University of Massachusetts, 1975.

12. *Grether, D. and Plott, C. "Economic Theory of Choice and The Preference Reversal Phenomenon," California Institute of Technology, 1977.

13. *Grossman, S. and Stiglitz, J. "Information and Competitive Price Systems," American Economic Review, 66 (May 1976), 246-253.

14. Hirshliefer, J. "The Private and Social Returns to Inventive Activity, American Economic Review, 61 (September 1971), 561-574.

15. *Horney, K. Neurosis and Human Growth, New York, 1950.

16. *Jencks, C. et al. Inequality, New York, 1972.

17. *Kagel, J., Battalio, R. et al. "Experimental Studies of Consumer Demand Using Laboratory Animals," Economic Inquiry,

18. *Keynes, J.M. "The State of Long-Term Expectation," (Chapter 12), The General Theory of Employment, Interest and Money, 1935.

19. *Laing, R.D. Sanity, Madness, and the Family, Tavistock Institute, 1964.

20. *Michael, R. and Becker, G. "On the New Theory of Consumer Behavior," Swedish Journal of Economics, 75 (December 1973), 378-396.

21. Muth, R. "Rational Expectations and the Theory of Price Movements," Econometrica, 29 (July 1961), 315-335.

22. *Nelson, P. "Information and Consumer Behavior," Journal of Political Economy, 78 (March-April 1970), 729-754.

23. *Nelson, P. "The Economic Value of Advertising," in Y. Brozen (ed.), Advertising and Society, New York, 1974, 43-66.

24. *Olson, J. "Theories of Information Encoding and Storage: Implications for Marketing and Public Policy;" this volume.

25. Phelps, E. and Winter, S. "Optimal Price Policy Under Atomistic Competition," in E. Phelps et al, Microeconomic Foundations of Inflation and Employment Theory, New York, 1970, 309-337.

26. Phelps, E.S. "The Statistical Theory of Racism and Sexism," American Economic Review, 62 (September, 1972), 659-661.

27. *Reich, W.R. Character Analysis, third edition, New York, 1972.

28. *Rothschild, M. "Models of Market Organization with Imperfect Information: A Survey," Journal of Political Economy, 81 (November 1973), 1283-1308.

29. Rothschild, M. "A Two-Armed Bandit Theory of Market Pricing," Journal of Economic Theory, 9 (1974), 185-202.

30. Rothschild, M. and Stiglitz, J. "Equilibrium in Competitive Insurance Markets: An Essay on the Economics of Imperfect Information," Quarterly Journal of Economics, 90 (November 1976), 629-650.

31. *Russo, J. "The Value of Unit Price Information," Journal of Marketing Research, 14 (May 1977), 193-201.

32. Salop, J. and Salop, S. "Self-Selection and Turnover in the Labor Market," Quarterly Journal of Economics, 90 (November 1976), 619-627.

33. *Salop, S. "Information and Monopolistic Competition," American Economic Review, 66 (May 1976), 240-245.

34. Salop, S. "The Noisy Monopolist: Imperfect Information, Price Dispersion and Price Discrimination," Review of Economic Studies, 1977, forthcoming.

35. Salop, S. ang Stiglitz, J. "Bargains and Ripoffs: A Model of Monopolistically Competitive Price Dispersion," Review of Economic Studies, 1977, forthcoming.

36. *Schelling, T. "Micromotives and Macrophenomena: A Lecture," Harvard University, 1976.

37. *Simon, H. "Theories of Decision-Making in Economics, American Economic Review, 44 (June 1959), 253-283.

38. *Spence, A.M. Market Signalling, Harvard University Press, 1973.

39. *Spence, A.M. "Time and Communication in Economic and Social Interaction," Quarterly Journal of Economics, 87 (November 1973), 651-660.

40. *Spence, A.M. "Informational Aspects of Market Structure: An Introduction," Quarterly Journal of Economics, 90 (November 1976).

41. Stigler, G. and Becker, G. "DeGustibus non est Disputandum," American Economic Review, 67 (March 1977), 76-90.

42. *Stiglitz, J. "Conceptual Approaches to the Economics of Discrimination," American Economic Review, 63 (May 1973), 287-295.

43. Stiglitz, J. "Information and Economic Analysis," in M. Parkin and A. R. Nobay, Current Economic Problems, Cambridge University Press, 1974.

44. *Tversky, A. "Assessing Uncertainty," Journal of Royal Statistical Society Series B, 36 (1974), 148-159.

THE ECONOMIC ANALYSIS OF ADVERTISING

Gerard R. Butters, Princeton University

INTRODUCTION

To a large degree academic disciplines are defined more by the tools employed by researchers than by the subject matter studied. This is particularly true in the social sciences, where such topics as crime, marriage, elections, and unemployment are each studied by economists, psychologists, sociologists, political scientists, historians, and anthropologists, each applying different insights and methods of analysis. Specialists in one field often have little awareness (and sometimes little regard) for the activities of researchers in closely related fields, even when they are studying the same phenomena.

This state of affairs is not without justification. One may very well develop a deeper understanding of human behavior by studying basic principles which apply in many apparently diverse and unrelated contexts than by bringing together many different points of view concerning a narrowly defined sphere of events. Moreover, effective research generally requires drastic simplification and abstraction from non-essential details. And it is not necessarily improper that what are regarded as "non-essential details" by one discipline are considered to be the "essential facts" in another discipline. After all, the dividing lines between disciplines are deliberately drawn so as to minimize the interdependence between them and thereby enable specialization to be productive.

Nevertheless, there remain a number of valid reasons why interaction between disciplines is important. First, in many cases the output of one discipline serves as the input of another. Most dramatically, it is increasingly important for economists and other social scientists to be able to use a substantial body of mathematical theorems, even though it is usually unnecessary for them to be mathematicians themselves, or even to understand the proofs of the theorems they use. Similarly, a good historian should be familiar with certain principles from economics, but need not necessarily be qualified to do economic research. Secondly, from time to time it is discovered that the tools of one discipline can be effective in answering questions previously studied only by a different discipline. Such a discovery may revolutionize a discipline or create a new academic specialty: recent examples are the growth of economic history and economic demography. Finally, public policy makers have a practical need to consider all the available knowledge and insights that different disciplines have to offer in order to make wise policy decisions.

The phenomenon of advertising is a perfect example of the preceding discussion. Consumer psychologists, experts in marketing, economists, and public policy makers (to make only a partial list) bring different methods and insights to bear on the same topic. What is the approach of the economist, and how does it compare, contrast, and interact with the approach of other specialists? To answer the question in some detail is my task in this paper. Here is a brief outline of my views:

(1) The consumer psychologist is primarily interested in the specific processes by which advertising affects consumer behavior. In particular, the cognitive psychologist examines how consumers perceive, process, encode, store, retrieve, and use the information contained in advertising; behaviorists and personality psychologists use different techniques to answer the same question. For the most part, consumer psychologists do not concern themselves with how or why corporate managers decide how much and what kind of advertising to use.

(2) The marketing expert, on the other hand, focuses on the role of the firm and its managers. Given the ways in which consumers will respond to different advertising appeals (he is quite willing to rely on the consumer psychologist to explain why the consumer responds as he does), what advertising strategy will most effectively increase sales? What overall level of advertising will be most profitable to the firm, what mixture of advertising media should be employed, and how should the firm respond to the advertising campaigns of competitors?

(3) The economist is primarily interested in the _interactions_ between the behavior of the various firms and the consumer. Although he occasionally uses the results of the consumer psychologist and the marketing expert, he is willing to take a simple, even superficial, view of the consumers' and firms' decision making processes, if it will help him understand how their decisions interact to determine the equilibrium level of advertising. He also has the audacity to advance views as to whether the amount and nature of advertising can be expected to be socially optimal or not, and to suggest potential remedies if he believes that advertising is excessive or misdirected.

(4) The public policy maker turns to each of the other specialists for practical advice. From the economist he may obtain general policy guidelines, but to put these into practice he needs the expertise of other disciplines as well. For example, the economist may point out the general conditions under which advertisers have the opportunity and incentive to air false or misleading advertising, but has no special expertise in determining which particular ads are misleading or in designing a corrective advertising campaign.

To elaborate upon the role of the economist in this outline, I begin in the following section by discussing the economist's basic paradigm of analysis. Section III contains a discussion of the particular problems economists have had in treating advertising within this basic paradigm. In Section IV I review a major debate in the economic literature on advertising which illustrates the way in which the economic paradigm has been applied and the possibilities for interdisciplinary research on advertising. Section V presents three simple insights which I think will be important in guiding new research and policy making, and Section VI considers in more detail some of my own attempts to follow these guidelines.

THE ECONOMIST'S PARADIGM

In approaching most problems, the economist uses some variant of the same fundamental paradigm. He believes that many aspects of human behavior can be understood by first considering separately the decisions made by economic units (such as individuals, families, firms, cooperatives, and groups of colluding firms), each of which takes as given certain features of its environment, and then analyzing how the decision-making rules of the units interact to determine simultaneously the actual behavior of each unit. To incorporate this paradigm into a mathematical model, he typically assumes that each economic unit acts as if it were solving a particular constrained optimization problem; the solution of this problem usually yields a single equation, or set of equations, which represents the unit's behavior as a function of other variables and parameters of the model. A simultaneous solution of all these equations, for every unit in the economy, is called a "market equilibrium."

The most important example of this paradigm in economics is the general equilibrium model of perfect competition, which summarizes mathematically the essence of two centuries of development of the central contribution of Adam Smith. In this model (and in many others) it is assumed that there are two types of economic units, consumers and firms. Certain characteristics of both the consumers' preferences, or "tastes," and the firms' production possibilities, or "technology," are simply taken as axioms of the model. For example, it is required that consumers be able to rank different bundles of goods according to their preferences in a consistent fashion, and it is assumed that firms' production technology has the property of constant returns to scale (i.e., doubling all inputs leads to a doubling of all outputs). If these axioms of consumer preferences are accepted, consumer tastes may be represented mathematically by a "utility function"; correspondingly, the technology available to firms plays a major role in determining their profit functions.

To complete the general equilibrium model, it is assumed that each consumer chooses the quantities of various "goods" to consume (one of these goods is his own leisure time) so as to maximize his utility function, conditional on the prices and wages given by the market. Similarly, firms choose quantities of goods to produce and to use as inputs in production, so as to maximize profits, again conditional on given prices and wages. The interaction of these choices by all consumers and firms determine the equilibrium prices, wages, and quantities of all goods produced and consumed.

In addition, many applied "partial equilibrium" models -- models which deal with only a single segment of the economy -- have a similar structure. Axioms about consumer's tastes and firms' technology form the bases of the demand and supply sides of the model, which together determine the price and quantity of the good in question. In such applied models the axioms concerning technology, in particular, often are the focus for productive interdisciplinary research. For example, in transportation economics the axioms of economists' models or the functional forms used in regression analysis are often given by an engineer's analysis of, say, the costs of operating airplanes or the traffic flow patterns on a highway.

Because many economic models require consumers to maximize their own utility functions and require firms to maximize their profit functions, economics has frequently been called the science of the rational, calculating, or selfish man. However, none of these adjectives is necessarily appropriate. Consumers may make their choices consciously or subconsciously, with foresight or on impulse, and for selfish or unselfish reasons, and yet exhibit identifiable and predictable patterns of behavior over time -- patterns which are adequately described by the utility maximization formalization. Firms may follow a policy of profit maximization not because all firm owners are selfish to begin with, but because those owners who do not maximize profits go out of business; alternatively, we may assume that firms maximize some other variable, such as sales or assets, in place of profits, and the economic paradigm remains intact.

In addition to "positive economics," which includes the study of the explanation, prediction, and control of economic behavior, economists are also concerned with "welfare economics," which deals with the evaluation of economic behavior. The single dominant concept of welfare economics is the notion of "Pareto optimality" or "Pareto efficiency": a technologically feasible allocation of resources is said to be Pareto optimal if and only if there is no feasible way to reallocate those resources in such a way that in the new equilibrium at least one consumer prefers his new level

of consumption to his old level and no consumer considers himself to be worse off. Intuitively, a situation is considered to be optimal if all potential improvements have already been made, so that no further improvement is possible.

In most economic models it is a straightforward and objective matter to find the Pareto optimal allocations and to check whether or not the market equilibrium allocation is Pareto optimal. It is the decision to use Pareto optimality as a measure of social desirability which is subjective and controversial. First, there is not just one Pareto optimal allocation in a given economy. There are many, some of which are highly inequitable. In particular, an allocation in which some individuals are starving may by Pareto optimal if additional food for the poor is available only at the minor inconvenience of the rich. Secondly, certain allocations of resources may be technologically feasible, but yet not attainable, because they require individuals to act altruistically. For example, the granting of patent rights results in the insufficient use of new products and processes, but it is considered to be necessary to provide adequate incentives to innovators. This point may be taken into account by modifying the definition of Pareto optimality by considering only those allocations which are both technologically and motivationally feasible. Thirdly, individuals are not always believed to be the best judges of their own self-interest, perhaps because they lack knowledge, foresight, or self-control. Finally, even if one is prepared to accept the individual's judgment of his own self-interest, how does one deal with situations in which his judgment changes over time? This last problem is especially important in the study of the welfare economics of advertising.

ADVERTISING AND THE ECONOMIST'S PARADIGM

Advertising poses particular difficulties for economists because it is difficult to fit into the usual paradigm of analysis. Since the main purpose of advertising appears to be to change consumers' preferences, it does not seem acceptable to retain the traditional assumption that tastes are fixed. If the individual himself has no consistent evaluation of his own self-interest, it seems impossible to even begin a welfare analysis of advertising. Traditional positive analysis is undermined as well, since it too depends on the assumption of fixed tastes. How then should the economist proceed?

The simplest way to incorporate advertising into an economic model is to replace the assumption that tastes are given by the assumption that consumers' responses to advertising are given. For example, it is commonly assumed that the sales of a particular brand are determined as a function of its price, the amount of advertising devoted to the brand, and perhaps other variables such as the prices and advertising of competing brands. It is then possible (see for example the works of Dorfman and Steiner [10], Nerlove and Arrow [16], and Schmalensee [20]) to calculate an individual firm's optimal advertising expenditure pattern and to analyze the game-theoretic interactions among competing firms' advertising strategies.

This mode of analysis, however, has two important flaws. The first is that unless one undertakes a more detailed investigation of the consumer's decision-making process, any assumptions regarding how consumers respond to advertising would appear to be highly arbitrary. The second is that since consumers' preferences are not explicitly treated in the model, there is still no foundation upon which to build a welfare economic analysis.

To illustrate the difficulties with making welfare judgments in the presence of advertising, consider the following example. Suppose that if there were no advertising a consumer would prefer brand X to brand Y, but that in the presence of advertising he would prefer brand Y to brand X. We might argue in favor of any of the following positions:

(1) The consumer is better off purchasing brand X, because advertising serves to manipulate his true tastes.

(2) The consumer is better off purchasing brand Y, because in the presence of advertising he makes a more carefully considered choice.

(3) The consumer is equally well off in either case because either way he chooses what he prefers.

(4) There is no way of saying how well off he is, because he does not have stable preferences.

In the absence of further information about the consumer's decision-making process, I know of no objective reason for preferring any one of these positions to any other. Nonetheless, this conceptual problem has not in fact deterred many economists from making value judgments about advertising.

The majority opinion among economists is that advertising is excessive. This position is supported on two grounds. First, it is held that the volume of advertising far exceeds that which could conceivably convey useful information. That portion of advertising which is non-informative is believed simply to be a waste of resources or to distort consumers' "true preferences," as in position (1) above. Secondly, it is believed that advertising creates an industry structure which is highly concentrated, in which entry is difficult, and therefore in which prices are too high and output is too low.

Both of these arguments have serious weaknesses. Although I have considerable emotional sympathy with the first position, I do not see how one can develop and elaborate it in a scientific manner. How can one distinguish between "informative" and "non-informative" advertising or issue a blanket condemnation of "non-informative advertising" when (1) advertising may serve to create a pleasant mystique surrounding an otherwise mundane product, (2) a large amount of advertising must be designed as entertainment if the consumer is to be enticed to pay sufficient attention to absorb the limited informational content of the ad, and when (3) simply the fact that a product is advertised intensively provides information in itself? The second position, although it is the basis for an interesting debate in positive economics which is reviewed in the following section, simply ignores the problem of changing tastes and appeals primarily to the indirect effects of advertising as a basis for condemning it. It addition, the two arguments for the view that advertising is excessive may easily lead to contradictions. According to the first argument, one might argue that advertising is excessive because it leads to excessive consumption of cigarettes and ready-to-eat breakfast cereals; according to the second argument, advertising results in too little consumption of these products.

Since the difficulties the economist faces in analyzing advertising arise from changing tastes, a straightforward, albeit radical, way to avoid these difficulties is to assume that, contrary to first impressions, advertising does not change individuals' tastes. In this view advertising acts to change the data upon which decisions are made, but not the criteria of judgment. Advertising may succeed in convincing you (truthfully or untruthfully) that a certain product has a lower price, is more durable, or has more sex appeal than another product, but it does not change your beliefs in the relative importance of low price, durability, or sex appeal as product attributes. This view of advertising, termed "advertising as information," is rapidly growing in popularity as a framework for both positive and normative analyses of advertising which preserves most features of the economists' basic paradigm.

The advertising as information approach, in common with all other approaches, has substantial drawbacks of its own. To begin with, it is questionable whether consumers can handle complex decision-making processes with the degree of rationality and sophistication that the models assume. More importantly, even if models of advertising as information are successful in predicting and explaining behavior, and even if they provide deductively rigorous welfare analyses, it does not follow that their welfare conclusions should serve as the basis for public policy making. As Milton Friedman [12] has argued in a famous article, the predictive success of a theory does not depend on the strict descriptive accuracy of its assumptions. It may be that the axiom that advertising works as information is faulty, that first appearances are indeed correct in that advertising acts in large part by manipulating the consumer's emotions, but that formal models of advertising as information might yet produce accurate predictions about observed behavior. In that case the welfare conclusions, based upon faulty axioms, could be wrong. The resolution of the matter rests on the development of objective, operational means of distinguishing informational from manipulative advertising, a problem which is far from being solved, and which is largely out of the realm of issues that economists have been trained to deal with. Nevertheless, the analysis of advertising as information is still justifiable on the ground that (1) it does provide a useful framework for positive analysis, appropriate for at least some forms of advertising, (2) if one is willing to accept the necessary axioms, it provides the only known rigorous framework for addressing welfare issues, and (3) if one is not sure which axioms are appropriate, or if one thinks that only certain varieties of advertising act to provide information, then one should welcome the chance to confirm (or throw doubt upon) one's policy views by checking whether or not different approaches yield the same policy conclusions.

Whether one views advertising as the provision of information or as a means of changing consumers' tastes, the role of interdisciplinary research remains essentially the same. In the same way that the technology of production is the interface between economics and engineering, so is the technology of information transfer (or persuasion) the interface between economics, psychology, and marketing. For example, just as engineers may provide useful information to economists concerning the existence of economies of scale in production, psychologists and marketing researchers may discover evidence supporting or rejecting the hypothesis that there are economies of scale in advertising. This example and others will be discussed in more detail in the following section.

THE ADVERTISING, CONCENTRATION, AND PROFITS DEBATE

A large portion of the economics literature on advertising has developed out of the attempt to identify and interpret statistical relationships between advertising intensity and two traditional measures of industry structure, concentration and profits. This debate exemplifies the economist's approach to advertising: primary attention has been devoted to the interaction of firms within an industry, and relatively little attention has been given to the precise mechanisms according to which consumers respond to advertising and the marketing strategies of firms which seek to expand sales.

On one side of the debate, following the tradition established by Nicolas Kaldor [14] and Joe Bain [2], it is argued that advertising creates barriers which discourage new firms from entering an industry; these barriers permit the industries in question to become more concentrated, and they allow firms in these industries to arrive at tacit understandings which lead to greater profitability. This position is buttressed by statistical evidence which shows that advertising is indeed positively correlated with standard measures of concentration and rates of return.

There are two prominent variants of the argument. The first holds that there are substantial economies of scale in advertising, so that in industries in which (perhaps due to the nature of the product) advertising is important only large firms can survive, resulting in a concentrated industry with high rates of return. The second holds that advertising creates or reinforces "brand loyalty," so that once a number of firms develop an established position, consumers' reluctance to try new brands makes entry difficult. In industries in which products are somehow more "differentiable" or "advertisable" (i.e., it is somehow easier in these industries to create brand loyalty through the use of advertising which convinces consumers that there are important differences among brands), both advertising expenditures (relative to sales) and rates of return might be expected to be higher.

This entire set of arguments has been attacked on several grounds. First, Julian Simon [21], Yale Brozen [7], and others have sought to demonstrate directly that there are no significant economies of scale in advertising and that advertising acts to remove barriers to entry rather than to create them. Secondly, it has been argued that the positive statistical relationships between advertising and concentration and between advertising and rates of return may simply be due to any one of several other causal relationships among advertising, concentration, and profits. Thirdly, Lester Telser [23, 24] and others have argued that the positive statistical relationships are mere artifacts of inappropriate data handling. All three of these lines of attack require examination in greater detail.

Let us consider first the issue of economies of scale in advertising. There are at least seven possible sources of such economies:

(1) It has been hypothesized that there is a threshold level of advertising per individual level which must be reached before the consumer will perceive or respond to the message. This position has never been supported empirically. Indeed, Julian Simon cites convincing evidence that there are substantial diseconomies of scale at this level.

(2) Stephen Glaister [13] and others have developed models indicating that there may be economies of scale due to word-of-mouth exchange of information among individuals. In analogy to nuclear fission, there may be a critical mass of informed consumers needed to sustain the growth in sales of a product. To the best of my knowledge, these models have not been tested empirically.

(3) There are undoubtedly some fixed costs associated with planning and producing advertising campaigns. It is uncertain, however, that these are of sufficient size to be empirically important.

(4) It is alleged that there are substantial quantity discounts available to large buyers of network television advertising time. This issue has been discussed at length in the Journal of Business and the Journal of Law and Economics, and it is questionable whether any real discounts remain after corrections for audience size and quality are made.

(5) Media advertising rates are usually lower for media which reach large audiences, but again this may be simply because smaller media are more specialized and therefore of higher quality to certain advertisers.

(6) Network television and magazine rates appear to be substantially cheaper than spot rates, for identical times and audiences. The underlying cause of this differential, if it does indeed exist, has not been established, and it might be the subject for worthwhile research.

(7) A second economy associated with nationwide advertising and distribution results from the fact that customer mobility is less damaging to a firm, the larger is the market area covered by any particular brand. It is at least plausible that the various economies to be obtained from nationwide operations, combined with regional economies of scale in production and distribution, might be sufficient to render entry impossible except for firms which can command huge amounts of capital. However, the details of this position remain to be established.

Turning to the brand loyalty issue, in Yale Brozen's view it is the characteristics of the brand and the costliness of obtaining information about alternative brands which creates loyalty, not advertising. He holds that advertising is effective in inducing consumers to try out different products and brands, and thus is essential as a means of entry or expansion; but that it has little effect on the patronage of steady customers of the advertised brand, who rely instead on their first-hand experience to make their decisions. The evidence Brozen cites for this position -- the correlation across industries of high advertising intensity and high brand turnover, the differences in firms' advertising within a given industry, and the patterns of advertising expenditure over the life cycle of the brand -- is indirect and is subject to contrary interpretations. It would be beneficial in this context for economists to draw on the experience of marketing specialists, who surely must have a wealth of knowledge about the effect of advertising upon inexperienced versus experienced buyers.

To elaborate upon the second line of attack on the barriers to entry theory, I will simply list a number of other plausible relationships among the three variables:

(1) Concentration and rates of return may be positively correlated with advertising because in concentrated industries firms are able to maintain tacit understandings that keep prices above marginal cost; the large profits to be gained from increasing one's market share induce the firms to engage in intensive nonprice competition, including advertising.

(2) Concentrated industries may advertise more heavily because they are less affected by the "free rider" problem. To explain briefly, advertising has two effects: to increase a firm's sales at the expense of its competitors and to increase the industry's sales as a whole. The less concentrated is an industry, the less firms are aided by the second effect of their own advertising, because they partake in such a small share of the industry a gain in sales which results from their own advertising.

(3) Industries in which new technological opportunities have arisen or in which consumer demand has expanded unexpectedly rapidly are likely to be both more profitable than average (due to temporary under-capacity) and to advertise more than average (to establish more new brands, to stake out a position in a market of future importance, and because there is a greater consumer demand for information).

Existing studies have not yet succeeded in sorting out the casual relationships, and I have serious doubts as to whether the issue can be entirely resolved by relying on industry level data exclusively.

Turning now to the third line of attack, many of the major statistical problems center around the measurement of rates of return. A firm's rate of return is defined in these studies as its profits (also called net earnings or net income) divided by the value of its assets. Annual profits (or losses) are simply the change in the value of a firm's assets from one year to the next. The measurement of rates of return thus depends solely on the measurement of the value of a firm's assets and its change over time. It is easy enough to keep track of a firm's financial assets, and (so it is claimed) even the value of its physical assets (plant, equipment, and inventories) may be reasonably approximated by the device of using historical cost data and making adjustments for depreciation, as is done in a firm's accounts. The difficulty lies in making a reasonable estimate of the value of intangible assets such as patents trademarks, know-how, and "goodwill." In conventional accounting intangible assets are all but ignored, unless they are acquired by a firm in a merger or some other market transaction. It is this omission, or faulty corrections for this omission, which may lead to serious biases in the statistical analyses.

To formalize this discussion, let us introduce a little notation. Let Y represent conventionally measured profits, let K represent the value of tangible assets, let C represent the value of intangible assets, and let I represent the annual change in value of intangible assets, which may be called the net investment in intangibles. Then the standard accounting rate of return, R, is given by Y/K, but the true rate of return is a different ratio, $R* = (Y+I)/(K+C)$. If I/C is less than Y/K, then the accounting rate of return, R, overstates the true rate of return. Furthermore, the greater is C relative to K, the greater is the overstatement of the true rate of return. Thus industries which have intensive advertising are likely to have grossly overstated rated of return, leading to a spurious correlation between advertising and measured rates of return across industries.

To correct for this bias, and to see whether or not a correlation between advertising and true rates of return remains, it is necessary to make estimates of the values C and I. In all studies to date of which I know, this has been done by following an accounting procedure analogous to the treatment of investment in physical assets. The value of intangible assets, C, is estimated by the accumulated, depreciated value of all past advertising expenditures. All other intangibles are ignored, and thus this value is simply termed "advertising capital." The value I, net investment in advertising capital, is measured by current expenditures on advertising minus depreciation on the existing stock of advertising capital. The controversy in the literature boils down to a choice of the rate of depreciation. The use of a very high rate amounts to assuming that the values of C and I are very small, so that the accounting rate of return is nearly correct. Only a very low depreciation rate, in the order of five to ten percent, but depending considerably on the data used, is small enough to eliminate entirely the correlation between advertising and "true" rates of return. A number of different techniques for calculating the depreciation rate have been explored, including the use of regressions of current sales on current and past advertising expenditure to measure the permanence of the effects of advertising, the use of the stock market's evaluation of firms as a second method for calculating the value of intangible assets, and the use of sales data on brands for which advertising has been discontinued. Unfortunately, the results which have been reached using these different methods vary markedly, (see references [1], [5], [9], and [25]) and are predictable only by the academic affiliation of the researcher.

Let us now take stock of this entire line of discussion about the measurement of rates of return. The generally accepted definition of the rates of return (also called the internal rate of return) of an investment project is the number r such that the value of the entire stream of cash flows associated with the project, discounted back to the beginning of the project, is zero. Any "snap-shot" method of estimating rates of return, namely by looking at ratios of profits to equity over a limited span of time, can only by justified by showing how it relates to the accepted definition just given. This analysis has been done fairly

thoroughly in the case of physical assets, identifying biases relating to differential inflation rates, differential growth rates, inappropriate depreciation accounting, and the marking up or down of capital assets according to market value. However, the case of "advertising capital" requires more sophisticated adjustments to deal with problems such as the following: (1) the effect of advertising is undoubtedly more lasting for better quality products, on which more research and development dollars may have been spent, than on low quality products; (2) "goodwill," if measured by sales or market share, can be produced by means other than advertising, such as simply offering a product at a low price, and it is not clear how to adjust for these other factors in estimating "advertising capital" and the appropriate depreciation rates; and (3) advertising of firms may increase the rate of depreciation of the advertising capital of other firms. Closely related to these conceptual problems is the practical matter of choosing what data to use, at what level of aggregation. Is it appropriate to look at rates of return associated with individual brands, firms, or industries? With a practically limitless supply of possible biases to account for in future papers, the literature on this topic is in little danger of dying out, unless it is due to the exhaustion of the researchers.

One important reason why the debate over the statistical literature which has grown out of the regression analysis of Comanor and Wilson [9] has been so inconclusive is that it uses data which is too highly aggregated. The effects of advertising are aggregated across media, across brands, sometimes across firms, and across the life cycles of brands, firms, and industries. No wonder it is hard to isolate the true causal relationships. Even if the existence of some barriers to entry involving advertising could be inferred, it would be of little value for public policy making, since different sources of the problem (say network advertising policies, trademark regulations, or capital market imperfections) would call for very different corrective actions. One exception to this rule is a series of regressions run by Michael E. Porter [18] which separates out the effects of advertising into different components according to the medium used. Although Porter does not make any corrections for rates of return bias or reverse causation in his regressions, the fact that the network television advertising variable has far more explanatory power than all other advertising variables suggests that he is picking up more than just errors in his data.

No matter how the rate of return debate comes out, however, I do not think that it will resolve the real issue which separates the two opposing camps. Suppose on one hand that it were proved conclusively that firms which advertise do not earn monopoly rates of return. In this case, I would expect to hear Harvard economists argue that the monopoly returns were simply frittered away by X-inefficiency or by non-price competition among oligopolists; George Stigler would reply that X-inefficiency doesn't X-ist, and the argument would be continued on other grounds. If on the other hand it were shown that rates of return were higher for firms which advertised intensively, then I would expect to hear from the University of Chicago or UCLA the argument that this high rate of return was simply the appropriate compensation for taking the huge risks associated with their initial entry into the market. The losses from the firms that failed in the effort to develop and sell new, improved products are not included in the biased sample of firms (the successful ones) that remain. In this case the argument has been shifted to the question of whether the (hypothetical) monopoly returns available to the firms which first firmly establish a sizeable market share are of the appropriate nature and size to encourage the optimal amount of product and marketing innovation.

What then is the real bone of contention? We may start by noting that there is at least one point on which everyone appears to be in full agreement, namely that the value of "goodwill" or "intangible capital" in high advertising industries is substantial. According to the traditional industrial organization view, with its emphasis on barriers to entry, the value of an established market position must be high; according to the Chicago position, rates of depreciation on advertising are low, and thus the accumulated capital value is high. The issue is whether the value of C is high or low compared to a social optimum level. Both sides must agree that these firms have substantial monopoly power, in the sense of being able to change price without incurring a large change in sales (otherwise, how could market share be so valuable? -- under pure competition, unlimited market share is obtainable by making the tiniest reduction in price). They disagree whether this monopoly power is due to real costs of providing useful information about products and to real differences in the products, or whether advertising misleads people into believing that essentially identical products are different. In the latter view advertising and "product differentiation" are generally non-productive; in the former view advertising serves a constructive role by lowering consumers' costs of obtaining information and thereby creating a market for improved products. The argument has returned to the quandaries raised in Section III.

The size of firms' stocks of goodwill is determined in large part by social choice. In particular, the ability to advertise profitably a specific brand name is established and protected by laws which grant exclusive rights to the use of a particular trademark. The purpose of these laws is to encourage firms to develop and maintain high quality products by preventing firms from selling shoddy goods under the same label, but they also have the effect of requiring manufacturers who are selling identical products to engage in duplicative advertising. Perhaps the appropriate focus of debate should be the nature and duration of trademarks, and the investigation of alternative public policies to ensure quality control, rather than the distracting arguments over rates of return.

At least one point should now be clear: if we are to resolve the very tricky issues of what determines the socially optimal level of advertising and how advertising is related to profits and concentration, we must first understand the more basic issue of how and why advertising affects sales. As I hope to illustrate in Section VI, this task may be accomplished in part by replacing our loose verbal models of advertising with more rigorous economic models of consumer behavior under uncertainty. Equally important, economists should pay more attention to the analytic techniques and the accumulated knowledge of marketing researchers and consumer psychologists, many of whom have devoted their careers to providing the answers we seek.

THREE TRUISMS

Drawing in part upon the lessons of the advertising-concentration-profits controversy, I will discuss three truisms which I believe should play an important role in guiding future research and public policy making concerning advertising.

The first truism is that advertising is just one of many means of promotion and information transfer. Other promotional techniques include the use of salesman, discounting, coupons, displays, attractive packaging, and games of chance; other sources of information include catalogs, the advice of friends, the advice of retailers, and the ratings of consumer groups and governmental agencies.

Keeping this simple fact in mind may change many of our established ways of thinking about advertising. Can we measure a firm's "goodwill" or "intangible assets" adequately by the accumulated, appropriately depreciated, value of its past expenditures on advertising? Perhaps not, because (in addition to reasons discussed earlier) if goodwill is defined as the number of satisfied customers who are potentially available for repeat sales, then these customers may have been attracted by any one of many other means of promotion. If we believe that advertising is excessive compared to some ideal standard, can we conclude that a tax to discourage advertising is appropriate? The answer must be no, unless we are assured that the tax will not simply induce firms to switch to some even more wasteful or otherwise objectionable substitute means of promoting their products.

The second truism, an immediate consequence of the first, is that any factor which affects any aspect of firms' promotional decisions or the information available to consumers will indirectly affect firms' advertising policy decisions. Indeed, I think it can be argued that much advertising, and in particular most of the advertising generally considered to be objectionable, arises as a response to "imperfections" in apparently different markets. The most important such imperfection occurs in the market for broadcast radio and television signals. Unlike the case in most markets, broadcast stations do not know the identity of those who are using the service they are providing, so they have no direct way to charge for this service. They do have an indirect way to charge, namely by providing advertising messages which listeners and viewers cannot totally avoid, and which bring in substantial advertising revenues. Newspapers and magazines, which can at least sell individual copies at a price, even if they cannot charge all readers individually, provide advertising which is generally considered to be more informative and less noxious, and which the reader can more easily choose to pay attention to or to avoid. Indeed, the economics of the media is a particularly fascinating and wide open area for prospective research. What determines the equilibrium duration and the degree of odiousness of television advertising? How will the development of cable and pay television change the advertising market? What determines the equilibrium market price for television and newspaper advertising space?

Another group of such market imperfections arise from general properties of the market for information. First, information is a prime example of a "public good": Unlike ice cream, housing, or most other goods, many types of information can be "consumed" by one person, or even simultaneously by many persons, without reducing its value to others. According to the principle of marginal cost pricing, information should be provided essentially free, at the cost of disseminating the information, not the cost of both gathering, or otherwise producing the information, and disseminating it. The need to charge for information to recoup all costs restricts the flow of information below the optimal level. Adding to this bias is the problem that it is difficult to prevent one's customers from cutting into one's market by reselling the information or giving it away free of charge to other potential customers. A final reason why information is difficult to sell for its true value is the fact that, almost by definition, it is difficult to judge the value of information prior to its acquisition. For all of these reasons the free market is limited in its ability to provide information in the most efficient manner. This leaves a vacuum to be filled by advertising, which may still be profitable because it provides only the part of the truth which favors the advertising firm, not the whole truth, and because it may also throw in something besides the truth for good measure.

The third truism is that advertising (in common with other forms of promotion and information transfer) is diverse. Advertising may convey information about the existence of a product or brand, its availability in a general location, or the identity of retailers carrying the item. Advertising may convey information about the price of the product, either absolutely or in relative terms. It may describe characteristics of the product, either truthfully or untruthfully, or it may even <u>create</u> such characteristics (advertising for drugs may create placebo effects in biologically inactive medications; advertising for cigarettes and whiskey seeks to make these products an integral component of a particular life style). It may be intended to induce individuals to try a product for the first time, or to induce repeat purchase. It may simply carry the information that the product is advertised, which indirectly provides information about its price and quality. Advertising may be conveyed through a variety of different media, each suitable for different techniques of drawing and sustaining consumers' attention. The nature of advertising used will depend on the characteristics of the product, the media used, and the intended audience. It is to be expected that different analytic models and different public policy considerations will be appropriate for each of the different forms of advertising.

TWO ILLUSTRATIVE MODELS

How can one use these three truisms to aid in the formulation of a coherent research strategy? One possible response is that there are so many factors involved in determining advertising and promotional behavior that only a correspondingly complicated model can be adequate to explain this behavior. Conceivably only a computerized simulation model can do the job. I disagree strongly with this point of view. The only cases I know of in which complex simulation models have been of proven value -- for example, meteorology, hydrodynamics, and aerodynamics -- are cases in which the underlying behavioral principles were already at least fairly well understood, and computational power was the major outstanding requirement for the solution to the problem at hand. When the basic elements of a model are in doubt, the "garbage in, garbage out" principle makes the computer's superior computational powers worthless. Scientific progress is achieved by finding ingenious experimental, statistical, or analytic devices to separate out unknown effects for individual study, and it is unlikely that this can be done by throwing many doubtful hypotheses into a single gigantic regression or simulation model. In the study of advertising, experimental data is available from marketing surveys and test market experiments. In addition, historical "accidents" such as the breaking up of large firms by antitrust action, the differential regulation of advertising across states and nations, and new technological developments in communications may serve as proxies for the controlled experiments that we are not able to make.

Indeed, the three truisms may be taken as evidence for a unity among various phenomena which justifies the use of simple models which have broad application. If advertising has characteristics in common with other forms of promotion, we may be able to explain important aspects of many types of promotion in a single model. If various forms of promotion achieve their effects by affecting the information available to consumers, we may be able to use established principles of the economics of information to explain promotional behavior. Since advertising is indeed diverse, a number of such models will be required. Admittedly, each single model will only deal with a single facet of advertising, and these models will play only one part in a comprehensive research program.

To illustrate the type of theoretical models I have in mind, I will summarize two models of my own which treat advertising as information. In each model one can rigorously compute both the market equilibrium amount of advertising and the Pareto optimal amount. It is thus possible to determine whether the market provides excessive advertising, and if so, why. To oversimplify a bit, if we make the Chicago assumptions (advertising serves as information; consumers are rational), do we get the Chicago conclusions (the free market provides the optimal amount of everything)?

The first model[1] concerns the role of advertising in providing information about the price and availability for purchase of a homogeneous product. It is assumed that consumers <u>must</u> know the "address" of a seller in order to buy the good. Each seller advertises this information, along with the price of his product. These advertising messages are distributed at random; the technology of communication makes it prohibitively costly for sellers to choose which consumers will be the recipients of their messages. Thus, some consumers may be unlucky enough not to receive any ads at all. These consumers may also obtain the same information, but only by engaging in costly search. To avoid extraneous complications, it is assumed that there are constant returns to scale in production of both the product itself and the advertising messages.

The market equilibrium under these conditions contains price dispersion. Consumers may either simply purchase from a firm whose advertising they have received, or they may engage in search for a better price. Firms must weigh the benefits of advertising at a high price, namely the higher advertising expenditures that must be incurred to reach customers who have no better alternative offer from another seller.

In general, it turns out that advertising is indeed excessive in this model. The same transfer of information could be achieved more efficiently if there were less advertising and more consumer search. Either a tax on advertising or a subsidy on consumers' search could achieve this objective. However, a prohibitive tax on advertising would destroy the market entirely. It is also interesting to note that if consumer search is not included in the model, so that advertising is the only possible means of conveying information, then the market equilibrium amount of information is in fact optimal. This fact indicates that the excessive advertising may be due to externalities in the search process rather than to any evil associated with advertising <u>per se</u>.

A major limitation of this first model is that heavy advertising is usually associated with products which are heterogeneous, not homogeneous. When products are subject to considerable variation in quality, price information alone does not provide the consumer with sufficient information to discriminate between competing brands, since he remains uncertain about the net utility associated with any given purchase. The next step in modeling should therefore be to treat advertising which improves the buyer's ability to choose by providing him with information about the product characteristics which matter to him.

Advertising may provide such useful information either directly or indirectly. Examples of directly provided information include automobile mileage figures, photographs or drawings of clothing in newspaper ads, and detailed job description provided in help-wanted advertising. However, advertising alone rarely provides all the information needed to make an intelligent choice, for the perfectly good reason that there are other, more efficient ways of exchanging this information. No conventional advertising medium will allow you to taste a product, feel it, smell it, or try it on for size. Television is suitable for providing vivid visual impressions, but not for giving detailed technical information. Print media may provide technical details, but will not allow the consumer to ask questions about the product.

For these reasons, I would argue that the information provided indirectly by advertising is far more important than the information provided directly. To be more specific, a

---

[1] For a full description of this model, see my forthcoming paper [8] in the <u>Review of Economic Studies</u>.

major role of advertising (and in fact of nearly all forms of promotion) is to reduce the consumer's cost of obtaining further information, and more generally to aid, encourage, and cajole the consumer in any manner to investigate the advertised product. Advertisements for retail stores, for example, by identifying the types of products carried by these stores, substantially reduce the number of abortive shopping trips undertaken by consumers. The proliferation of retail stores themselves is a form of promotion which reduces the search and transportation costs borne by consumers who are shopping around for the best buys. Advertisements which attract the consumer's attention, drum in a brand name, identify the general nature of a product, and create positive emotional associations with the product are designed in large part simply to draw the consumer into the showroom (for an expensive, durable good) or to encourage trial purchase. Free samples and introductory sales are the most obvious forms of promotion which reduce the consumer's cost of trying out a product; the periodic discounts on grocery items which form the bulk of weekly supermarket advertising serve the same purpose. Even directly informative advertising may be thought of as reducing, not eliminating, the cost of consumer search, because it requires time and effort to obtain and absorb technical information, no matter how conveniently it is packaged. All of these examples indicate that a model which emphasizes the indirect role of advertising in providing information would be useful in providing us with insight about one important facet of many types of promotion, even though it may not treat any single form of promotion in precise detail.

I will now outline the major features of a model I have constructed to analyze this type of advertising.[2] To begin with, it is assumed that each consumer must engage in search in order to be able to locate a firm from which he can purchase the desired product. This search is described analytically by a Poisson process: in each unit of time Δt, a consumer has probability $\lambda \cdot \Delta t$ of finding a firm. Once a consumer succeeds in locating a firm, he learns everything relevant about the firm's product, and then must decide if he wishes to make a purchase or to continue to search for a better buy. There are a large number of firms which carry different varieties of the desired product, and these firms compete on the basis of both price and advertising. Advertising works by increasing the rate, λ, at which consumers make contact with the advertising firm, and thus it reduces each consumer's expected cost of search.

The precise nature of product heterogeneity is of central importance in the model, because it provides the prime motivation for firms to advertise. In particular, I find it useful to make a distinction between product variety and product quality. A product may be said to be of higher quality than another if consumers can agree, perhaps with some minority dissent, that they prefer the first product to the second. In contrast, product variety indicates a situation in which consumers have different tastes, so that they cannot agree on any ranking of brands according to desirability. If products differed only according to quality, it would be cheap and easy to certify and report an appropriate quality index. It is therefore product variety, not product quality, which is responsible for the high cost of obtaining useful consumer information, and therefore is responsible for the importance of promotional practices which serve to reduce this cost. To capture this notion of product variety in the model, I introduce a somewhat technical assumption.[3] Letting U_{ij} refer to the utility, measured in dollars, of consumer i for one unit of the product variety

sold by firm j, I assume that there is a continuous probability distribution function F, such that:

(1) for any given firm indexed by j, F represents the distribution of the values U_{ij}, where i varies across all consumers, and

(2) for any given consumer indexed by i, F represents the distribution of the values U_{ij}, where j varies across all firms.

The central economic problem in this model is the matching of consumers possessing different tastes with firms selling different products. The longer consumers search, and the more firms advertise, the more contacts will be made between the two groups, and the greater will be the chance that consumers will find products well suited to their tastes. However, both consumers' search and firms' advertising are costly, so it would not be worthwhile to find a perfect match. There are actually two related problems to be solved: what is the optimal degree of matching to be achieved, taking into account the costs, and what is the optimal combination of search time and advertising expenditure to be devoted to creating this degree of matching?

In the main variant of the model, it turns out once again that in the market equilibrium there is too much advertising. Compared to the optimal situation, this excessive advertising makes search too cheap, thereby leading consumers to search too much and to find products which match their tastes more closely than can be justified, considering the expenditures required. In one example, namely when the distribution F is uniform, a tax of 100% on advertising will create the proper incentives to induce the market to function efficiently. There is nothing magic about this particular number. When other forms of the distribution F are used, the size of the corrective tax varies enormously; in some extreme cases it can even be the case that the market produces insufficient advertising, and that the optimal corrective policy is to subsidize advertising. All things considered, however, this model captures the popular notion that firms, in their individual attempts to increase sales and thereby earn high mark-up profits, may easily waste money collectively. In the end, as in most models of "monopolistic competition," firms make zero profits anyway, and it is the consumers who end up footing the bill for the excessive promotional expenditures in the form of higher prices. They get a better product, it is true, but not good enough to make up for the extra expense.

These models represent only a small beginning in the attempt to understand more clearly the multiple facets of advertising and promotion. Next on the agenda should be models which treat the economic incentives behind truthfulness versus deception in advertising and which treat the interactions between advertising and the amount of product variety. The ultimate goal, still far out of reach, is to develop a close integration between this theoretical research and the accumulating body of empirical work on advertising.

REFERENCES

1. Ayanian, Robert. "Advertising and the Rate of Return," Journal of Law and Economics, 18 (October 1975).

2. Bain, Joe S. Barriers to New Competition. Cambridge: Harvard University Press, 1956.

3. Benham, Lee. "The Effects of Advertising on the Price of Eyeglasses," Journal of Law and Economics, 15 (October 1972), 337-352.

---

[2] Complete details are contained in an unpublished paper, which I will make available upon request.

[3] This same formulation, arrived at independently, has been used in the unpublished work of John Cross.

4. Blank, David M. "Television Advertising: the Great Discount Illusion, or Tonypandy Revisited," *Journal of Business*, 41 (January 1968), 10-38.

5. Bloch, Harry. "Advertising and Profitability: A Reappraisal," *Journal of Political Economy*, 82 (March/April 1974), 267-286.

6. Boyer, K.D. "Informative and Goodwill Advertising," *Review of Economics and Statistics*, 56 (November 1974), 541-548.

7. Brozen, Yale. "Entry Barriers: Advertising and Product Differentiation," in H. Goldschmid, et. al. (eds.), *Industrial Concentration: the New Learning*. Boston: Little Brown and Co., 1974.

8. Butters, Gerard R. "Equilibrium Distributions of Sales and Advertising Prices," *Review of Economic Studies*, forthcoming, 1977.

9. Comanor, William S. and Thomas S. Wilson. *Advertising and Market Power*. Cambridge: Harvard University Press, 1974.

10. Dorfman, Robert and Petero O. Steiner. "Optimal Advertising and Optimal Quality," *American Economic Review*, 44 (December 1954), 826-836.

11. Ferguson, J.M. *Advertising and Competition: Theory, Measurement, Fact*. Cambridge: Ballinger, 1974.

12. Friedman, Milton. "The Methodology of Positive Economics," in *Essays in Positive Economics*, the University of Chicago Press, 1935.

13. Glaister, Stephen. "Advertising Policy and Returns to Scale in Markets Where Information is Passed Between Individuals," *Economica*, 41 (May 1974), 139-156.

14. Kaldor, Nicolas. "The Economic Aspects of Advertising," *Review of Economic Studies*, 18 (1949-50), 1-27.

15. Nelson, Phillip. "Advertising as Information," *Journal of Political Economy*, 82 (July/Aug. 1974), 729-754.

16. Nerlove, Marc and Kenneth J. Arrow. "Optimal Advertising Policy Under Dynamic Conditions, *Economica*, May, 1972.

17. Peterman, John L. "The Structure of National Time Rates in the Television Broadcasting Industry," *Journal of Law and Economics*, 11 (October 1965), 77-131.

18. Porter, Michael E. "Interbrand Choice, Media Mix, and Market Performance," *American Economic Review*, 66 (May 1976), 398-406.

19. _____. *Interbrand Choice, Strategy, and Market Power*. Cambridge: Harvard University Press, 1976.

20. Schmalensee, Richard. *The Economics of Advertising*. Amsterdam: North Holland, 1972.

21. Simon, Julian L. *Issues in the Economics of Advertising*. Urbana: University of Illinois Press, 1970.

22. Stigler, George S. "The Economics of Information," *Journal of Political Economy*, 69 (June 1961), 213-225.

23. Telser, Lester G. "Advertising and Competition," *Journal of Political Economy*, 72 (December 1964), 537-562.

24. _____. "Comment (on Comanor and Wilson," *American Economic Review*, 59 (May 1969), 121-123.

25. Weiss, Leonard W. "Advertising, Profits, and Corporate Taxes, *Review of Economics and Statistics*, 51 (November 1969), 421-430.

INFORMATION, UNCERTAINTY AND ADVERTISING EFFECTS

Robert B. Avery and Andrew A. Mitchell, Carnegie-Mellon University

INTRODUCTION

Developing models of market behavior that include advertising has proven difficult within the economic paradigm. There is a general belief that since firms advertise, advertising must have a positive effect on demand. In addition, there are many legends within the industry that attribute the large sales increases of a particular product or service to its advertising (e.g. Marlboro cigarettes, Avis car rental, Miller beer). If advertising causes a change in the demand for a particular product, however, a subset of buyers must change their evaluation of the product. In a world of perfect information, this could only occur if advertising changes the utility functions of these buyers. This, in turn, implies that buyers are unsure about their own desires and makes the determination of the welfare implications of advertising difficult, if not impossible.

An alternative approach is to assume that buyers have imperfect information about alternative products in the marketplace and advertising conveys information about these products. If a buyer's evaluation of a product is a function of his knowledge about the product, then, advertising may change this evaluation by either adding new information or changing stored information. A change in the evaluation of a product may, in turn, change the consumer's behavior toward the product.

In this paper, we use this latter approach to examine how the type of information transmitted with advertising may affect the market behavior of firms. We recognize that firms may provide information about their product through advertising or by inducing a purchase by other means. In some situations, however, advertising may provide information that cannot be obtained by inspection or use of the product. Consequently, we examine situations where advertising transmits the same information that would be obtained through inspection and use of the product and when it provides information that cannot be obtained through these means. The results indicate that the market behavior of firms will differ under these two situations.

Models of Consumer Demand

Classical economic models of purchase behavior assume that buyers have perfect information about all the alternatives in the market, consequently a buyer's evaluations of these alternatives remain fixed over time. Since evaluations cannot change, there is no need to include factors which may cause changes in evaluations. If, however, we want to examine the effect of advertising on market behavior and we recognize that advertising may change a buyer's evaluations of products, then, these models must include factors which effect these evaluations. An initial step in this direction was taken by Lancaster [5]. In his model, a buyer's evaluation of a product is a function of the characteristics, properties or attributes of that product. Buyers purchase those products or combination of products that produce the amounts of the different product characteristics or attributes that yield the greatest satisfaction at the lowest possible cost. In operationalizing his model, Lancaster uses a linear utility function and suggests that only product attributes that can be objectively measured should be used as the arguments of the utility function.

Lancaster did not use his model of consumer demand to examine advertising effects. It should be noted, however,

that under his formulation only advertising that conveys information about product attributes that can be objectively measured (e.g. calorie content of a food) can have an effect on the evaluation of products. In almost all situations, this same information could be obtained through inspection and use of the product.

Stigler and Becker [9] have developed a similar model of consumer demand and have used it to examine advertising effects. In their model, the arguments of a buyer's utility function are a number of different commodities. Although they do not clearly define what they mean by commodities, their examples indicate that they might be thought of as the consumption goals of the buyers such as social prestige or fresh breath. Consequently, in the Stigler and Becker model, the arguments of the utility function may include product characteristics that cannot be objectively measured. As in the Lancaster model, different products may produce different amounts of a commodity or characteristic.

Stigler and Becker assume a linear relationship between the number of units of a particular product that is purchased and the amount of a commodity produced. In their model, advertising may affect the conversion rate of a particular product into a commodity. For instance, advertising may convince a particular buyer that ownership of a Cadillac will produce 100 units of social prestige instead of 80 units. This change in the conversion rate will increase the value of the product to the buyer which may, in turn, increase the amount of the product demanded.

Both the Lancaster model and the Stigler and Becker model assume that a buyer's evaluation of a product is a function of the buyer's knowledge of the product. As mentioned previously, Lancaster uses only objectively measured product knowledge while Stigler and Becker allow for the use of the buyer's perceived knowledge. This latter formulation is consistent with a number of behavioral models relating an individual's evaluation of concept (e.g. product) to his knowledge about the concept (e.g. Fishbein [3] [4], Rosenberg [8]).

Finally, it should be noted that neither of these models includes the possibility that a buyer's information about a product may be imperfect. For instance, in purchasing an automobile a buyer may not know the repair rate of a specific automobile with certainty. If a buyer's knowledge of a particular product is imperfect, then his assessment of the utility of that product may take the form of a probability distribution. If the buyer is risk averse, then his willingness to purchase a particular product may be a function of more than just the first moment of the probability distribution (see Cox [1]).

The Supply of Advertising

Information about a product may be obtained from two sources: (1) by inspecting or using the product and (2) from external sources such as advertising, friends or or Consumer Reports. Most economists make the implicit assumption that a consumer's evaluation of a product after usage is independent of whether or not he or she has seen any advertising for the product (e.g. Nelson [6]). If this were true, then the only influence that advertising would have on the demand for a product would be the provision of information to non-purchasers of the product. After this information had been transmitted, advertising should have no effect on the demand for the product from current users or nonusers. Therefore, the advertising expenditures of frequently purchased products that have been on the market for a number of years should be low. The only effect that advertising could have for these types of products would be on new buyers entering the market or if forgetting occurs between purchases.

Empirical evidence, however, does not support this contention. Many frequently purchased products that have been on the market for a number of years have large advertising expenditures. Examples of these products include cigarettes, beer and soft drinks. If one wishes to maintain the assumption that advertising does not change utility functions, then the implication is that advertising is providing information that affects a consumer's evaluation of the product beyond that obtained through inspection, purchase and use of the product.

One possible interpretation is that much of this latter information is what is frequently called the "image" of a product. An example of this type of information is the amount of masculinity contained in a brand of cigarettes. Consumers purchase masculinity when they purchase this particular product, however, usage of the product without advertising will provide little or no information as to the amount of masculinity purchased. Since purchase and use provides little information with respect to these attributes, continual advertising is required to provide this information.

In this case, then, we can view a consumer's evaluation of a brand as the joint product of the actual physical product and its advertising. Consequently, advertising may add utility to the product. In some cases, advertising may develop prior expectations about a product so that after usage a consumer may evaluate a product differently than if no advertising would have been observed. This has recently been demonstrated empirically by Olson and Dover [7].

The previous discussion illustrates the difficulties in achieving a concensus view of the role of advertising in market behavior. Without taking a position on the "correctness" of any particular view, we believe it would be useful to examine whether these alternative approaches are likely to give rise to different market behavior. We propose to examine this issue with a simple model of two products with significantly different roles for advertising. Advertising for one product is assumed to supply the same information that would be obtained from inspection and use of the product. Thus, consumers who purchase the product are no longer affected by advertising. The second product is identical to the first except that advertising has a continuing affect on purchase behavior. Consequently, in this latter case, advertising contributes to consumer's evaluation of the product in a way which cannot be duplicated by purchase or actual use of the good. Obviously, these two types of information are polar characterizations that are selected to demonstrate how these differences will affect the behavior of firms. Most product advertising probably falls between these extremes. In the next section we present our model and derive implications for market behavior.

A SIMPLE MODEL

We want to illustrate via a simple model that the type of information advertised can influence market behavior of firms. We do this by distinguishing between two different types of products. The first type, which we term a "quality" product, can be evaluated perfectly by use. Thus the only purpose of firm advertising can be to induce a first purchase of the product. The second product type, which we term "image", cannot be evaluated perfectly by usage. In fact, we shall assume that usage provides no information to the consumer. This type of a product has

been called a "credence good" by Darby and Karni [2]. Advertising, therefore, is assumed to provide information not only relevant for first purchase, but all subsequent purchases as well. We recognize that this characterization is an extreme polarization. Most products, in fact, will have characteristics of both quality and image.

The critical difference between our image and quality product lies in the repurchase decision. Product usage will provide the consumer perfect information on the quality product eliminating all future need for advertising. Advertising, however, has a continuing role for the image product. This suggests that a multi-period model is necessary to examine product differences. In keeping with our goal of simplicity we propose a two period model of products identical in all respects except one is an image product and one a quality product. Each product is a new product produced and marketed by a firm viewed as either a monopolist or Cournot Oligopolist. The firm is assumed to face a known demand curve which is linear in the product's price and consumers' evaluation of the product. The firm produces the product at constant average cost and maximizes profits for two periods without discounting.

Consumers are assumed to have identical tastes and during each period purchase either one or zero units of the product. The representative consumer's probability of purchasing the product is assumed to be a linear function of their evaluation of the product and price. More explicitly,

$$PR_t = \theta H(A) - \Psi P_t$$

where the subscript $t = 1, 2$ denotes time period; PR is the probability of purchase; A is advertising; $H(A)$ is the consumer's evaluation of the product based on advertising information; P_t is the price; and θ and Ψ are fixed positive parameters.

In most situations, information from advertising will provide only imperfect information about a product. As mentioned previously, this uncertainty as to the amount of utility that a product will provide may take the form of a probability distribution. In these cases, $H(A)$, the consumer's evaluation of the product based on advertising information may be thought of as the certainty equivalent of this distribution. In other words, it is the expected utility of the product which has been discounted to take into account higher moments of the distribution.

The primary difference between the quality product and the image product occurs in the second time period. For the quality product, we assume that usage provides perfect information, which leads to an evaluation Q. In the second time period, therefore, the probability of purchase for a repeat purchase is assumed to be:

$$PR_2 | \text{purchase in period one} = \theta Q - \Psi P_2$$

where $\theta Q > \theta H(A)$ for all A. Thus perfect information is assumed to increase the probability of purchase. For the image product, the probability of purchase in period two will be independent of whether or not the product was purchased in period one.

The firm's decision variables are the number of advertising messages sent in periods one and two--A_1, A_2--and price in each of the two periods. We assume that each advertising message reaches a total market of N consumers, and that each advertising message costs N dollars. Each additional advertising message is assumed to increase a consumer's evaluation of the product since each additional message presumably provides more information. However, the incremental effect decreases because the consumer gets less information with each additional message. Consequently, increases in the number of advertising messages seen by a consumer increases the probability of purchase; however, with diminishing returns, i.e.

$$\frac{\partial PR_t}{\partial A_t} > 0, \quad \frac{\partial^2 PR_t}{\partial A_t^2} < 0$$

We now use this formulation to examine the differential effects on the market behavior of firms advertising either a quality or image product for two different cases. In the first case, no forgetting of the advertising information occurs between time periods. For the second case, forgetting of the advertising information occurs.

Case 1: No Forgetting

For the quality product, expected firm profits are the sum of expected sales for the two periods minus production costs, C, and advertising. Recalling that,

$$PR_1 = \theta H(A_1) - \Psi P_1$$

expected firm profits for the quality product are:

$$E(\pi_Q) = N[PR_1][P_1-C] + N[(PR_2|\text{purchase in period one})$$

$$PR_1 + (PR_2|\text{no purchase in period one})(1-PR_1)]$$

$$[P_2-C] - N[A_1+A_2]$$

$$E(\pi_Q) = N[PR_1][P_1-C] + N[\theta Q-\Psi P_2)PR_1 +$$

$$(\theta H(A_1+A_2) - \Psi P_2)(1-PR_1)]$$

$$(P_2-C) - N(A_1+A_2)$$

Notice that the middle term has two components -- the first, the probability of repurchase for a consumer who purchases the product in period one,

$$PR_2' = \theta Q - \gamma P_2.$$

The second, the probability of purchase for consumers who have not purchased in period one,

$$PR_2'' = \theta H(A_1+A_2) - \Psi P_2$$

with,

$$PR_2' > PR_2''.$$

Maximizing with respect to A_1, A_2, P_1, P_2 yields first order conditions,

$$\frac{\partial E(\pi_Q)}{\partial A_1} = \frac{\partial PR_1}{\partial A_1}[P_1-C] + \frac{\partial PR_1}{\partial A_1}[PR_2' + [1-PR_1]$$

$$- PR_2''][P_2-C] - 1 = 0$$

$$\frac{\partial E(\pi_Q)}{\partial A_2} = \frac{\partial PR_2''}{\partial A_2}[1-PR_1][P_2-C] - 1 = 0$$

$$\frac{\partial E(\pi_Q)}{\partial P_1} = PR_1 + [PR_2''-PR_2'][P_2-C]\gamma - [P_1-C]\gamma = 0$$

$$\frac{\partial E(\pi_Q)}{\partial P_2} = PR_1[PR_2'-PR_2''] + PR_2'' - [P_2-C]\gamma = 0$$

The following observations follow directly from the first

order conditions. First, $\frac{\partial E(\pi_Q)}{\partial A_1}$ and $\frac{\partial E(\pi_Q)}{\partial A_2}$ cannot both be

zero unless $\frac{\partial PR_2''}{\partial A_2} > \frac{\partial PR_1}{\partial A_1}$, which contradicts our assumption

of diminishing returns. Thus A_2 must be a corner solution, $A_2=0$. This makes obvious intuitive sense. If it pays to advertise, one should advertise in the first period where the payoff is two periods of purchase rather than one. Second, price in period two will be strictly greater than price in period one. This can be derived as follows. Since $PR_2'<PR_1'$, it follows directly from the third and fourth first order conditions that,

$$\gamma[P_2-C] > PR_2''$$

$$\gamma[P_1-C] < PR_1.$$

If $[P_2-C] \leq [P_1-C]$ this would imply $PR_2'' < PR_1$. Since there is no additional advertising in period two this could only happen if $P_2 > P_1$, which leads to a contradiction. Again this conclusion makes intuitive sense. It will pay the firm to lower price in period one to induce the consumer to purchase the product, which results in a higher probability of purchase in period two. This inducement is not present in period two. We speculate that in a multiperiod model price would monotonically increase over time, as the fraction of consumers who have not tried the produce would monotonically decrease. It is also interesting to speculate what would happen if the product were inferior, i.e., probability of repurchase lower for previous users, or the company lies in its advertising. It is now conceivable (though unlikely) that the firm would advertise in period two. It also follows that price will monotonically decrease over time.

The above model can also be applied to a product characterized entirely by image. Assume the same parameters, prior consumer uncertainty, product and advertising costs, but make one important change. Assume that product usage provides no information on the expected utility of the product. Thus the probability of purchase in period two will be independent of whether or not the product was purchased in period one. Denoting image by I, expected firm profits for the image product are:

$$E(\pi_I) = N[PR_1][P_1-C] + N[PR_2][P_2-C] - N[A_1+A_2],$$

where,

$$PR_1 = \theta H(A_1) - \Psi P_1$$

and,

$$PR_2 = \theta H(A_1+A_2) - \Psi P_2$$

Again first order conditions follow as:

$$\frac{\partial E(\pi_I)}{\partial A_1} = \frac{\partial PR_1}{\partial A_1}[P_1-C] + \frac{\partial PR_1}{\partial A_1}[P_2-C] - 1 = 0$$

$$\frac{\partial E(\pi_I)}{\partial A_2} = \frac{\partial PR_2}{\partial A_2}[P_2-C] - 1 = 0$$

24

$$\frac{\partial E(\pi_I)}{\partial P_1} = PR_1 - [P_1-C]\gamma = 0$$

$$\frac{\partial E(\pi_I)}{\partial P_2} = PR_2 - [P_2-C]\gamma = 0$$

Again note that $\frac{\partial E(\pi_I)}{\partial A_1}$ and $\frac{\partial E(\pi_I)}{\partial A_2}$ can both be zero only

if $\frac{\partial PR_2}{\partial A_2} > \frac{\partial PR_1}{\partial A_1}$ which violates the assumption of diminish-

ing returns to advertising. Thus again A_2 must be zero,
i.e., if it pays to advertise, do it in the first period.
The implications with respect to price, however, are
different than for the quality product. Suppose that
$P_1 > P_2$, this implies $PR_1 > PR_2$, since the contribution to
the probability of purchase from advertising is the same
in both periods this implies $P_1 < P_2$. A similar contradiction is reached if we assume $P_2 > P_1$. Thus price will
be the same in period one as period two. Again this is an
intuitive result since unlike the quality product, there
is no inducement to lowering price in period one.

Case 2: Complete Forgetting

The above model may be somewhat unrealistic in that consumers remember all advertising. It can be argued that
over time consumers, particularly those who did not purchase the product, are likely to forget at least a portion
of the information from advertising. Realistically, only
a portion of the information from advertising is likely to
be forgotten. To demonstrate the importance of information retention to our model, however, we shall examine a
model identical to model one in all respects, except that
all advertising is forgotten between periods. Product
usage, however, is still assumed to provide perfect information for the quality product.

The equation for expected profits for the image product is
identical to model one. First order conditions, however,
are somewhat different:

$$\frac{\partial E(\pi_I)}{\partial A_1} = \frac{\partial PR_1}{\partial A_1}[P_1-C] - 1 = 0$$

$$\frac{\partial E(\pi_I)}{\partial A_2} = \frac{\partial PR_2}{\partial A_2}[P_2-C] - 1 = 0$$

$$\frac{\partial E(\pi_I)}{\partial P_1} = PR_1 - [P_1-C]\gamma = 0$$

$$\frac{\partial E(\pi_I)}{\partial P_2} = PR_2 - [P_2-C]\gamma = 0 .$$

Solving first order conditions implies $P_1=P_2$ and $A_1=A_2$.
This is not surprising, as complete forgetting implies no
carryover from period to period. Thus the firm's optimal
behavior would be the same in period one as period two.

The expected profit equation for the quality product is
also identical to model one. First order conditions,
however, are different:

$$\frac{\partial E(\pi_Q)}{\partial A_1} = \frac{\partial PR_1}{\partial A_1}[[P_1-C] + [P_2-C][PR_2'-PR_2'']] - 1 = 0$$

$$\frac{\partial E(\pi_Q)}{\partial A_2} = \frac{\partial PR_2}{\partial A_2}[[1-PR_1][P_2-C]] - 1 = 0$$

$$\frac{\partial E(\pi_Q)}{\partial P_1} = PR_1 - [PR_2'-PR_2''][P_2-C] - \gamma[P_1-C] = 0$$

$$\frac{\partial E(\pi_Q)}{\partial P_2} = PR_2'' + PR_1[PR_2'-PR_2''] - \gamma[P_2-C] = 0$$

Solving for the first order conditions, surprisingly yields
ambiguous results. Intuitively, since advertising in
period two has an effect only on those who did not use the
product in period one, it seems logical that A_2 would be
less than A_1. Similarly since there is no price inducement
effect in period two, and period one users will value the
produce more highly, it also appears that P_2 should be
greater than P_1. We have tried several simple numerical
solutions and found that this intuitive result always
holds. It is possible, however for A_2 to be greater than
A_1 or (not both) P_2 to be less than P_1. A necessary
condition for A_2 to be greater than A_1 is that for a given
price, the probability of purchase with perfect information
(repurchase) be substantially larger than the probability
of purchase with imperfect information (no previous purchase). The intuitive explanation is that the significant
increase in purchase probability for the period one users
allows the firm to charge a substantially higher price in
period two, warranting a higher level of advertising. For
this effect to occur it is also necessary for the probability of purchase in period one to be very low. Extreme
conditions in the other direction, i.e., little gain to
perfect information and a high probability of purchase in
period one, can lead to P_2 being less than P_1. The normal,
and reasonable conclusion, however, is that P_2 will be
greater than P_1 and A_2 less than A_1. If we allow only
partial forgetting, A_2 will decrease and P_2 increase.

It is interesting to compare the image and quality product
markets. Given the same initial parameters, customer uncertainty and advertising response, the period one advertising for the quality product will unambiguously be
greater than the image market. Similarly, the price in
period one will unambiguously be lower for the quality
product. In period two, in the absence of the extreme
conditions cited above, advertising expenses will be lower,
and price higher for the quality product.

CONCLUSIONS

The results of this analysis suggest that the marketing
programs for new quality products will be characterized by
large initial marketing efforts--high levels of advertising
and lower prices. However, once a stable market has been
established, prices may be expected to rise and advertising
expenditures to substantially decrease. The marketing
programs for new image products should show stable prices
since there is no long term payoff to inducing purchase by
special price promotions. We would expect some reduction
in advertising over time, however maintenance advertising
to combat consumer forgetting would be higher than quality
product markets. We can also speculate on market behavior
if advertising were turned off. Since image product
"loyalty" is based solely on advertising, market share
would erode rapidly as consumers forget. For the quality
product, however, usage would provide continual affirmation

of a quality product's worth. Thus we would expect market share to depreciate more slowly in the absence of advertising.

REFERENCES

1. Cox, Donald (ed.), <u>Risk Taking and Information Handling in Consumer Behavior</u>, Boston: Graduate School of Business Administration, Harvard University, 1967.

2. Darby, Michael and Edi Karni, "Free Competition and the Optimal Amount of Fraud," <u>The Jounal of Law and Economics</u>, 16 (April, 1973), 67-88.

3. Fishbein, Martin, "A Consideration of Beliefs and Their Role in Attitude Measurement," in Martin Fishbein (ed.), <u>Readings in Attitude Theory and Measurement</u>, New York: John Wiley and Sons, Inc., 1967, 389-400.

4. Fishbein, Martin and Icek Ajzen, <u>Belief, Attitude, Intention and Behavior</u>, Reading, Mass.: Addison-Wesley, 1975.

5. Lancaster, Kevin, <u>Consumer Demand: A New Approach</u>, New York: Columbia University Press, 1971.

6. Nelson, Phillip, "Advertising as Information," <u>Journal of Political Economy</u>, 81 (July/August, 1974), 729-754.

7. Olson, Jerry and Philip Dover, "Cognitive Effects of Deceptive Advertising," <u>Journal of Marketing Research</u>, 15 (February, 1978), 29-38.

8. Rosenberg, M. J., "Cognitive Structure and Attitudinal Affect," <u>Journal of Abnormal and Social Psychology</u>, 53 (November, 1956), 367-372.

9. Stigler, George and Gary Becker, "De Gustibus Non Est Disputandum," <u>The American Economic Review</u>, 67 (March, 1977), 76-90.

COMMENTS ON THREE PAPERS ON "THE EFFECT OF INFORMATION ON MARKET BEHAVIOR"

George H. Haines, Jr., University of Toronto

PREFACE

The first comment is one of information. There exists a large and possibly enlightening literature on Optimal Search in the Management Science-Operations Research literature which someone ought to look at sometime. A reasonable starting place, for example, might be Bernard O. Koopman, "Search", pp. 40-83 in Notes on Operations Research: 1959, The Technology Press, Massachusetts Institute of Technology, 1959.

This fulfills the mandatory obligation of a discussant to present a relevant reference not given in any of the papers. Having done this, it is appropriate to move on to a discussion of substance.

WHAT IS INFORMATION?

There seems to be a bit of a tradition to be very careful never to define clearly what information is. The same tradition, incidentally, appears to exist among people interested in "management information systems".

All the same, it seems reasonable to inquire whether what is being studied can be defined. For example, Jacob Marschak defined it this way: "A purposive processing chain is often called an information system, the word information presumably bearing some relation to transformations from and into symbol sets" [20]. George W. Ernst and Allen Newell state: "The representation of an object is given by a set of information units. Each information unit has the same generic form: a Boolean function of several arguments (in most cases two). The arguments can be atomic constants-either symbolic or numeric. An argument can also be a feature of an object, which is a function whose domain is objects and whose range is values... An example of an information unit is the number of missionaries at the left bank of the river equals 3.

In this information unit,

    the Boolean function is "equals"
    the feature is "the number of missionaries at the left"
    the atomic constant is "3".

This information unit represents the fact that there are three missionaries at the left bank of the river in the object [7]". This point of view appears to assert that information is concerned with the representation of reality.

Once upon a time a working definition of information was put forward as:

"information is a preliminary concept of a product that induces a consumer to decide to (1) alter his or her decision process for the relevant product category, or (2) if the product category is one the consumer had not previously bought, construct a decision process" [11]. However, it seems appropriate to point out that if information is a means to the representation of reality, then there must be a more general definition than one which deals merely with consumption decisions. One such definition is: "When data are processed and encoded into a symbol, the raw data have been converted into information" [12]. Although this is an improvement, it is still not utterly satisfactory, for it is only in context that one can clearly understand that these symbols were meant to be a representation of reality. One custom has been to display descriptive studies of how

people represent reality symbolically in terms of a decision tree, although it would be entirely inappropriate to say that this is the "best", or even a completely satisfactory, method for reporting such data.

Where does all of this lead? Let us suspend judgment temporarily and grant that information is the symbolic representation of reality, and such symbolic representation is often undertaken to enable decisions to be made. (It may, of course, also be undertaken for artistic purposes, but I take these sorts of goals as beyond the range of the present discussion.)

The first thing that is immediately clear is that much of what is labelled the "economics of information" is not that at all. Rather, it is the "economics of data". The traditional economic model of man models man's or soman's representation of reality for consumption purposes in terms of revealed preferences, or, what is equivalent, a utility function. Data from the task environment in the form of prices and self-knowledge of income, are then used, in conjunction with this representation of reality, to make consumption decisions. Only if prices enter the utility function could it be said that a study of price data relates to the information a consumer uses in making consumption decisions. Yet the tradition in some parts of the "economics of information" has been to fail to make this distinction clearly.

Thus, for example, it is quite customary to assume people have fixed, stable, and transitive preference orderings. When this is done the problem or at least most of it, has been assumed away. What is left is the study of the "economics of data". This assumption says, in effect, that people have complete information. They may not have complete data. So the economics of data are studied: how best to acquire the data required, given complete information (i.e., an entirely adequate representation of reality), so as to be able to make "optimal" decisions. Optimal is placed in quotes to indicate there are a substantial variety of assumptions that can be make in constructing the resulting optimization model. The preceding papers give a representative overview of the methodology and technology for studying this problem.[1] The issue really is: why is the state-of-the-art such that a restricted subproblem is focussed on? Therefore, this paper will review first, why the study of the economics of information is difficult, and then a little bit of what is known about it. Under "what is known about it" whall be placed two headings: an extremely brief review of models designed to remove the central difficulty, and then a review of what is known about the economics of the representation of reality.

Why is it difficult?

One argument for the central reason why so many people have worked so hard on the economics of data rather than the economics of information rests in the need for an analytical framework. It has been well known in economics, ever since Basmann's thesis and perhaps well before that, that

_____

[1]Steven Salop, "Parables of Information Transmission in Markets;" Gerard R. Butters, "The Economic Analysis of Advertising." Robert B. Avery and Andrew A. Mitchell, "Information, Uncertainty and Advertising Effects."

if arbitrary shifts in a consumer's utility function occur,
it is in general impossible to make any predictions about
consumer behavior in the framework of the traditional economic theory of consumer behavior [2, 10]. This simply
means the theory is totally inapplicable to such a situation. Alas, it provides no guidelines as to what to do a-
bout it! The classical response to all this has been to
assume such arbitrary shifts do not occur. The problem with
this response is that it ignores what happens in reality.
For example, a lot of advertising (not all) has as its goal
achieving such arbitrary shifts. Whether this is generally
accomplished is another matter, but we all know fairytales,
such as Hathaway Shirts, which describe its occurrence.
The reason for this problem is the weak measurement properties assumed in the traditional economic theory of consumer
behavior. This theory assumes that an external observer
can only measure the consumer's information ordinally.

Another difficulty, of course, is the assumption of a fixed
number of choice alternatives. The traditional economic
theory of consumer has no very satisfactory way of handling
the introduction of Oranges into an economy where they were
previously unknown. Cross sectional applications, however,
avoid this problem.[2]

WHAT ABOUT THESE DIFFICULTIES

A sensible response is to strengthen the measurement properties. Von neumann-Morgenstern utility is one example:
it not only assumes utility can be measured on an interval
scale, it also provides a constructive method for actually
doing so. From this, indeed, has sprung one sub-brand of
the "economics of information", exemplified by the Economic
Theory of Teams [21]. The requirements for such measurement are quite strict. It is not difficult to find situations where it is not possible to construct von neumann-
Morgenstern utilities. These situations arise because such
utilities require transitive preferences for their construction [19, 21, 23]. Therefore, some researchers next proposed even stronger measurement properties: ratio-scale
measurement of consumer utility (or, if you prefer, infor-
mation-for remember we have agreed that information is the
symbolic representation of reality, measured by what is
called utility). This line of research is associated with
Kuehn's parameterization of Luce Choice Axiom, and much of
the early research on it was done at Carnegie-Mellon University [17, 18]. This has become one of the standard models of markets and consumer behavior in the tool kits of
marketers.

A second approach, based on interval scaled measures of attitudes, has also been widely studies in marketing. This
goes under the Fishbein-Rosenberg two component model name
and appears to have some promise [22]. Much of the work to
date has been methodological: developing reasonble measurement techniques. The promised land, in terms of understanding information and its effects using this theoretical
approach, is still in the future.

One last approach has been to directly study, via collection
of protocols and human information processing, consumer decision making. This approach also has some merits and difficulties. Since these problems and promises have been
discussed elsewhere, this paper will not review them [13].

THE UNASKED QUESTION - AND WHAT IS KNOWN ABOUT IT

The simplest way of stating the unasked question is: are
peoples preferences for alternatives transitive? The reason for calling this an unasked question is simply to describe the state of the research. Before presenting some
empirical evidence, however, it is useful to pause a moment
and consider the matter theoretically. Since Dr. Salop has
utilized the statistical decision theory framework in his
paper I shall use it also to exemplify the basic paradox.
The basic paradox is that if we assume "individuals rationally choose from a complete and transitive set of preferences", then we are assuming individuals are utterly irrational [23].

This is so because the "first" thing one learns from statistical decision theory is that a rational decision maker
will not collect data unless the expected benefits from doing so exceed the expected costs. Since statistical decision theory is normative in nature, this paradox is no
problem. If a decision maker finds it is not rational to
have complete information in the form of a representation
of reality that will allow a utility function to be defined
then statistical decision theory is simply not an appropriate tool for making decisions. Now, of course, some
people have argued that statistical decision theory is a
positive theory. However, there seem to possibly be difficulties in arguing that "everyone should have white skin
because it is to your advantage to have white skin". The
simple fact, from a theoretical point of view, is that in
general it is irrational for people to pay the costs of
having such complete information that they "choose from a
complete and transitive set of preferences". Therefore,
what exists in the literature is a discussion of "rational"
decision making by irrational people.

But, of course, a theoretical argument may be factually incorrect if the premises are in error. Therefore, it is of
some interest to ask whether there exist any empirical
studies of the matter.

A Review of Empirical Studies

The first empirical study I am aware of was that of A.Y.C.
Koo in 1963 [15]. Koo, using panel data, studied 215 households, using 13 major food groups as the consumption alternative. 0.93% (2 out 215) had transitive preference orderings for the 13 major food groups. Koo also developed a
procedure for finding the "maximal consistent subset"; applying this, he found that there did exist a subset of the
13 alternatives for which a transitive preference ordering
existed for all households. The subset size ranged from 4
alternatives to 12.

A second empirical study done by myself and William S.
Whittaker dealt with attributes of careers. The percentage
of respondents with transitive preference orderings in this
study varied from 90% to 80% depending on the attribute
[25].

Finally, a third empirical study done by Dan Greeno and myself, using data collected during the act of consumption,
found that, in the 1973 data, 63% percent of the respondents had transitive preferences for modes of travel between cities. When the survey was repeated in 1975, 74%
percent of the respondents had transitive preferences for
the four modes of travel between cities investigated [9].

Probably not a great deal can be said from four studies,
except that it is clear not all people have transitive preferences all the time.

---

[2]The example of Oranges is taken from Duncan Ironmonger [14], who dates the existence of data on a commercial
market for Oranges in the United Kingdom from 1854.

WHAT IS KNOWN ABOUT THE ECONOMICS OF
THE REPRESENTATION OF REALITY

One might inquire whether people could have stable intransitive preferences. What horrible fate might befall a person so inconsiderate as to have incomplete information, and therefore intransitive preferences? The truth, sad to say, is that the fate of such a person does not appear to be very horrible. Such a person is merely doomed to have the order in which alternatives are presented affect his or her choices. This is hardly a terrible fate; indeed, it can be argued it is desirable to keep lifes little incidents, such as purchasing a bag of frozen peas, interesting.[3]

Therefore, it seems of some interest to inquire whether inconsistency of preferences affects consumer search. Here one moves into uncharted waters, so the study to be reported should be prefaced with a plea of humility. First, it should be said that this work was co-authored with William S. Shittaker, who should receive credit for any virtue it has.

Let us suppose, for the sake of argument, that intransitivities arise from incomplete information, and that consumers actually desire (if the perceived cost-benefit ratio is favorable) to be able to choose from alternatives for which a well defined preference ordering exists. This may not be very likely, but lets pretend. Then the existence of intransitivities would lead the decision maker to seek data which is convertible into information in an effort to resolve the intransitivities into a transitive preference ordering.

It should be noted that psychological consistency theory would also lead to this conclusion under certain conditions [8]. This would be the case when people engaged in choice behavior are uncertain as to their preferences.

While this may seem a straightforward proposition, the methodological problems involved in empirically testing this proposition are formidable. People may be uncertain about alternatives because they have no way of evaluating the relative merits of the choice available to them (the rat, having free will, may refuse to even attempt to go through the maxe), or, more importantly, beacuse it might be very rational for them to be either uncertain and/or intransitive.

People might be inconsistent because the phenomena, within the cognitive framework of the individual, is perceived as irrelevant or because the individual has never considered the phenomena within his or her cognitive framework. Under both circumstances there are no motivating tensions caused by the inconsistency to warrant undertaking activities designed to reduce the tension. The experiment to be reported was designed to attempt, however, to avoid these potential difficulties by choice of a choice problem perceived by the experimenters to be relevant, and one which was known to have been considered before by the subjects.

Method

The Braustein Career and Organization preferences scale was administered to an entire entering freshman class at the University of Rochester [5]. This instrument uses paired comparison scaling. It asks the respondent to choose

between a pair of alternatives, and to repeat this decision process for a series of all possible pairs of alternatives to be compared. The respondent also indicates a rank order of importance of criteria. There are ten criteria, rated for five occupations and for five different types of organizations.[4]

A random sample of 73 students was then offered an opportunity to purchase additional information about the careers and organizations covered in the Braunstein Career and Organization preference scale. Twenty-one of the 73 students responded to this opportunity positively. The students rank-ordered the careers and/or organizations they would like to receive information about on the response sheet. The original experimental design included a final phase of making up packets on information and offering them at different prices to the responding students. This last part of the experiment was never performed, however, as research funds necessary to do it were not available.

Analysis

The Koo-Dobell procedure was applied to the organizational preferences of each of the 73 students on the criteria they ranked first and second in importance [6, 16]. These would be the criteria which would really matter if importance were a measure of what attributes really mattered [17]. Unfortunately, it is not clear that this is the case. There is evidence that importance may also measure social norms and/or order effects in the process of decision making (that is, the "most important" criteria may be the one which is applied first to discard clearly irrelevant alternatives) [5].

Therefore, the Koo-Dobell [6, 16] procedure was also applied to the salary criteria.[5] There are good reasons, in terms of economic theory, to expect this criteria to have an influence on career choice [25]. Fifteen subjects stated that salary was either the first or second most important criteria. All other subjects listed other criteria as first and second in importance.

Each subject, based on the Koo-Dobell procedure, was classified as having either a transitive or an intransitive ordering.[6] Since the Braunstein Career and Organization preference scale uses only five different organization types, and any intransitive preference ordering involves at least three, no attempt was made to see if there existed a transitive subset.

The hypothesis stated above would predict that a higher proportion of those students whose preference ordering was intransitive would request information than of those students whose preference was transitive.

The data from the experiment are presented in Table 1. Table 2 presents similar data, combining the three responses. If a subject was intransitive in either his or her first criterion, his or her second criterion, or his or her salary criterion, then the respondent is classified as intran-

---

[3] I am indebted to Steven Salop, for pointing out that in any market where the potential buyer haggles or bargains with potential sellers over prices, a consumer with intransitive preferences can expect, sooner or later, to be taken advantage of by the seller. In such markets, of course, there is then a greater economic incentive for transitivity than in markets where there is a fixed (in a market period sense) price.

[4] Discussion of another application of this instrument may be found in [4].

[5] The salary criteria was "you would earn the highest salary". This criteria, as well as the other nine, was added to the following pair of questions: "On your first job in which [type of organization] do you think [criteria]"; "On your first job doing which [type of job] do you think [criteria]." [5, p. 381].

[6] This preference ordering might also be called an "information subset". The reader might prefer this terminology, because the subjects were sevrral years away from actually having to make a choice.

sitive in Table 2. The basis for this is the possibility that more than one criteria might enter in the decision, and that any intransitivity might cause the person to seek further information.

TABLE 1

Most Important Criteria

Entries indicate number of subjects in each category

	Respond to Offer	
	Yes	No
Transitive	20	45
Intransitive	1	7

Second Most Important Criterion

	Respond to Offer	
	Yes	No
Transitive	14	46
Intransitive	7	6

Salary

	Respond to Offer	
	Yes	No
Transitive	15	43
Intransitive	6	9

TABLE 2

Logical "Or", All Three Criteria

Entries indicate number of responses in each category

	Respond to Offer	
	Yes	No
Always Transitive	10	33
Intransitive at least once	11	19

The data were analyzed using the normal test for the difference between two percentages [3]. The null hypothesis is no difference in proportion requesting information exists between the transitive and intransitive groups. The proportion intransitive is subtracted from the proportion transitive; thus the alternate hypothesis (which is not numerically specifiable) is a large negative value of the test statistics.

Results

The test statistics are given in Table 3.

TABLE 3

Case	Normal Test Statistics	Significance Level
First Criterion	1.08	——
Second Criterion	-2.20	.0139
Salary	-1.08	.14
Logical "Or"	-1.25	.105

The First Criterion results would tend to indicate that transitive subjects, rather than intransitive ones, tend to seek information. The Second Criterion results strongly to support the theory; the Salary and Logical "Or" results tend to support the theory, but not as strongly.

OVERVIEW

Information was defined as the symbolic representation of reality, where the symbols results from the processing and encoding of data. The implications of this definition were then discussed.

It was argued that because information is not te be a free good, it is then in general not rational for a consumer to necessarily have a transitive set of preferences. This argument was supported by results from four empirical studies which showed that not all people have transitive preferences all the time. Finally, the issue of whether intransitivity of preferences affects information search was explored by presenting some experimental data. The results indicate that it may be possible that indeed people would be more likely to seek additional data if they have intransitive preferences. A detailed discussion of the experiment was presented in the hope that future work could be done avoiding some of the problems of this first, exploratory, study.

REFERENCES

1. Banks, Seymour. "The Relationship Between Preference and Purchase of Brand" Journal of Marketing, 14 (Oct., 1950), 145-157.

2. Basmann, R.L. Application of Several Econometric Techniques to a Theory of Demand with Variable Tastes, Iowa State College, Ames, Iowa: PhD Thesis, 1955.

3. Braunstein, Daniel N. and George H. Haines, Jr. "Preference Scaling of Careers and Organizations" Journal of Applied Psychology, 52 (October, 1968), 380-385.

4. Braunstein, Daniel N. and George H. Haines, Jr. "Student Stereotypes of Business" Business Horizons, XIV (February, 1971), 73-80.

5. Bryan, Joseph G. and George P. Wadsworth. Introduction to Probability and Random Variables, New York: McGraw-Hill, 1967, Ch. 9.

6. Dobell, A.R. "A Comment on A.Y.C. Koo's 'An Empirical Test of Revealed Preference Theory'" Econometrica, 33 (April, 1965), 451-455.

7. Ernst, George W. and Allen Newell. GPS: A Case Study in Generality and Problem Solving, New York: Academic Press, 1969, p. 93.

8. Feldman, S. Cognitive Consistency, New York: Academic Press, 1966.

9. Greeno, Dan W. and George H. Haines, Jr. "Predicting Product Choice Behavior From Attitudes," Working Paper, University of Toronto, Faculty of Management Studies, June, 1976.

10. Haines, George H. Jr. Consumer Behavior: Learning Models of Purchasing, New York: Free Press, 1969, Ch. 1

11. Haines, George H. Jr. "Information and Consumer Behavior," in Jagdish N. Sheth, ed., Models of Buyer Behavior: Conceptual, Quantitative, and Empirical, New York: Harper and Row, 1974.

12. Haines, George H. Jr. "A Prologue to Four Papers on Information Search," in G. David Hughes and Michael L. Ray, eds., Buyer/Consumer Information Processing, Chapel Hill: University of North Carolina Press, 1974, p. 17.

13. Hughes, David G. and Michael L. Ray, eds., Buyer/Consumer Information Processing, Chapel Hill: University of North Carolina Press, 1974, esp. Part I.

14. Ironmonger, Duncan S. New Commodities and Consumer Behavior, Cambirdge: Cambridge University Press, 1972, p. 139.

15. Koo, Anthony Y.C. "An Empirical Test of Revealed Preference Theory," Econometrica, 31 (October, 1963), 646-663.

16. Koo, Anthony Y.C. "Reply" Econometrica, 33 (April, 1965), 456-458.

17. Kuehn, Alfred A. "A Model for Budgeting Advertising," pp. 315-348 in Bass, F.M. et. al., eds., Mathematical Models and Methods in Marketing, Homewood: Richard D. Irwin, 1961.

18. Kuehn, Alfred A. and Doyle L. Weiss. "Marketing Analysis Training Exercise" Behavioral Science, 10 (Jan., 1965), 51-67.

19. Luce, Duncan R. and Howard Raiffa. Games and Decisions: Introduction and Critical Survey, New York: John Wiley and Sons, 1957, Ch. 13.

20. Marschak, Jacob. "Economics of Information Systems," Working Paper No. 153, Western Management Science Institute, University of California, Los Angeles, November, 1969, p. 2.2.

21. Marschak, Jacob and Roy Radner. Economic Theory of Teams, New Haven" Yale University Press, 1972.

22. Mazis, Michael B., Olli T. Ahtola, and R. Eugene Klippel. "A Comparison of Four Multi-Attribute Models in the Prediction of Consumer Attitudes" Journal of Consumer Research, 2 (June, 1975), 38-51.

23. Pollay, Richard W. "Only the Naive Are Transitive Decision Makers" Journal of Business Administration, 2 (Fall, 1970), 3-8.

24. Whittaker, William S. and George H. Haines, Jr. "A Search for an Explanation of Consumer Search," Working Paper, University of Rochester, Graduate School of Management, 1971.

25. Wilkinson, R.W. "Present Values of Lifetime Earnings for Different Occupations" Journal of Political Economy, 74 (August, 1966), 556-572.

PART II: THE EFFECT OF INFORMATION ON CONSUMER BEHAVIOR

CONSUMER INFORMATION ACQUISITION AND
SEARCH STRATEGIES

James R. Bettman, University of California, Los Angeles

INTRODUCTION

The major purposes of this paper are to provide a framework for discussing the processes of consumer information
acquisition and to review the relevant research on consumer acquisition and search for information. The paper
is structured as follows: first, an overview and framework for considering information acquisition is presented.
This overview is followed by a general discussion of each
of the major aspects of information acquisition considered: internal search and external search. Then more
detailed considerations are examined: measures of information search, influences on the amount of internal
search and on the direction and degree of external search,
analyses of detailed patterns of information acquisition,
and a brief comparison of the consumer research and economic
views of search.[1]

A FRAMEWORK FOR EXAMINING CONSUMER
INFORMATION ACQUISITION

Acquisition of information is viewed at its most general
level. Information can be acquired by actively seeking it
while engaged in some choice process, or by being
confronted with it during the course of other activities,
as in television commercials [17]. Thus, information
acquisition is not synonymous with information search,
but includes information consumers obtain without actively
looking for it. Information search is further broken down
into two components: information sought from memory, or
internal search and retrieval; and information sought
through outside sources, external search.[2] A brief overview of the major phenomena involved in consumer information acquisition is now presented. The focus is first
on active search for information, and then information
acquisition without active search is briefly discussed.

In making a choice, the consumer examines relevant information in memory, and in some cases may acquire additional
information from the external environment (e.g., from
friends, salesmen, packages, advertisements) if the information in memory is not sufficient. In general, the
specific goals being pursued by the consumer will exert a
strong influence on the particular pieces of information
attended to and perceived. For example, if the consumer
has chosen a brand and is trying to decide where to buy
that brand, information about which retailers carry that
brand and their prices for it, store hours, and so on may
be sought. If, on the other hand, the consumer has not
chosen a brand, then information relevant to the evaluation of alternative brands may be sought.

It is proposed that information search generally begins
with internal search, with memory examined for relevant
information. The degree to which this internal search is
a conscious process varies with the type of choice being

considered. In choice situations where the consumer has a
great deal of experience, a simple habitual choice may be
made. In such a case, no information may be needed beyond
that necessary to actually implement the choice (e.g.,
recall of the brand name or recognition of the package),
and such implementation may be virtually automatic. Thus
the internal search process is essentially trivial in such
cases. However, for more complex choice situations, the
consumer may need to actively think about what is in memory, to exert more conscious processing effort.

As the consumer examines information in memory, that information may prove to be sufficient for the purposes at hand,
and no further search may be undertaken. However, in some
cases that information may not be sufficient. Several
pieces of information may conflict, information may be
lacking, and so forth. These phenomena are instances of a
more general concept, that of an interrupt [73]. Consumers do not usually pursue goals methodically and single-
mindedly, with no sidetracks or detours. Rather, consumers are distractable. If events require, or if something
interesting is noticed, consumers can and will interrupt
what they are doing and pursue other activities. Such
interrupts are often due to departures from expectations
(e.g., price changes, out of stock conditions, new brands,
conflicting information, "interesting" information) or
things which remind one of plans which had been temporarily
forgotten. Thus the major distinguishing feature of an
interrupt is that the flow of ongoing processing is temporarily disrupted, that what the individual was planning to
do has been momentarily sidetracked. Responses to interrupts can vary from deciding to ignore the interrupting
event after it has been noticed to stopping what one is
doing to consider the interrupt in more detail. Thus,
although the consumer's responses to such conflicts or lack
of information will vary, one major type of response to
insufficient or conflicting information is external search.

During external search, the consumer examines the environment to see if relevant information is available. Consumers, in general, use different detailed search patterns
and search for different amounts of information in different choice situations. Information acquired during
external search will lead to further internal search to
interpret or elaborate that information. Thus, there is a
continual cycling between internal and external search
processes. Interrupts due to conflicting information or
lack of information will also arise during external
search. Again, the consumer's reactions will vary, but
more external search may ensue. Eventually, of course, the
consumer will cease searching for information and make a
decision.

This proposed sequence of internal search possibly followed by external search applies only to cases where
information is actively sought. The consumer can also be
confronted with information, as in an overheard conversation, a billboard, or a television commercial, for
example. In general, consumers are continually learning
about their purchasing environments, even though such
learning may not be directly relevant to any current purchases. For example, a consumer may be generally aware of
which brands of appliances a discount store carries,
because he has noticed these brands while shopping in that
store for some other purchase. As another example, the
consumer may be aware, from seeing several newspaper ads,
that a certain store has the lowest price for a particular

---

[1]This paper is largely based upon Chapter 5 of the
author's book, An Information Processing Theory of Consumer Choice, to be published by Addison-Wesley.

[2]Engel, Kollat and Blackwell [21] also distinguish
between internal and external search. In addition,
Hansen [25] uses the term deliberation to refer to phenomena related to internal search, and the term exploration to refer to external search phenomena.

item, say an electronic calculator, even though the consumer is not actively in the market for a calculator. Such learning about the environment can arise in two basic ways. First, the consumer may learn about the environment through interrupts, when something happens to attract the consumer's attention because it "looked interesting." Thus the consumer may notice some piece of information and explore it further, even though it is not related to any current choice. This type of learning about the environment involves attention to the information once it is noticed.

A second basic type of learning about the environment may occur in cases where the consumer is devoting little active attention to the information presented. Krugman [38] has proposed that consumers learn about which attributes to consider and some other aspects of products through low involvement, essentially passive processes. The consumer may pay little attention to many television commercials, for example, but over time may learn some of what is in these commercials (see also [62]).[3]

The above discussion implies that decisions are made after all information deemed necessary has been gathered. That is too simplistic a view. Choice and information acquisition processes occur simultaneously. That is, as information is acquired, comparisons of alternatives and development of rules for selecting alternatives are being carried out as well.

This completes the presentation of the framework for viewing consumer information acquisition used in this paper. Figure 1 depicts the basic phenomena to be considered and lists some of the determinants of each. These phenomena are considered below, in broad terms at first and then in more detail.

Internal search refers to the acquisition of information that is available in memory. It is hypothesized that when faced with a choice to make, consumers, in general, first engage in internal search, examining memory for available information.[4] There are two aspects of internal search: direction and degree. The first aspect, direction of search, is concerned with which pieces of information are examined, and the second, degree of search, is concerned with how much information is sought. The direction of internal search is in large part determined by the particular goals currently relevant to the consumer, by what is useful for the choice at hand. Although what is in memory clearly depends upon the structure of the particular choice environment within which the consumer acts, the course of search through memory is more under the control of current goals and less directly influenced by choice environment structure. In addition to generally examining which pieces of information are sought from memory, one can also characterize details of the actual sequences of data retrieved during search, the patterns of memory search. The consumer's general strategies for searching memory would influence these patterns.

Various degrees of internal search are possible, ranging from virtually automatic responses in habitual choice situations to more extensive searches of what is in memory. In many cases, the initial internal search may not be exhaustive or comprehensive; the purpose of the search may be to ascertain what is not known, to provide a guide for external search. Then there may be cycles between external and internal search, as noted above. In general, it is proposed that the major determinants of the degree of internal search are the amount of information stored in memory; the

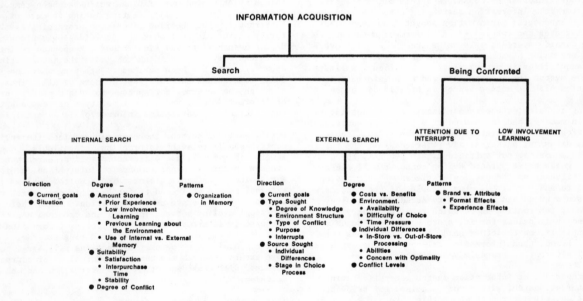

Figure 1

A Framework for Viewing Consumer Information Acquisition

[3]These learning about the environment phenomena have also been studied in psychology. For cases where active attention is involved, work in latent learning is relevant [29]. The low involvement, more passive cases have been considered in the literature on incidental learning [47,61], and spectator learning [60].

[4]In situations where the consumer has no prior knowledge, or where an interrupt has occurred (e.g., a commercial has just come on which caught the consumer's attention), then external search with little or no internal search may ensue.

suitability of that information or its usefulness for the current choice; and level of decision conflict.

In the course of internal search, interrupts may occur. Information may be found to be lacking, for example. The lack may not be recognized until some processing is done. For example, the consumer may discover that he cannot remember a price. In addition, conflict may be aroused in other ways during internal search. For example, if the consumer's weights for various attributes have changed since the last choice in a product class, and if previously preferred brands would not be preferred given these current attribute weightings, perceived conflict would increase. The consumer might not even be aware of this conflict until the actual internal search was performed. Finally, during the course of internal search, the consumer may be reminded of goals other than those relevant to the purchase being considered. Such interrupts may lead to restructuring of goals. Although responses to interrupts will vary in general, one major type of response to such interrupts arising during internal search is to form a goal for external search.

EXTERNAL SEARCH

External search is the acquisition of information from sources other than memory, such as friends, packages or other in-store displays, advertisements, magazines such as Consumer Reports, and so forth. External search is postulated to follow internal search. As mentioned above, internal search need not be complete to lead to external search. A brief internal search may suffice for the consumer to ascertain what is not known, or an interrupt of internal search due to a lack of information or conflict may lead to external search. Periods of external search, followed by internal search, then more external search, and so on, are probably typical. In many cases, however, the decisions to be made are trivial and habitual, and very little internal or external search may ensue for such choices where there is a great deal of prior knowledge and experience. As with internal search, both direction and degree aspects can be examined for external search, as can more detailed strategies for information acquisition.

As was the case for internal search, the influence of current goals is a major factor determining which pieces of information are sought by the consumer. That is, those pieces of information most useful for the current choice will be sought. Several influences other than current goals on the direction of external search can also be considered, such as prior experience or structure of the choice environment.

External search can be of varying degrees, as well as in different directions. The influences upon degree of search are numerous (e.g., costs vs. benefits of search, choice environment factors, individual differences, conflict), and the amount of research on these influences is substantial. External search is also subject to interrupts due to novel or surprising events, conflicting information, lack of information, and so on. Such interrupts may lead to further external search; some of the determinants of degree of search discussed below, particularly conflict and reactions to it, are relevant.

One final aspect which must be considered is the relationship between internal and external search, particularly with regard to the amount of search. The most simplistic conception is that internal and external search are compensatory, that the more is done of one, the less must have been done of the other. However, it is also possible that the degrees of search are positively correlated, that if one tends to do a good deal of internal search, one also tends to do a good deal of external search. The relationship found may depend upon level of conflict. It might be hypothesized that under low perceived conflict, internal

and external search would be compensatory. In high conflict choices, however, it may be that degree of internal and external search are positively, rather than negatively, correlated. The relationship would also presumably depend upon individual differences.

This completes the general characterization of internal and external search. Now we consider more detailed aspects of search: measures of search, influences on the amount of internal search engaged in, influences on the direction and amount of external search, and detailed patterns of information acquisition.

DETAILED ASPECTS OF INFORMATION ACQUISITION

Measures of Information Search

In order to examine influences on search, measures of the degree of search undertaken must be developed. This has proven to be a difficult undertaking. In one of the rare attempts to measure phenomena related to internal search, Hansen [25, p. 281] used the scale, "When faced with a problem of this kind, how carefully would you think that most people would consider the alternatives." This measure does not directly examine internal search, however, but deliberation, and includes several other aspects of prechoice processing in addition to internal search.

More work has been carried out in attempting to measure external search. Many measures of degree of external search have been used: number of stores visited, number of shopping trips, time spent, number of sources of information used, and so on [53]. Several studies have also combined scores on items such as those above to form an overall index. For example, Newman and Staelin [55] measured the number of kinds of information sought (e.g., for various attributes or stores), the number of sources of information consulted, and the number of retail outlets visited. They then combined these measures into an overall search index. Although such measures seem relatively straightforward, recent research has indicated that these measures may be suspect. Newman and Lockeman [53] measured degree of external search using both the typical survey methods described above and an unobtrusive in-store direct observational method for a sample of women's shoe buyers. They found very low correlations between the observational and survey measures, with the highest of eight such correlations being .12. In addition, the survey measures severely understated the amount of search actually observed. Future studies should thus be very careful in attempting to measure degree of external search. Standard survey techniques seem inadequate.[5] It should also be noted that measures of the sheer amount of search do not take into account that some consumers will be more efficient searchers than others. Thus, measurement of search is not an easy task, and is one that should receive more research.

As noted earlier, the relationship between the degree of internal and external search carried out is not clear. Partially due to the lack of measures for both processes, only one study has measured phenomena related to both internal and external search [25, p. 291]. Hansen found that the average amount of deliberation (related to internal search) was perfectly rank correlated with the average amount of external search over six situations varying in level of perceived conflict. Data on the correlation of the search and exploration indices within each conflict situation were not

---

[5]The information monitoring and eye movement techniques discussed in [4] provide measures of external search, but these techniques are not readily applicable for measuring search in actual choice environments.

reported. Also, as stated above, Hansen does not actually
measure internal search itself.

Influences on the Degree of Internal Search

Three general determinants of degree of internal search are
the amount of information stored in memory, the suitability
of that information for making the choice, and degree of
conflict. The greater the amount of stored information
[86], the more suitable that information is, and the
greater the degree of conflict (if not too high), the
greater the amount of internal search. Each of these
three factors is now examined in more detail. One difficulty in most of the research reported below is that internal search was not directly measured, so only indirect inferences can be attempted.

Amount of Stored Information. The more relevant information one has in memory, the greater the degree of internal search which can be undertaken. The amount of stored
information in memory reflects the degree of prior learning
relevant for the choice in question. There are several
sources of information in memory about a product class.
First, past purchase experiences in a product class may
lead directly to learning about criteria and/or alternatives. Bennett and Mandell [1] examined search behavior
for new car purchases and found that the number of previous
purchases of the same make as that eventually bought was
negatively related to the degree of external search. This
may imply a greater reliance on internal search. As noted
above, however, lower external search need not imply
higher internal search; unfortunately such indirect evidence is all that is available. Bennett and Mandell [1]
found, however, that the total number of previous purchases,
without regard to make purchased, was not related to
degree of external search. Thus, not all previous purchase experience is necessarily instructive.

A second source of information in memory is low involvement learning [38]. This is information with which the
consumer is confronted (e.g., in television commercials),
rather than information which is actively sought. Such
information, Krugman hypothesizes, would mainly affect
attribute saliences, or whether attributes come to mind
during the choice process.

A third source of information in memory is from previous
learning about the environment, or learning about the product class currently under consideration that has been
gleaned in previous situations where that product was not
itself being considered. Brands available and general
price levels for specific retail stores are among the types
of information which might be gathered in this manner.

Finally, the amount of information actually stored in memory as a result of prior experiences is influenced by an
individual differences variable, the degree of reliance upon in-store displays as an external memory [52]. That is,
a consumer may not remember items of information, but may
use the package or shelf tags while in the store. Thus,
these become an external memory, making efforts to remember data internally less crucial. Consumers undoubtedly
differ in terms of the degree to which they use the product
display in this manner. Some individuals may prefer to do
as much decision processing as possible outside of the
actual store, and hence would attempt to retain more information memory; others would prefer to process in the store
itself, and might retain less.

Thus there are four main sources of information stored in
memory: prior purchase experiences (including previous acquisition activities, word of mouth, etc.), previous low
involvement learning, previous learning about the environment, and the degree to which one uses internal (one's own
memory) as opposed to external (packages or lists) memory.
All of this stored information can of course be used by
consumers to generate new information by deduction or

inference.

Suitability of Stored Information. The sheer amount of information stored is not the only determinant of degree of
internal search. As pointed out above, for example,
Bennett and Mandell [1] showed that the total amount of
prior purchasing experience was not necessarily related to
degree of search. Another crucial determinant is the perceived suitability, appropriateness, or usefulness of the
stored information for the current decision [21, p. 377].
One factor influencing suitability is satisfaction with
previous purchases. Presumably, the more satisfactory
these purchases, the more relevant is one's stored information based upon past purchases. Newman and Staelin [54]
show that satisfied users take less time to make a decision. They also show in a later study [55] that buying
the same brand as before is associated with less external
search. Again, this evidence is only indirect about degree of internal search.

A second factor influencing suitability is length of interpurchase time. The longer the interpurchase time, the
greater the likelihood of forgetting relevant information.
In addition, the longer the interpurchase time, the greater the likelihood of changes in the mix of alternatives,
such as new brands or changes in price or other attributes.
Swan [78] found that more external search ensued when different mixes of brands were offered over time in his experiment than when the mix of brands remained the same. Also,
Krugman [38] hypothesizes that under low involvement learning, which attributes are salient can change. The longer
the interpurchase time, the greater the likelihood of such
switches in salience of attributes. These switches might
lead to the necessity for more external search if different
attributes than the consumer had previously considered are
of increased salience. Thus the two major determinants of
information suitability are satisfaction with previous
purchases and interpurchase time. Interpurchase time is
related not only to ease of remembering, but also to the
degree of stability one might expect in the choice
environment. To reiterate, the evidence for these assertions is only indirect, as internal search has not been
measured.

Degree of Perceived Conflict. Hansen [25, pp. 280-94]
found that the amount of deliberation (which may be related to internal search), as measured by a projective
question, was higher under higher perceived conflict.
Hansen also found somewhat weaker support for more external
search under high conflict.

Influences on the Direction of External Search

As noted above, the influence of current goals is a major
factor in understanding the direction of external search,
which specific information is sought. However, other
factors are relevant as well. In this section two areas of
research on the direction of external search are considered.
In one stream of research, different types of information
(e.g., how to weight criteria, attribute ratings, available
retail outlets) are sought, depending upon several factors; in the second stream, influences on which sources
(e.g., stores, mass media, friends, salesmen) of information are used is considered. Each of these streams is
now considered in turn.

Influences on Type of Information Sought. There are five
major classes of influences on the specific type of information to be sought: the amount and type of knowledge in
memory; the structure of the particular choice environment;
the type of conflict; the purpose for which the information
will be used; and the nature of interrupt events. Each of
these is now considered below. One factor which influences how useful a particular kind of information is relative to current goals is the degree of knowledge already
held about the product class being considered. If the consumer has little knowledge about a product class, then

Howard and Sheth [30] hypothesize that information that aids in weighting and assessing criteria for evaluating brands is most desired (this is their phase of extensive problem solving). Only after such criteria are developed is information on properties of alternatives gathered. However, this notion may be too narrow, as information on properties may help to shape the criteria.

If the consumer knows what criteria are to be applied, but does not know which alternative best meets these criteria (limited problem solving), then data on how the alternatives perform relative to the criteria would be sought. Howard and Sheth postulate that search aimed at developing plans (i.e., ascertaining criteria) can be separated from the search needed to implement those plans (i.e., comparing alternatives on the criteria). These processes to some extent will tend to go on in parallel, however, since determining what the attributes or criteria are for a product class often involves examining some set of alternatives. Finally, if the alternative desired is known (Howard and Sheth's routinized response behavior phase), the consumer may search for information about stores where that alternative is available (e.g., price levels, hours, locations, service capabilities).

The Howard and Sheth analysis thus provides some notions about what types of information are sought when knowledge about the product class due to prior experience is lacking. These notions may be too specific, however. In choice situations where the consumer has had little prior experience and has only broad, vague goals, the consumer may engage in a relatively general search for information relevant to the choice, in hopes that such information may later prove useful. In such a situation the consumer may not know at the time exactly how, or even if, the information will be used later [24]. The point is that, in general, the type of information sought depends upon what is already known.

A second factor influencing what type of information is sought is the structure of the particular choice environment, the relative availability of various kinds of information. For some product classes there may be only a few attributes and many alternatives, or vice versa. Particular alternatives may only be carried at one particular store. These features of the environment would limit search for various types of information. For example, if one desired to buy a particular make of automobile for which there was only one dealer in the area, search for a retailer would be trivial. On the other hand, in a large city, where usually many dealers for any particular make are available, the search for a dealer from whom the car should be purchased might be quite extensive.

In addition to these general factors of the task environment structure, there are factors specific to individual stores. Some consumers, as noted earlier, tend to rely on little prior planning, and keep little product information in memory. Instead, decision-making is done within the store, using the in-store display as an external memory and making only general plans a priori. This individual difference variable affects the degree of environmental influence on the type of information sought. For individuals who make decisions in the store itself, the type of data sought will be greatly influenced by the particular set of alternatives available. If few alternatives for a particular product class are available in the store, processing may tend to concentrate on more attributes, relative to alternatives, than if the store carried a wide assortment of brands.

The type of conflict occurring in a particular choice situation (e.g., approach-approach, approach-avoidance, avoidance-avoidance) is a third factor that influences the type of information sought. March and Simon [45, pp. 116-18] discuss these influences. Approach-approach conflicts, where a number of competing alternatives are desirable, should result in short decision times, with situational factors relating to what captures one's attention in the moment or order of presentation of alternatives influencing choice. Thus, little search would be performed; rather, some feature of the particular situation would tip the balance for one alternative or the other. For avoidance-avoidance conflicts, where alternatives are all relatively undesirable, the tendency would be to search for new alternatives. These alternatives might be other alternatives for the same product class choice, or alternatives to choice of the product class itself. For example, if a consumer is attempting to choose between two outfits for a baby present, neither of which is really liked, the consumer may decide to search for more outfits, perhaps at a different store, or decide to choose a toy instead of an outfit. March and Simon make no direct hypotheses about approach-avoidance conflicts.

A fourth influence on the type of information sought is the purpose for which the information will be used. Mazis [46] used a framework developed by Zajonc [89] to study this issue. Zajonc differentiated between transmission tuning, where a person expects to communicate to others; and reception tuning, where the individual expects to use the information himself. Earlier research [7, 12] had shown that receivers accepted more discrepant information than transmitters. Receivers tried to process as much information as they could to form an accurate impression, whereas transmitters structured the message to present it to others. Mazis manipulated the expectations of his subjects by telling "decision makers" they would be asked for an evaluation of a car after acquiring information and by telling "non-decision makers" they would communicate their impression of the car to another person who would then make an evaluation; Mazis also gave subjects control over how much familiar or novel information they sought. The results showed that "decision makers" chose significantly more novel information than "non-decision makers." Thus the task for which the information will be used affects what type of information will be gathered. This finding can also be applied to word of mouth: consumers who engage in word of mouth but do not intend to buy a product themselves may differ in the kinds of information they transmit from those consumers who both buy the product and transmit word of mouth.

Finally, a fifth influence on type of information examined is that interrupt events can lead to goals for external search. In general, the interrupting event itself provides the focus for which information would be examined (e.g., for an interrupt due to a novel stimulus, the initial focus is presumably on that stimulus and its surrounding context).

Influences on the Source from which Information is Sought. Consumers can choose varying mixes of sources of information: advertisements, in-store shopping for several brands, multiple store shopping for one brand, and so on. Several studies have examined aspects of these patterns. Two major factors appear which influence these patterns of sources sought: individual differences and stage in the choice process.

Several studies show that consumers display wide individual differences in the patterns of sources they consider. For example, Donnermuth [16] proposed that consumers could be classified by a two-fold classification scheme, number of brands considered and number of retail outlets shopped. By combining these two dimensions, he developed a "shopping matrix." Some consumers may shop in many stores for a single brand, others in one store for many brands, or some may consider both several stores and brands. In an empirical study using the matrix, Donnermuth found that in general there was little shopping across stores for one brand, but there was some amount of examination of many brands in one store for appliances. Many consumers visited one store and examined one brand; where more effort was expended, it usually led to consideration of both more brands and more stores.

Claxton, Fry, and Portis [11] examined patterns of information source usage, using a cluster analysis based upon three major variables: total number of sources used, number of stores visited, and total deliberation time (time from first consideration until purchase). Furniture buyers and appliance buyers formed two samples for their analyses. The results were similar in both cases. One group (roughly 5% of both samples) was labeled "thorough (store intense)." This group took a long time to decide, used many sources, and visited a very large number of stores. The second major group was labeled "thorough (balanced)," 44% of the sample for furniture and 27% for appliances. This group took a long time and used many sources, but only a moderate number of stores. There were two subgroups of this group, slow and fast. These subgroups are interesting, in that the slow group took more time but visited fewer stores, and the fast group was the opposite. This suggests trade-offs between deliberation over time and store visits, although Claxton, Fry and Portis point out that long decision time may simply indicate procrastination. Finally, the third main group, labeled non-thorough, was 34% of the sample for furniture and 65% for appliances. This group used few sources, made few store visits, and took less time. Again, subgroups were found based upon deliberation time.

These groupings were then related to other variables. Higher income and education were associated with thoroughness, as were price paid and concern with selecting the right product. Immediacy of need was related to lack of thoroughness, and existence of financial constraints with thoroughness. This research is important in emphasizing the idea of a multidimensional profile of search activities, rather than a single summary measure.

One final set of findings on source patterns is the temporal patterns of source usage found in innovation research. Rogers [63] states that mass media sources are most used during the earlier awareness and interest stages of adoption, whereas word-of-mouth communication is most used during later evaluation and trial stages. Kohn Berning and Jacoby [37] reviewed the evidence for this proposition and found mixed support. They then applied a new methodology to study this issue. Five product categories were selected and subjects were asked to select a brand from a set containing both "old" and "new" (recently introduced) alternatives for each category (actual brands were used). Information of five types could be obtained: 1) ads; 2) price; 3) package information; 4) comments attributed to "friends"; and 5) comments attributed to sales personnel. This information was available on index cards which could be selected by the subjects in any order desired. When the subject was ready to choose a brand, she stopped searching the available information and made her choice. There were no limits set on degree of search. The findings showed that innovators (those who chose a new brand) selected more information than non-innovators, mostly attributable to greater use of the "friends" cards. Also, it was found that more personal information was acquired in later portions of the total card sequence, supporting Rogers [63].

Influences on the Degree of External Search

Many factors influence the amount of external search performed by the consumer. The major determinants of the degree of external search are now presented, followed by a summary of the research related to each determinant.

Costs vs. Benefits of the Information. A common notion, developed from economic theories of search (discussed further in a later section), is that consumers weigh the costs of obtaining information against the benefits which might be expected from using that information. Although the trade-offs implied by rational theories of search [75] may not be made in such an optimizing fashion, there is evidence that consumers do heuristically consider costs and benefits. Costs of search may include time and effort, money, frustration and other psychological costs, and delay of the decision [21, p. 380]. Benefits might include increased satisfaction with the purchase or psychological benefits such as feeling one did a thorough job. The consumer must assess whether the information is beneficial. Finally, note that one form of search is to simply _buy_ the product and try it. For low cost products, the costs versus benefits of this strategy may be appealing.

Several models exist which are related to costs versus benefits of search. Burnkrant [9] proposes and presents a preliminary test of an expectancy-value model which focuses on benefits from a source of information. In particular, need for information on a topic, expectancy that processing a stimulus will lead to information on that topic, and the value of that information on the topic determine search tendency. Literature is reviewed which supports the notion that more useful information is preferred, regardless of whether or not it is supportive of the individual's beliefs. In preliminary research testing the theory, Burnkrant found only an effect due to need for information. Feather [22] presents evidence for a different expectancy-value model which focuses on seeking consistency and avoiding inconsistency.

These two expectancy-value models, although considering elements of a costs versus benefits approach, do not provide complete examples of that approach. Pollay [58, 59] presents an explicit Bayesian model of costs versus benefits related to decision time. This model predicts that if difficulty of discriminating alternatives is high, decision time will shorten, as the higher costs of processing will outweigh the benefits at an earlier time. This notion is partially borne out by Pollay's studies and those of Kiesler [36] and Hendrick, Mills, and Kiesler [27].

Other empirical work has focused on the components of the cost-benefits model, particularly the cost component. Lanzetta [40] and Lanzetta and Kanareff [42] found that as cost of information increased, less information was purchased. Bucklin [8] found that lower shopping costs (as inferred from the geography of the area where shopping was done) were related to greater external search of stores. Swan [79] found that if trying a brand were the only means of gathering information, a greater cost for switching brands led to less switching and hence less search. Lutz and Reilly [44] found that in purchase situations where perceived risk was low, and hence costs of search relative to benefits might be high, the subjects' stated preferences were for simply buying and trying a brand rather than seeking information from other sources. Green [23] reported similar results. Finally, Winter [85] found that greater search ensued if subjects had no attractive alternative task to search behavior (and hence opportunity costs were lower).

Some work has also been done relative to benefits from search. Swan [78] found that if subjects received payoffs only if optimal rather than satisfactory choices were made, search increased. In his study, benefits were thus directly related to search. Donnermuth [16], Bucklin [8], and Katona and Mueller [35] found consumers searched more for higher priced products. Also, Claxton, Fry and Portis [11] showed that the presence of financial constraints for a consumer implied more search. If finances are tight, presumably cost savings (a benefit) are more important, and search may be seen as potentially leading to cost savings.

Finally, there is work which suggests that costs and benefits are weighed against each other. Lanzetta [40] and

Driscoll and Lanzetta [18] found that search continued until uncertainty was reduced to a certain level, when a decision was made. Lanzetta [40] calls this a "commitment threshold." Hansen [25] postulates that conflict will either be reduced to a tolerable level, or search will stop when the conflict generated in choosing search alternatives is greater than the product choice conflict. These notions imply that there is a point below which it simply is not worth the effort to further reduce uncertainty or conflict, indirectly supporting the notion that perceived benefits and costs are weighed against one another.

Choice Environment Factors. Since humans adapt their behavior to reach goals, and goals are sought in particular choice environments, the characteristics of the choice environment may greatly influence the amount of information search. This influence of the shopping environment will be more potent for external search than for internal search. In general there are three major properties of choice environments considered below: availability of information, difficulty of the choice task, and time pressure.

The first major influence, availability, is to be taken in its most general sense. That is, availability refers not only to whether the information actually exists, but whether it is more or less accessible. One obvious influence on amount of search is how much information exists in the choice environment. If there is little or no information relevant to a consumer's goals, extended search is not possible. The consumer may need to modify goals for search, change his acceptable level of conflict, postpone the purchase, and so on. All of these involve modification of some goal. Even if there is a great deal of information, it may not be in the form desired by the consumer. For example, there may be many alternatives, each with values for several attributes, but no information relevant to determining which criteria or attributes should be used to evaluate alternatives; or there may be much information relevant to determining criteria, but few available alternatives. If the consumer wants information on criteria in the former case and on alternatives in the latter, then even though there is information available, it is not the type needed, and thus search would be reduced.

A second choice environment factor influencing degree of search is difficulty of the choice task. Two types of research are relevant here: research related to how easy the information itself is to process, and research related to the sheer amount of information presented, the information load. Ease of processing is heavily impacted by the format utilized for presenting information. Information may be present, but in a form in which consumers cannot process it effectively. This would lower information search. Russo, Krieser, and Miyashita [66] show that the lack of use of unit price information may be due in part to the difficulties inherent in processing such information as it is typically presented. By changing the mode of presentation to make the unit price information more processable, usage (and hence external search, presumably) increased.

Another aspect related to the difficulty of the choice task is the amount of information available. Typical measures of amount of information available used in consumer research are the total number of brand alternatives available and the number of attributes given for each alternative. Several researchers have argued that as task difficulty (measured in this case as the total amount of information, or information load) increases, there will first be increases in search, but then eventually decreases as too high an information load is imposed. Studies reporting such an 'information overload' include Schroder, Driver, and Streufert [68], Streufert, Suedfeld, and Driver [76], and Sieber and Lanzetta [72].

However, not all researchers find that search eventually declines as load increases. Lussier and Olshavsky [43],

for example, in a design which included up to twelve brands with fifteen attributes per brand, found that the number of pieces of information referenced increased as the numbers of attributes and brands increased. These conflicting results are difficult to reconcile. However, Seibel, Christ, and Teichner [69] present results supporting the notion that high input rate in itself is not the crucial factor. Rather, the factor limiting performance is if a high rate of internal processing is required. Thus, the more complex the manipulations required for a set of data in some fixed time span, the greater the potential for an information overload. In several types of consumer situations (e.g., where the in-store display may be used as an external memory or where the consumer is reading print advertisements) the time available for processing and hence the rate of internal processing can be controlled by the consumer, and processing can be done at a more leisurely rate. The sheer amount of information may not be a crucial factor, since consumers can select subsets of the information and can devote as much time as they desire to processing it. On the other hand, in cases where the required internal processing may be complex and the rate of information input cannot be controlled by the consumer, as in listening to radio or television commercials, for example, performance may deteriorate as load increases [87]. However, even in these cases the consumer may select some subset of the information which can be processed in the time available. This notion of whether or not the rate of processing required is controllable seems to reconcile the results of the studies cited above, as the tasks of all of the studies seem to require high internal processing. Lussier and Olshavsky [43] allowed subjects to control rate of information input, whereas most of the other studies had some aspect of the flow of information outside of the subjects' control. Shwartz [71] presents other evidence that processing time is a crucial element. Thus, the amount of information processing necessary per unit time seems to be the crucial factor in leading to information overload effects, not the sheer amount of information itself. This coincides with the first factor related to choice task difficulty discussed above, in that in both cases the ease of processing information, processability, is positively related to amount of search.

Finally, the third choice environment factor related to degree of search is time pressure. Since time pressure influences the degree of control the consumer can have over internal processing rate, such pressure will affect search behavior. In general, as time pressure increases, search should decrease. Several researchers have shown that the more immediate the need for purchase (e.g., because the currently owned product has broken down), the less the information search [11, 35]. Also, Donohew and Tipton [17] point out that in many situations search is cut off by running out of time, rather than by a decision on the part of the individual about whether or not information is sufficient.

Thus, three factors, related to difficulty of the choice task, influence amount of external search. The more easily available the information is, the more processable information is, and the less time pressure there is, the more external search there will be.

Individual Difference Factors. Several types of individual differences are related to degree of external search. First, individuals may use the external memory provided by in-store displays to different extents, and differ in the amount of prior planning done before entering the store. Individuals who rely on in-store processing to a greater extent will tend to display greater external search. However, one cannot imply that this necessarily means greater overall search for such individuals as compared to individuals who rely on out-of-store processing, since those relying on in-store processing may use less internal search. A related issue is the fact that individuals differ in terms of the degree of prior learning about the environment for different purchases. The fact that low external search has been observed in studies of durable purchases [35, 55] may mean only that internal search is used, not that consumers are irrational or lazy. Measures of the total amount of search carried out, both internal and external, need to be utilized in such studies.

A second source of individual differences is the abilities of consumers. Abilities which seem particularly relevant are those Mischel [49] refers to as cognitive and behavior construction competencies. By this is meant the ability needed to ascertain and carry out appropriate behaviors. There is a good deal of research on ability factors associated with carrying out external search. Several researchers have found that more educated and affluent consumers engage in more search [11, 35, 48, 80]. However, Newman and Staelin [55] found that external search was not monotonically related to education. Those consumers with advanced degrees engaged in little external search. This may be due to increased time pressures; a higher degree of past knowledge and hence higher internal search; or great efficiency of search for such consumers; or that such consumers don't care as much about the choices studied. The Newman and Staelin data do not allow for tests of these hypotheses.

Other factors related to processing abilities have been examined in studies not related to consumer research. For example, Sieber and Lanzetta [72] show that degree of conceptual complexity is related to search with more complex subjects searching more. Lanzetta and Kanareff [42], in related research, show that for tasks with a fixed time span, processing abilities are related to external search. For low speed processors, less information will be gathered. Time needed for processing competes with time available for acquisition. Thus, in general, greater abilities, defined in various ways, lead to greater search. The main caveat to this generalization is that greater abilities may also mean more efficient search or more use of internal search. These factors might in some cases lead to lower external search.

A third major type of individual difference variable related to degree of external search is the consumer's concern with optimality of the choice. Consumers develop criteria for determining when activity related to goals should be stopped. One criterion is satisfying or stopping when an alternative is "good enough" even if it is not necessarily optimal. Individuals with higher standards for what is "good enough" will tend to engage in more external search. Both Swan [78] and Claxton, Fry and Portis [11] found that greater concern with optimality of choice was associated with greater amounts of search. Other individual difference factors related to external search are summarized in Engel, Kollat and Blackwell [21, pp. 380-83].

Thus, in general, greater use of in-store processing, less prior knowledge, greater abilities, and greater concern with finding an optimal alternative are associated with higher external search.

Conflict Levels. A great deal of research has attempted to relate conflict and conflict response strategies to degree of external search. Several theories propose that there are optimal levels of conflict (or some related variable), and that if conflict is below the optimal level or moderately above the optimal level information will be sought. If conflict is far above the optimal level, simple strategies will be used, and information may not be sought [3, 20, 25, 30, 31].[6] For moderate levels of conflict,

---

[6]Howard and Sheth [30] use variables of Confidence and Stimulus Ambiguity, not conflict per se. However, lower Confidence and higher Stimulus Ambiguity would seem to imply higher conflict.

external search is seen as a way out of the dilemma posed by the conflict, as a way of reducing the general level of conflict (e.g., [30] or [25]), although some researchers note that information can increase conflict as well as decrease it [86]. Under low levels of conflict, novel or discrepant information may be sought [25, 30, 84]. Most of the research cited below has examined the moderate conflict case.

A large body of research by Driscoll, Lanzetta and their associates has examined level of conflict and external search behavior. In these experiments, conflict is defined as uncertainty times importance. Uncertainty was usually measured by the entropy measure suggested by Berlyne [2]. That is, if P_i is the probability of choice of alternative i, then uncertainty is measured by

$$H = -\sum_i P_i \log P_i \qquad (1)$$

Various experimental manipulations were carried out to vary importance. Sieber and Lanzetta [72] found that search was directly related to uncertainty, but curvilinearly related to importance: the high importance condition had lower search levels. Hawkins and Lanzetta [26] found that search increased with uncertainty, but decreased with importance. There was also no interaction between uncertainty and importance, contrary to the hypothesis of a multiplicative model for conflict. Driscoll, Tognoli and Lanzetta [19] found that search was directly related to the H measure of uncertainty and also to subjective measures of uncertainty generated by the subjects. Finally, Lanzetta and Driscoll [41] showed that search increased with uncertainty and importance, but again found no importance by uncertainty interaction. This series of studies supports uncertainty as a determinant of search, but obtains varied results for importance. Heslin, Blake and Rotton [28] criticize these studies for using responses of different judges to the same stimuli to compute the H measure of uncertainty (i.e., P_i was estimated from how many judges chose response i). Thus inter-judge disagreement was used to measure a construct which purportedly reflects within-subject uncertainty. Heslin, Blake and Rotton performed a study using a within-subject method to measure uncertainty, and also varied response importance. The results showed that both uncertainty and importance led to higher search, and that interactions between uncertainty and importance did occur. Thus, the relationship of uncertainty and importance to conflict and search is still uncertain. Criterion measures for perceived conflict and more standardized measures of importance and uncertainty are needed to clarify these issues.

In consumer research settings, Hansen [25] related conflict (measured as uncertainty times involvement) to internal and external search. Internal search increased with perceived conflict, but the support for increases in external search was weaker. Although perceived risk is a different phenomenon from conflict, it is related to conflict. There has been some research relating risk to information search which shows weak evidence that word-of-mouth is sought more by high risk perceivers [13, p. 610; 44]. Sheth and Venkatesan [70] also report high risk perceivers search for more information. Again, the relationships are weak and varied. The nature of conflict and the theory underlying it need to be studied in more detail, and appropriate measures devised for conflict and related variables. There is no clearly supported relationship between level of conflict and degree of external search.

This ends the discussion of determinants of amount of external search. In all of the research cited, the implicit assumption that degree of internal search could be assumed to be either constant or to not affect degree of external search has been made, since conclusions were drawn about degree of external search without measuring degree of internal search. This assumption seems suspect, and should be directly researched in future studies by attempting to measure both internal and external search.

Analysis of Detailed Patterns of Information Acquisition

The above discussions have concentrated on broad features of the information acquisition process: how much information is acquired, or broad characterizations of what types of information are selected. However, recent research has begun to examine in detail the strategies individuals use in acquiring information from information displays, the sequences of information examined and the structure of such sequences. This research, more detailed in focus than that discussed above, is now examined.

Some recent research in both cognitive psychology and consumer decision making has begun to examine detailed patterns of external information search. Simon and Barenfeld [74] examined how an expert chess player perceives the features of a position, and developed a program, PERCEIVER, based upon information about relations among pieces and recognition of learned configurations of pieces (chunks). In Russ's [64] study of small appliance choices, protocols were gathered and subjects obtained information by requesting it from the experimenter. Svenson [77] examined protocols obtained from six subjects in making a decision among seven hypothetical houses, where information on houses was presented in booklets. Lussier and Olshavsky [43] studied decisions among hypothetical typewriter brands, where information on each brand was typed on a card. Jacoby, Szybillo, and Busato-Schach [33] studied brand choice, with information covered by tape on a display arranged as a brands x attributes array. The information could be examined by removing the tape from any given attribute row in the array. Russo and Rosen [67] examined choices among six used cars, each characterized by three attributes, by studying sequences of subjects' eye fixations over the data, displayed on a cathode ray tube. Russo and Dosher [65] also examined choices among several sets of alternatives by examining eye movements. Jacoby, Chestnut, Weigel, and Fisher [32] and Bettman and Jacoby [5] studied choice of brands of cereal by using an information display board, where cards containing information on cereals were arranged in a brands x attributes array. Subjects could select as many cards as desired. Finally, Payne [56, 57] studied choices of apartments in two experiments, where information was presented in a number of envelopes attached to a board in brands x attributes array. He varied number of alternatives and number of attributes to study task effects on processing.

In all of this research, the data include a detailed description of the sequence of information actually acquired by the subject. Thus external information seeking responses are measured, but not necessarily internal processing, although the two may be congruent [34]. These external search sequences can be analyzed to see if any patterns emerge. Some stable findings have emerged from these studies. First, there are individual differences in the order of external information search. Some subjects search by examining one "brand" (strictly speaking, alternative) at a time. That is, they choose a brand and gather information on several attributes of that brand. Then they choose a second brand and gather information on several attributes (not necessarily the same as those for the first brand) and so on. This strategy may be called Choice by Processing Brands (CPB). A second group of subjects acquire information by choosing an attribute and determining values for each of several brands on that attribute, choosing a second attribute and determining values for several brands and so on. This may be called a Choice by Processing Attributes (CPA) strategy. Other strategies exist, but the two major strategies are those related above. Several of the studies have found more processing by attribute than by brand (e.g., [64, 65, 67]), but others have found more brand processing (e.g., [6]).

The results seem to indicate that where there is little prior experience with the alternatives, attribute processing is used; where there is a great deal of experience, brand processing is used. These findings relate to the decision rules used by consumers, as some rules (e.g., linear compensatory, conjunctive, disjunctive) are characterized by brand processing; others (e.g., lexicographic, additive difference [81], elimination by aspects [82]), are characterized by attribute processing (see [4] for more details).

A second set of findings from several of the above studies is that some subjects use one of the basic strategies above in a uniform manner, i.e., they do not change their strategy during the course of the search. Other subjects use phased strategies [88], where the type of processing varies over the search. A particularly common type of phased strategy is one where the first phase is information input, either by brands or attributes, and the second phase is a set of paired comparisons among specific alternatives [43, 56, 57, 67, 77].

Third, some studies have attempted to relate processing strategy to other consumer behavior variables. For example, Jacoby, Chestnut, Weigl and Fisher [32] found that processing by brands was related to high consumption frequency, and processing by attributes to low consumption frequency and low brand loyalty.

Finally, a fourth factor which needs to be considered is the effect of the structure of the task environment (i.e., how the information display is arranged) on search processes in the above studies. The tasks in many of the studies (e.g., matrix displays or tables) make it equally easy, in terms of the effort needed to acquire the information, to process by brands or by attributes. However, this property is not true of the real world, except for perhaps tasks such as reading a table in Consumer Reports. For a choice of brands from a supermarket shelf, information is organized by brand, facilitating brand processing. Bettman and Kakkar [6] attempted to directly test the effect of display format on the structure of the resulting acquisition sequences. They examined three groups of consumers, each presented with a different display format: one which was the standard matrix array, with either brand or attribute processing equally easy; one display which encouraged attribute and discouraged brand processing; and one display which encouraged brand and discouraged attribute processing. The results showed quite strongly that consumers acquired the information in the fashion which was easiest given the display. For example, attribute processing was observed where the format encouraged it, and not where the format discouraged it. Given the relationship between form of processing and decision rules discussed above, format can thus influence the rules used to compare alternatives.

The above discussion documents impacts on the structure of external search processes. Processing in internal search can also be influenced by various factors. Perhaps the most important of these is how information is stored in memory. As Calder [10] points out, the type of processing used may depend very closely on the way information stored in memory is organized. Payne [56] distinguishes between two possible ways of representing attribute-brand data in memory: where the organization is by brand or by attribute. Internal search would presumably proceed in ways congruent with this organization -- i.e., if information is stored by brand, internal search would be by brand; if stored by attribute, search would be by attribute. These internal storage patterns might also impact external search, as the external search pattern might agree with the internal structure, so that processing the incoming data in light of what is in memory is made easier.

This completes the discussion on consumer research results relating to information acquisition and search. Now a brief comparison of this view of information acquisition to the view implicit in economic treatments of search is presented. It is beyond the scope of this paper to engage in a detailed comparison. Instead, only a limited analysis of some major issues is attempted.

CONSUMER RESEARCH AND ECONOMIC VIEWS OF CONSUMER INFORMATION ACQUISITION

Beginning with early work by Stigler [75], economists have analyzed consumer information acquisition in increasing detail. In this section, we will concentrate largely on recent work done by Philip Nelson [50, 51], as it is in many ways the most explicit of the economic views, and seems to include the most well developed behavioral notions.

Nelson's Framework

Nelson [50, 51] distinguishes two types of attributes a good may possess: search qualities and experience qualities. Nelson defines search in a limited way: actual inspection of an option before purchasing. Search qualities are then those which can be determined by such inspection prior to purchase (e.g., price, color, size). Experience qualities are those the consumer can only evaluate by actually buying and gaining experience with the option (e.g., taste). Darby and Karni [14] add a third type of quality, credence qualities, which cannot be evaluated in normal use, but can only be assessed by gathering additional information from some diagnostic expert (e.g., whether an appendix operation was a good one or was even necessary, whether repairs were needed and done well). Nelson assumes that <u>products</u> can also be classified as search or experience products. We will return to this assumption below.

Nelson then assumes that consumers will engage in search or sampling (to gain experience) by trading off the expected costs and benefits of these actions. As noted below, Nelson views search very narrowly, as physical inspection. He asserts that advertising, word of mouth, consumer rating publications, and so forth act to <u>guide</u> searching, to enable the consumer to determine <u>which</u> brands to actually search [50]. In consumer research terms, these guides are seen as determining the evoked set the consumer searches once in the store.

Finally, advertising is viewed by Nelson [51] as being of two sorts. Advertising for search goods is seen as providing direct, "hard" factual information. Advertising for experience goods, since hard factual information cannot help the consumer assess quality, will be "soft" and will concentrate on enhancing the reputation of the seller. Nelson [50, 51] then uses this framework to derive and test various hypotheses about market structure. Given this very brief treatment of Nelson's framework, let us now consider various aspects of his models in the light of the consumer research findings noted above. The major areas considered are aspects of acquisition and search; cost-benefit trade-offs; classification problems; and contradictory behavioral evidence for some assumptions. Then a consideration of the benefits to consumer research from considering some of Nelson's notions is presented.

Aspects of Acquisition and Search Considered

The purposes and foci of consumer research and economic analysis are clearly quite different. Consumer researchers are concerned with choices among brands and the detailed phenomena that underlie these choices. Economists are often concerned with overall market structure, and hence concentrate more on aggregate-level analysis. This difference in focus is evident in Nelson's work. Nelson only implicitly considers many of the phenomena discussed in the above sections. The distinctions among internal search, external search, and low involvement processes, for

example, are mentioned in his verbal text, but are not a formal part of his models. Detailed patterns of information acquisition (e.g., brand versus attribute processing) are not considered, nor are effects of the format of information, although these factors relate to the choice rules used by consumers and hence presumably to the brands chosen. Phenomena such as conflict, changes in the suitability of information in memory because of changes in alternatives, the specific types and sources of information sought, the purposes for which information will be used, time pressure, and processing abilities are again not considered directly. Most of these can be argued to affect either the costs or benefits derived from search or sampling, however, so they could thus be argued to be implicitly included.

Views of Cost-Benefit Trade-offs

There are two basic views of cost-benefit trade-offs in the economic search literature. In one case, the consumer is assumed to decide, prior to actually searching, how much search will be engaged in (e.g., [75]). In the other case, the consumer decides sequentially, based on the results of each search or product sampling, whether or not to search further. Nelson [50] develops analyses for both cases. The behavioral literature, as exemplified by the Lanzetta [40], Driscoll and Lanzetta [18], Pollay [58], and Hansen [25] research, typically assumes a sequential perspective.

Another aspect of cost-benefit trade-offs, where the economists and behavioralists differ more substantially, is the now well-worn distinction between the optimal search rules used in the economic models and the heuristic, simple rules of thumb assumed by many behavioralists. As innumerable authors have previously pointed out, humans have limited computational and processing abilities, and hence tend to use simplifying devices (e.g., look at what is here on the shelf) rather than optimal rules. For example, consumers may attempt to analyze an ad to see "what's in it for me" [39], but this process seems very simple compared to assertions that the consumer rigorously assesses the marginal revenue of various advertisements [51].

Classification Problems

Nelson's [50] classification scheme for search and experience goods seems non-intuitive (e.g., automobiles are experience goods, but it seems as though there is a great deal of hard information in many automobile ads or obtainable by search). The basic problem seems to be the focus on the product as the entity, rather than keeping the focus on the individual attributes. This is understandable, given an interest in aggregate level phenomena, but causes problems in practice.

It seems more reasonable to take an attribute focus, which allows any product to be viewed as having some mix of search, experience, and credence qualities. Then some kind of sequential model may apply, where consumers first use search for those attributes where they can, and then move to sampling or surrogates to sampling (such as the repair records presented for automobiles in Consumer Reports) to evaluate experience and credence qualities. This is certainly more intuitive, but it may not lead to workable models capable of generating aggregate-level results.

Competing Behavioral Explanations

There are some interpretations made in Nelson's models which behavioral findings suggest may be incorrect. Without dwelling on too many pedantic distinctions, let us consider one such instance.

One case where behavioral interpretations might disagree with Nelson's analysis is in the explanation of why advertisements with hard information are found more in newspapers and magazines. Nelson argues that this is true because the marginal opportunity cost of reading an ad in a newspaper or magazine is higher than that of sitting through a television or radio ad. Hence ads with higher marginal revenue (hard information) will be found there. A behavioral explanation which seems more intuitive is based on the notions, described earlier, that consumers can only process a limited amount of information per unit of time. Television and radio ads require the consumer to do whatever processing is desired within a fixed limited time span, whereas the consumer can decide how much time to spend on a newspaper or magazine ad. Hence, consumers are not able to process as much information from a radio or television ad as they can from a print ad. More hard information is put in print ads because that is the only way consumers can process it. These two views may be merely two ways of saying the same thing, but it seems that the information processing view is more intuitively plausible.

Benefits from Considering Economic Theories of Search

Although there are some problems with economic theories of search, as discussed above, there are some important benefits and insights which can be gained from examination of this literature. Nelson's work makes an important contribution in pointing out that an emphasis on the properties of the tasks consumers must perform can help clarify analyses, both economic and behavioral. The economist's view of the structure of choice situations is a helpful perspective. For example, the notion that attributes are of inherently different types, which may require different information acquisition strategies, is an extremely useful one. While one may not agree with Nelson's particular classification of products, or even with the idea that products rather than attributes are the focus, the basic idea of search, experience, and credence qualities seems to be a good one. The structure of the kinds of attributes present in any particular choice situation may then influence search and other aspects of choice behavior. For example, one might hypothesize that products where actual quality is most heavily related to experience attributes would be those where surrogate, "search attribute" indicators of quality would be found most often (e.g., price).

Another task property implicitly emphasized by Nelson is the distinction between in-store examination of options (what he calls search) and out-of-store deliberations. These represent different kinds of information processing tasks, as noted in earlier sections. This is another distinction worth pursuing, therefore.

Others have noted that analyses of the properties of choice tasks can yield a great deal of information about how choices are made [4, 6, 52]. The economic search theories reinforce this notion from a very different perspective, and Nelson's work provides some useful insights into which task properties might be considered.

CONCLUSIONS

The framework presented above and the research reviewed suggest that a good deal is known about consumer information acquisition. However, there are some glaring gaps in this knowledge. The most significant, perhaps, is the lack of measures for and direct findings about internal search. It is difficult to interpret much of the previous research in the field without making some assumption about internal search. Solid knowledge about internal search would be preferable.

A second gap in prior knowledge is our understanding of low involvement processes. Characterizations of what kinds of information, if any, are acquired during low involvement choice processes and of how often choices are low involvement are needed. Finally, more knowledge of the relationship betwen internal and external search is needed.

Thus, the terrain, although well traversed, has not been fully mapped. Researcher information acquisition about consumer information acquisition is still a fertile area for exploration.

REFERENCES

1. Bennett, Peter D. and Robert M. Mandell. "Prepurchase Information Seeking Behavior of New Car Purchasers-- The Learning Hypothesis," Journal of Marketing Research, 6 (November 1969), 430-33.

2. Berlyne, D. E. "Uncertainty and Conflict: A Point of Contact between Information - Theory and Behavior - Theory Concepts," Psychological Review, 64 (November 1957), 329-339.

3. Berlyne, D. E. Conflict, Arousal, and Curiosity. New York: McGraw-Hill, 1960.

4. Bettman, James R. "Data Collection and Analysis Approaches for Studying Consumer Information Processing," in William D. Perreault, Jr., ed., Advances in Consumer Research, Volume 4. Chicago: Association for Consumer Research, 1977, 342-48.

5. Bettman, James R. and Jacob Jacoby. "Patterns of Processing in Consumer Information Acquisition," in Beverlee B. Anderson, ed., Advances in Consumer Research, Volume 3. Chicago: Association for Consumer Research, 1976, 315-20.

6. Bettman, James R. and Pradeep Kakkar. "Effects of Information Presentation Format on Consumer Information Acquisition Strategies," Journal of Consumer Research, 3 (March 1977), 233-40.

7. Brock, Timothy C. and Howard L. Fromkin. "Receptivity to Discrepant Information," Journal of Personality, 36 (March 1968), 108-25.

8. Bucklin, Louis P. "Testing Propensities to Shop," Journal of Marketing, 30 (January 1966), 22-27.

9. Burnkrant, Robert E. "A Motivational Model of Information Processing Intensity," Journal of Consumer Research, 3 (June 1976), 21-30.

10. Calder, Bobby J. "The Cognitive Foundations of Attitudes," in Mary Jane Schlinger, ed., Advances in Consumer Research, Volume II. Chicago: Association for Consumer Research, 1975, 241-47.

11. Claxton, John D., Joseph N. Fry, and Bernard Portis. "A Taxonomy of Prepurchase Information Gathering Patterns," Journal of Consumer Research, 1 (December 1974) 35-42.

12. Cohen, Arthur R. "Cognitive Tuning as a Factor Affecting Impression Formation," Journal of Personality, 29 (June 1961), 235-45.

13. Cox, Donald F., ed., Risk Taking and Information Handling in Consumer Behavior. Cambridge, Massachusetts: Harvard Business School, 1967.

14. Darby, Michael R. and Edi Karni. "Free Competition and the Optimal Amount of Fraud," Journal of Law and Economics, 16 (1973), 67-88.

15. Day, George S. and William K. Brandt. "Consumer Research and the Evaluation of Information Disclosure Requirements: The Case of Truth in Lending," Journal of Consumer Research, 1 (June 1974), 71-80.

16. Donnermuth, William P. "The Shopping Matrix and Marketing Strategy," _Journal of Marketing Research_, 2 (May 1965), 128-32.

17. Donohew, Lewis and Leonard Tipton. "A Conceptual Model of Information Seeking, Avoiding, and Processing," in Peter Clark, ed., _New Models for Communications Research_. Beverly Hills, California: Sage Publications, Inc., 1973, 243-68.

18. Driscoll, James M. and John T. Lanzetta. "Effects of Two Sources of Uncertainty in Decision Making," _Psychological Reports_, 17 (1965), 635-48.

19. Driscoll, James M., Jerome J. Tognoli, and John T. Lanzetta. "Choice Conflict and Subjective Uncertainty in Decision Making," _Psychological Reports_, 18 (1966), 427-32.

20. Driver, Michael J. and Siegfried Streufert. "The 'General Incongruity Adaptation Level' (GIAL) Hypothesis: An Analysis and Integration of Cognitive Approaches to Motivation," Paper No. 114, Krannert Graduate School of Industrial Administration, Purdue University, 1964.

21. Engel, James R., David T. Kollat and Roger D. Blackwell, _Consumer Behavior, Second Edition_. New York: Holt, Rinehart, and Winston, Inc., 1973.

22. Feather, N. T. "An Expectancy-Value Model of Information-Seeking Behavior," _Psychological Review_, 74 (1967), 342-60.

23. Green, Paul E. "Consumer Use of Information," in Joseph W. Newman, ed., _On Knowing the Consumer_. New York: John Wiley and Sons, Inc., 1966, 67-80.

24. Greeno, James G. "Indefinite Goals in Well-Structured Problems," _Psychological Review_, 83 (November 1976), 479-91.

25. Hansen, Flemming. _Consumer Choice Behavior: A Cognitive Theory_. New York: Free Press, 1972.

26. Hawkins, C. K. and J. T. Lanzetta. "Uncertainty, Importance, and Arousal as Determinants of Pre-Decisional Information Search," _Psychological Reports_, 17 (1965), 791-800.

27. Hendrick, Clyde, Judson Mills, and Charles A. Kiesler. "Decision Time as a Function of the Number and Complexity of Equally Attractive Alternatives," _Journal of Personality and Social Psychology_, 8 (1968), 313-18.

28. Heslin, Richard, Brian Blake, and James Rotton. "Information Search as a Function of Stimulus Uncertainty and the Importance of the Response," _Journal of Personality and Social Psychology_, 23 (1972), 333-39.

29. Hilgard, Ernest R. and Gordon H. Bower. _Theories of Learning_, 3rd Edition, New York: Appleton-Century-Crofts, 1966.

30. Howard, John A. and Jagdish N. Sheth. _The Theory of Buyer Behavior_. New York: John Wiley and Sons, Inc., 1969.

31. Hunt, J. McV. "Motivation Inherent in Information Processing and Action," in O. J. Harvey, ed., _Motivation and Social Interaction-Cognitive Determinants_. New York: Ronald Press, 1963, 35-94.

32. Jacoby, Jacob, Robert W. Chestnut, Karl C. Weigl, and William Fisher. "Pre-purchase Information Acquisition: Description of a Process Methodology, Research Paradigm, and Pilot Investigation," in Beverlee B. Anderson, ed.,

Advances in Consumer Research, Volume III. Chicago: Association for Consumer Research, 1976, 306-14.

33. Jacoby, Jacob, George J. Szybillo, and Jacqueline Busato-Schach. "Information Acquisition Behavior in Brand Choice Situations," _Journal of Consumer Research_, 3 (March 1977), 209-16.

34. Just, Marcel A. and Patricia A. Carpenter. "Eye Fixations and Cognitive Processes," _Cognitive Psychology_, 8 (October 1976), 441-80.

35. Katona, George and Eva Mueller. "A Study of Purchase Decisions in Consumer Behavior," in Lincoln H. Clark, ed., _Consumer Behavior: The Dynamics of Consumer Reaction, Volume 1_. New York: New York University Press, 1955, 30-87.

36. Kiesler, Charles A. "Conflict and Number of Choice Alternatives," _Psychological Reports_, 18 (1966), 603-10.

37. Kohn Berning, Carol A. and Jacob Jacoby. "Patterns of Information Acquisition in New Product Purchases," _Journal of Consumer Research_, 1 (September 1974), 18-22.

38. Krugman, Herbert E. "The Impact of Television Advertising: Learning Without Involvement," _Public Opinion Quarterly_, 29 (Fall 1965), 349-56.

39. Krugman, Herbert E. "Why Three Exposures May Be Enough," _Journal of Advertising Research_, 12 (December 1972), 11-14.

40. Lanzetta, John T. "Information Acquisition in Decision Making," in O. J. Harvey, ed., _Motivation and Social Interaction-Cognitive Determinants_. New York: Ronald Press, 1963, 239-65.

41. Lanzetta, John T. and James M. Driscoll. "Effects of Uncertainty and Importance on Information Search in Decision Making," _Journal of Personality and Social Psychology_, 10 (1968), 479-86.

42. Lanzetta, John T. and Vera T. Kanareff. "Information Cost, Amount of Payoff, and Level of Aspiration as Determinants of Information Seeking in Decision Making," _Behavioral Science_, 7 (1962), 459-73.

43. Lussier, Denis A. and Richard W. Olshavsky. "An Information Processing Approach to Individual Brand Choice Behavior," Paper presented at the ORSA/TIMS Joint National Meeting, San Juan, Puerto Rico, October, 1974.

44. Lutz, Richard J. and Patrick J. Reilly. "An Exploration of the Effects of Perceived Social and Performance Risk on Consumer Information Acquisition," in Scott Ward and Peter Wright, eds., _Advances in Consumer Research, Volume I_. Chicago: Association for Consumer Research, 1974, 393-405.

45. March, James G. and Herbert A. Simon. _Organizations_, New York: John Wiley and Sons, Inc., 1958.

46. Mazis, Michael B. "Decision-Making Role and Information Processing," _Journal of Marketing Research_, 9 (November 1972), 447-50.

47. McLaughlin, Barry. "'Intentional' and 'Incidental' learning in Human Subjects: The Role of Instructions to Learn and Motivation," _Psychological Bulletin_, 63 (1965), 359-76.

48. Miller, Stephen J. and William G. Zikmund. "A Multivariate Analysis of Prepurchase Deliberation and

External Search Behavior," in Mary Jane Schlinger, ed., *Advances in Consumer Research, Volume II*. Chicago: Association for Consumer Research, 1975, 187-196.

49. Mischel, Walter. "Toward a Cognitive Social Learning Reconceptualization of Personality," *Psychological Review*, 80 (July 1973), 252-83.

50. Nelson, Phillip. "Information and Consumer Behavior," *Journal of Political Economy*, 78 (March/April 1970), 311-29.

51. Nelson, Phillip. "Advertising as Information," *Journal of Political Economy*, 81 (July/August 1974), 729-54.

52. Newell, Allen and Herbert A. Simon, *Human Problem Solving*. Englewood Cliffs, New Jersey: Prentice-Hall, Inc., 1972.

53. Newman, Joseph W. and Bradley D. Lockeman. "Measuring Prepurchase Information Seeking," *Journal of Consumer Research*, 2 (December 1975), 216-22.

54. Newman, Joseph W. and Richard Staelin. "Multivariate Analysis of Differences in Buyer Decision Time," *Journal of Marketing Research*, 8 (May 1971), 192-98.

55. Newman, Joseph W. and Richard Staelin. "Prepurchase Information Seeking for New Cars and Major Household Appliances," *Journal of Marketing Research*, 9 (August 1972), 249-57.

56. Payne, John W. "Heuristic Search Processes in Decision Making," in Beverlee B. Anderson, ed., *Advances in Consumer Research, Vol. III*. Chicago: Association for Consumer Research, 1976a, 321-27.

57. Payne, John W. "Task Complexity and Contingent Processing in Decision Making: An Information Search and Protocol Analysis," *Organizational Behavior and Human Performance*, 16 (August 1976b), 366-87.

58. Pollay, Richard W. "A Model of Decision Times in Difficult Decision Situations," *Psychological Review*, 77 (1970a), 274-81.

59. Pollay, Richard W. "The Structure of Executive Decisions and Decision Times," *Administrative Science Quarterly*, 15 (December 1970b), 459-71.

60. Posner, Michael I. *Cognition: An Introduction*. Glenview, Illinois: Scott, Foresman and Company, 1973.

61. Postman, Leo. "Verbal Learning and Memory," *Annual Review of Psychology*, 26 (1975), 291-335.

62. Robertson, Thomas S. "Low-Commitment Consumer Behavior," *Journal of Advertising Research*, 16 (April 1976), 19-24.

63. Rogers, Everett M. *Diffusion of Innovations*. New York: The Free Press, 1962.

64. Russ, Frederick A. "Consumer Evaluation of Alternative Product Models," Unpublished doctoral dissertation, Carnegie-Mellon University, 1971.

65. Russo, J. Edward and Barbara A. Dosher. "Dimensional Evaluation: A Heuristic for Binary Choice," Unpublished working paper, Department of Psychology, University of California, San Diego, 1975.

66. Russo, J. Edward, Gene Krieser, and Sally Miyashita. "An Effective Display of Unit Price Information," *Journal of Marketing*, 39 (April 1975), 11-19.

67. Russo, J. Edward and Larry D. Rosen. "An Eye Fixation Analysis of Multi-Alternative Choice," *Memory and Cognition*, 3 (May 1975), 267-76.

68. Schroder, Harold M., Michael J. Driver, and Siegfried Streufert. *Human Information Processing*. New York: Holt, Rinehart, and Winston, Inc., 1967.

69. Seibel, Robert, Richard E. Christ, and Warren E. Teichner. "Short-Term Memory Under Work-Load Stress," *Journal of Experimental Psychology*, 70 (1965), 154-62.

70. Sheth, Jagdish N. and M. Venkatesan. "Risk-Reduction Processes in Repetitive Consumer Behavior," *Journal of Marketing Research*, 3 (August 1968), 307-10.

71. Shwartz, Steven P. "Capacity Limitations in Human Information Processing," *Memory and Cognition*, 4 (1976), 763-68.

72. Sieber, Joan E. and John T. Lanzetta. "Conflict and Conceptual Structure as Determinants of Decision-Making Behavior," *Journal of Personality*, 32 (1964), 622-41.

73. Simon, Herbert A., "Motivational and Emotional Controls of Cognition," *Psychological Review*, 74 (1967), 29-39.

74. Simon, Herbert A. and Michael Barenfeld, "Information Processing Analysis of Perceptual Processes in Problem Solving," *Psychological Review*, 76 (1969), 473-83.

75. Stigler, George J. "The Economics of Information," *Journal of Political Economy*, 69 (June 1961), 213-25.

76. Streufert, Siegfried, Peter Suedfeld, and Michael J. Driver. "Conceptual Structure, Information Search, and Information Utilization," *Journal of Personality and Social Psychology*, 2 (1965), 736-40.

77. Svenson, Ola. "Coded Think Aloud Protocols Obtained When Making A Choice to Purchase One of Seven Hypothetically Offered Houses; Some Examples," Unpublished paper, University of Stockholm, 1974.

78. Swan, John E. "Experimental Analysis of Predecision Information Seeking," *Journal of Marketing Research*, 6 (May 1969), 192-97.

79. Swan, John E. "Search Behavior Related to Expectations Concerning Brand Performance," *Journal of Applied Psychology*, 56 (1972), 332-35.

80. Thorelli, Hans B., Helmut Becker, and Jack Engeldow. *The Information Seekers*. Cambridge, Massachusetts: Ballinger Publishing Co., 1975.

81. Tversky, Amos. "Intransitivity of Preferences," *Psychological Review*, 76 (January 1969), 31-48.

82. Tversky, Amos. "Elimination by Aspects: A Theory of Choice," *Psychological Review*, 79 (July 1972), 281-99.

83. Udell, Jon G. "Prepurchase Behavior of Buyers of Small Electrical Appliances," *Journal of Marketing*, 30 (October 1966), 50-52.

84. Venkatesan, M. "Cognitive Consistency and Novelty Seeking," in Scott Ward and Thomas S. Robertson, eds., *Consumer Behavior: Theoretical Sources*. Englewood Cliffs, New Jersey: Prentice-Hall, Inc., 1973, 354-84.

85. Winter, Frederick W. "Laboratory Measurement of Response to Consumer Information," Journal of Marketing Research, 12 (November 1975), 390-401.

86. Woodruff, Robert B. "Measurement of Consumers' Prior Brand Information," Journal of Marketing Research, 9 (August 1972), 258-63.

87. Wright, Peter L. "Analyzing Media Effects on Advertising Responses," Public Opinion Quarterly, 38 (1974a), 192-205.

88. Wright, Peter L. "The Use of Phased, Noncompensatory Strategies in Decisions Between Multi-Attribute Products," Research Paper 223, Graduate School of Business, Stanford University, 1974b.

89. Zajonc, Robert B. "The Process of Cognitive Tuning in Communication," Journal of Abnormal and Social Psychology, 61 (1960), 159-67.

THEORIES OF INFORMATION ENCODING AND STORAGE:
IMPLICATIONS FOR CONSUMER RESEARCH

Jerry C. Olson, The Pennsylvania State University[1]

"It has been suggested that, after the discovery of particles by the physicists and the breaking of the genetic code by the molecular biologists, the next major scientific problem of our time is how the brain encodes, stores and retrieves information (Murdock, 1974, p. 312)."

INTRODUCTION

The steadily increasing interest in information processing and cognitive phenomena among consumer behaviorists (e.g., Bettman, 1970; Bither and Ungson, 1975; Jacoby, 1974; Payne, 1976; Russo and Rosen, 1975; Wilkie, 1975), and even economists (e.g., Nelson, 1970, 1972), reflects a general trend of several years duration in psychology (cf. Mahoney, 1977; Newell and Simon, 1972; Postman, 1975). Much of the work in marketing/consumer behavior settings has focused on information integration processes, that is, how consumers combine or integrate informational cues in making a decision such as a purchase choice (Bettman, 1971; Chaffee and McLeod, 1973; Wright, 1975), or in forming a product judgment such as like-dislike, or high-low quality (Bettman, Capon, and Lutz, 1975; Olson and Jacoby, 1972). More recently, consumer researchers have become interested in the so-called "process" of information acquisition (see Jacoby, Chestnut, Weigl, and Fisher, 1976) and have examined sequences of informational cues selected under various experimental conditions (Bettman & Jacoby, 1976; Jacoby, Speller and Kohn-Berning, 1974; Jacoby, Szybillo and Busato-Schach, 1977). In addition to these obvious examples, a wide variety of other consumer research issues such as advertising effectiveness involve information processing phenomena, although they are not often studied from an explicit cognitive processing perspective. This paper considers the implications of information encoding and storage processes for selected examples of such phenomena, as well as for the integration and acquisition research areas.

A major point made in this paper is that, in general, the enthusiastic research programs mentioned above have ignored certain critical issues related to the basic cognitive processes that underlie the phenomena of interest. Consequently, our understanding of the information integration process or the process of information acquisition (or any other cognitive process) is limited, and may in fact be misleading or even totally inaccurate. This paper focuses on two of these basic cognitive processes--information encoding and information storage.[2] Theoretical ideas regarding these two major "sub-processes" in information processing are briefly reviewed and their heuristic implications for research issues are identified and discussed.

It should be emphasized that this "review" is not intended to be broadly inclusive of either consumer research problems or encoding and storage theories. In fact, the magnitude of the burgeoning information processing literature precludes even a shallow review of all the recent theories dealing with encoding and storage processes. Rather, selected "convenient" issues and theories are examined (i.e., those both obvious and familiar to this author). A major goal of this paper is simply to introduce consumer researchers to some of the fascinating ideas from the cognitive psychology literature in hope that these ideas will find their way into our own work on consumer information processing.

OVERVIEW OF INFORMATION PROCESSING

An information processing approach presumes that cognitive phenomena such as perception, learning, remembering, and deciding can be conceptualized as a series of stages during which certain "mechanisms" perform transformations or recodings of information (cf. Bower, 1975). Each stage is considered to receive the informational output of the preceding stage as input, which in turn is operated upon and passed on to the next stage. In this view, the term "information" refers not to the external reality but rather (a) to the internal, symbolic representation of the external stimulus and, moreover, (b) to the interrelationships between these symbolic representations, as organized into symbolic structures. In the present paper, these informational concepts are frequently referred to as cognitions and cognitive structures, respectively.

Newell and Simon (1972), among others, have identified specific structural components or mechanisms involved in information processing (e.g., a sensory system, response generator, memory, and central processor) and elementary information handling processes (e.g., discrimination, symbol creation, and writing, designating, and storing symbol structures). These considerations are not explicitly dealt with here. Rather, because of time and space limitations, the level of specificity taken in this paper is more abstract. The encoding and storage processes involved in information processing are described in broad conceptual terms, but precisely how, in structural and mechanistic terms, such processes occur is not discussed. However, citations are usually given to which the reader interested in greater specificity can refer.

WHY BOTHER WITH ENCODING AND STORAGE PROCESSES?

For many frustrated researchers trying to keep current in their own immediate areas of interest, the present call to delve into a new and massive body of literature dealing with apparently complex and somewhat nebulous cognitive processes is not likely to be accepted eagerly. Thus, it seems advisable to present several examples of research problems and areas that would benefit from a focus on information coding and memory processes.

Information Integration

A major focus of information processing interest in marketing, virtually to the exclusion of other aspects of cognitive processing, is on the processes by which consumers combine or integrate information in making purchase choices or evaluative judgments (Chestnut and Jacoby, 1977). This

---

[1]The author is Associate Professor of Marketing at The Pennsylvania State University. I am grateful for the impetus provided by my students Aydin Muderrisoglu, Rajesh Kanwar, and Sik Shum in preparing myself to write this paper and to Andrew Mitchell for the opportunity to present it at his stimulating conference.

[2]Another basic process, that of information retrieval from storage, is the focus of a massive body of research literature. However, because of space constraints, retrieval processes are not examined in this paper.

emphasis on decision-making by applied, marketing-oriented consumer researchers, although understandable, has led some to suggest that cognitive decision rules constitute the basic content of consumer information processing (Bettman, 1970; Haines, 1974; Wright, 1972). Others (Bettman, 1974 Wilkie, 1974; Jacoby, 1974; Jacoby and Olson, 1977) have argued that how the information is acquired, represented in cognitive symbolic form, stored in relationship with other information, and retrieved from storage are also important, particularly since these processes precede information integration processes for the most part. However, few of these more "basic" processes have been empirically examined in current consumer research or even in our theorizing (see Bettman, in press, or Chestnut and Jacoby, 1977 for excellent overviews of consumer information processing research). Thus, our inferences regarding how consumers combine information are based on several untested assumptions.

For example, in a typical study consumers might be presented with several informational stimuli regarding a product or products and asked to make a judgment or a choice response. The responses are then related (correlationally or experimentally) to specific stimuli and inferences made about the integration processes that underlie the response (e.g., Bettman, Capon, and Lutz, 1975). A number of typically unstated and untested assumptions underlie this inference, however. For example, it is assumed that all the information presented to subjects was encoded. This assumption probably is valid, particularly for studies involving limited amounts of information and forced exposure and attention. A second and more problematic implicit assumption is that the cues are encoded in a form essentially isomorphic to the external stimulus. For instance, several researchers have presented consumers with various price levels for a product and obtained overall evaluative judgment responses (e.g., Peterson, 1970; Woodside, 1974). These studies must implicitly assume that the actual prices are encoded in a way that maintains not only the rank ordering of the price levels but also their relative distance.[3]

The fact is, however, that neither marketers nor economists know how price stimuli are encoded by the consumer (Jacoby and Olson, 1977). It may well be that consumers do not represent an actual price in terms of an exact numerical amount of money. Rather, consumers may encode a given price in terms of some general category of meaning (see the extensive work on categorizations by Wyer, 1973, 1974). Moreover, it is quite likely that the specific code assigned to a price is strongly influenced by some internal reference price level or price range (cf. Rosch, 1975). For instance, a given price might be first encoded at a sensory level as 79¢ and then (re)coded and stored as "cheap" or "expensive," depending upon one's frame of reference. If rather "broad" codes (categories of meaning) of this nature are used to represent price, one might expect little or no differences in overt response to prices that are encoded similarly. Unfortunately, this relatively simple and basic question regarding the encoded form of a stimulus or how information is represented in terms of symbolic meaning has received little attention in integration research, or in consumer research generally.

Information Acquisition

Similar issues are salient for other areas of consumer research. One is the information acquisition procedure adapted by Jacoby (1975), which shows signs of becoming a research paradigm for studying consumer information acquisition and search behavior. Typically, subjects are shown a large board on which are placed cards, each containing an item of information about one of the alternatives. Subjects are usually asked to make a choice among the several alternatives and may select as much information as they wish in accomplishing this objective. Again, a number of implicit and therefore untested assumptions underlie the inferences usually drawn from such data. First, it is assumed that each item is encoded. This no doubt is correct since subjects do select cards and apparently read them, behavior which requires that the information be encoded. However, it is not necessarily true that a given stimulus is encoded in a form isomorphic to the original stimulus nor in a way that will be useful or influential in reaching a purchase decision. Since it is the form of the encoded information-- not the physical cue itself--that influences the task response and, in fact, subsequent search strategy, it is important that we know the form of the cognitive representation or code. As mentioned above, it appears likely that consumers encode discrete levels of specific product dimensions into a relatively few broad categories (cf. Wyer, 1974). Thus, the price of a bottle of wine may be represented as cheap, moderate, or expensive, while the sweetness of a wine might be encoded as "dry, medium dry, sweet, or sugary." In both cases the code is related, but not isomorphic to the physical stimulus.[4]

Information Storage

Issues involving the storage of coded information and, by implication, its retrieval and subsequent use are similarly important to the practice of consumer research. For instance, in the information acquisition paradigm (Jacoby et al., 1976) it is not at all clear or even likely that all the information selected by a consumer is stored in memory in an accessible form. More broadly, since most marketing stimuli (e.g., ads) seem designed to create a relatively long-lived cognitive impact, it would seem important to establish that some "permanent" storage in fact took place. Although studies of ad copy retention are occasionally used in advertising effectiveness research, studies of what information is stored in memory or of the structure in which this information is stored are rarely encountered in other types of consumer research.

In sum, it is important that consumer/marketing researchers consider the potentially critical implications of information encoding and storage processes for their research designs and for the interpretation of their research results. A more proactive recommendation is for marketers to begin to explicitly examine such phenomena in their research on consumer information processing. We now turn our attention to several specific theoretical ideas which appear relevant in helping accomplish these suggestions.

SELECTED IDEAS ABOUT ENCODING PROCESSES

Cognitive psychologists have been strongly interested in encoding and memory/storage processes for nearly a decade. The literature on both topics is voluminous and is certainly larger than anyone not single-mindedly devoted to the area can hope to become more than generally familiar with. Therefore, of necessity, this "review" is highly selective. The primary criterion used to select theories and/or theoretical ideas was that they appeared useful in a heuristic sense for guiding future research or for understanding certain issues in our present research on consumer information processing.

---

[3]Occasionally, however, it is assumed that the differences between encoded price levels are logarithmically related to actual prices.

[4]Ahtola (1975) has incorporated this basic notion in attitude research by considering multiple belief levels or amounts of product attributes as belief vectors in an expectancy-value attribute model. However, few consumer researchers have incorporated the idea into their own research or thinking (cf. Mitchell and Olson, 1977; Olson and Dover, in press).

50

Before proceeding, it should be explicitly noted that, for the most part, the theories described below are not widely accepted by cognitive psychologists. Although one can muster a number of studies which have produced data consistent with predictions derived from each theory, there have been few critical tests between competing theories. In fact, it appears that the rate of cognitive theory development is far outstripping that of theory testing. At least part of this state of affairs is due to the severe methodological problems in studying complex, transient cognitive processes. Despite such difficulties, however, the notions discussed below are quite interesting and may stimulate ideas about the reader's own research.

Encoding

An information processing approach tends to treat phenomena such as perception, comprehension (McGuire, 1976), concept formation (Dominowski, 1974), or even learning (Johnson, 1972) as the encoding of information. It is widely accepted that people do not necessarily react to the external world "as it is," but rather respond in terms of their own perceptions of the world. Encoding refers to the processes by which a person selects and assigns a cognitive symbol (perhaps a word or visual image) to represent a perceived object. The cognitive symbol used as representative of some concept has been termed a code (Johnson, 1972), cogit (Hayes-Roth, 1977), cognitive unit (Frijda, 1975), or simply cognition. It is what most researchers mean by information.

There are a wide variety of conceptual ideas, models, and theories in the current literature regarding information codes and the encoding process. Although even a brief discussion of all of these notions is beyond the scope of this paper, several of the more interesting of these ideas are briefly identified below.

Form of Code. As discussed earlier, a very basic issue involves the form of an encoded cognition. At least three broad possibilities exist. First, the encoded information may be essentially isomorphic with the external stimulus. Second, the code may be similar to the external stimulus but modified somewhat. For instance, the code may represent a simplification of the stimulus (elements are "subtracted" to form the code), or an elaboration (elements/meanings are "added" to the code). Third, the code may be quite different from the stimulus such as a visual image code for a printed word or a verbal language code for a visual stimulus.

Recodings. It is widely accepted that recodings of coded information can occur. The phenomenon of chunking introduced by Miller (1956) clearly illustrates one type of recoding. Chunks tend to develop as one's experience with a complex stimulus increases and patterns of stimuli come to be recognized, organized together, and recoded by a single symbol. The chunk then comes to "stand for" all the information contained therein and is handled as if it (the chunk) was a single information code (Simon, 1974). It has been suggested that brand names may serve as an index to a chunk of brand information for consumers who are familiar with a product category (Jacoby, Olson and Haddock, 1971; Olson, 1977). Related issues include the degree to which consumers tend to recode correlated or redundant product attributes into related clusters or chunks, and the subsequent effects such higher order codes have in decision making (see Geistfeld, Sproles, and Bradenhop, 1977).

Although calls have been made for research into the process by which consumers recode information into higher-order structures or chunks, no studies of this issue have been published. Of course, development of appropriate methodologies is a major stumbling block. One procedure that may be useful for investigating the chunking of attributes involves looking for "clustering" of attributes or related concepts obtained in free elicitations (e.g., "Tell me

whatever comes to mind when I say 'Tide detergent'"). Clustering can be indicated by the order of responses (meaningfully related attributes within a chunk may tend to be elicited together) and in terms of response latencies between elicited concepts (presumably attributes within a chunk ought to be elicited rapidly with minimal time delays, whereas longer delays between responses may represent chunk boundaries, (cf. Buschke, 1976).

Multiple Codings. One notion in the cognitive literature is that incoming stimuli tend to be encoded (virtually instantaneously) in terms of several different codes (cf. Wickens, 1970). For example, a variety of different codes or meanings may be assigned to an automobile stimulus, e.g., some dealing with the physical object--"it's a red car, it's big, etc.;" some dealing with more abstract meanings--"it represents high status;" and others which represent the visual image of the car.

In contrast, common-coding theories (cf. Pylyshyn, 1973) suggest that cognitive representations are neutral with respect to the input modality. That is, regardless of whether the stimulus was exposed verbally, visually, or through some other sense, these theories propose that the code is of the same nature. Typically, the cognitive representation is considered to be coded in semantic, linguistic terms. Alternatively, a dual-coding theory (Paivio, 1975, 1976) postulates two different coding processes, verbal and imaginal, and two types of codes, semantic/linguistic and visual, respectively. Although the distinction between semantic and visual/imaginal encoding is highly relevant to consumer research issues, particularly those related to advertising effectiveness, in only a few studies have researchers examined differential cognitive effects of ads involving verbal claims and ads high in visual imagery (Mitchell and Olson, 1977; also see Rossiter, 1976.

Automatic Encoding. Related to the above notion is that much, but not all encoding occurs essentially automatically, outside our conscious awareness for the most part (cf. Chestnut and Jacoby, 1977; Wickens, 1970). Thus, much encoding may involve parallel processing. In fact, most theoretical ideas regarding encoding propose that as experience and familiarity with a stimulus increases, encoding becomes more automatic and less available to conscious introspective awareness. Conversely, without a base of experience, exposure to unfamiliar stimuli requires conscious levels of attention to encoding operations. Obviously, these notions are relevant to advertising, particularly to the differences in consumer response to advertising for innovative vs. familiar products and to issues involving repetition effects (cf. Mitchell and Olson, 1977; Sawyer, 1977).

Cognitive Reference Points. It is well known that peoples' judgments are highly influenced by reference points and adaptation levels. It would seem obvious then that how one encodes an incoming stimulus also depends critically upon one's frame of reference or one's cognitive reference point (Rosch, 1975; Wyer, 1974). However, in consumer research, little attention has been directed toward such issues. In cognitive psychology, broader notions to be discussed later such as memory frames (Minsky, 1975; Kuipers, 1975) or memory schemata (Norman and Bobrow, 1975) appear to be useful notions in explaining how previous experience influences the encoding process.

We now examine the theory of encoding selected for major emphasis in this paper--the "depth" of processing notion.

DEPTH OR LEVELS OF PROCESSING

In 1972, Craik and Lockhart presented the now-popular idea that the encoding operations and processes applied to a stimulus in "converting" it from sensation to encoded cognition were critically determinant of the code's "durability" in memory. Their emphasis on the process of encoding, in contrast to a more typical structural approach to memory reflected an increasingly popular process perspective in cognitive psychology. Similar emphasis on the processes involved in consumer behavior has been called for and is beginning to be evidenced in consumer research (Bettman, 1971; Jacoby et al., 1976; Jacoby & Olson, 1977; Olson & Mitchell, 1975; Wright, 1972, 1973).

Craik and Lockhart's ideas regarding the encoding process are consistent with a large body of literature which has demonstrated that memory performance (typically level of recall) is substantially enhanced when subjects perform cognitive tasks on the incoming information that require their consideration of the meaning of the stimuli (Hyde, 1973; Hyde & Jenkins, 1969, 1973; Walsh & Jenkins, 1973). In fact, subsequent unanticipated recall of information encoded under such conditions typically was as high as recall under intentional learning conditions (i.e., when subjects were forewarned that they would be asked to remember. See Jenkins, 1974, for a readable overview of this research program). Many other studies have found that the cognitive activity involved in making semantic (meaning-related) or affective judgments results in better memory performance than non- or less semantic tasks (e.g., judgments regarding physical aspects of the stimulus, e.g., "Is this word in upper case type?"). Interestingly, instructions to form mental images of the physical stimulus also lead to high levels of retention (Paivio, 1971; Sheehan, 1971). All of these data suggest that the encoding processes--that is, the type of cognitive operations carried out during encoding--are critical determinants of memory performance as measured by later ability to retrieve the information from storage. More specifically, it appears that conscious attention to the meaning or semantic aspects of a stimulus is a critical type of encoding operation.

Craik and Lockhart's (1972) description of the "depth of processing" theory was an attempt to explain these phenomena. Aspects of their basic ideas have been modified somewhat in later writings (especially see Craik and Tulving, 1975) and this more recent form of the theory is presented here. The essential notion is that certain types (or domains) of encoding operations exist which can be ordered in terms of "depth," from less semantic to "deeper," more semantic levels of processing. For instance, given a price stimulus of $1.49, a consumer might encode the stimulus at essentially a sensory level as "$1.49" or verbally as "one dollar and forty-nine cents." If, however, the stimulus were encoded as "very cheap," a more semantic level of encoding processing would be evidenced. An even "deeper" level of processing might be indicated by relating the encoded price information to other knowledge, such as "very cheap" means "low status, others might laugh at me, may be of poor quality, likely to have poor functional performance," etc. In sum, the encoding process is considered to become successively "deeper" as the degree of semantic analysis or involvement with the meaning of the stimulus becomes greater.

In a number of studies (Craik and Tulving, 1975), deeper levels of initial (encoding) processing were found to be related to higher performance on subsequent memory tasks, measured by both recall and recognition. As expected, more semantic processing tended to require more time than less semantic encoding. However, a series of studies demonstrated that the effect on recall from episodic memory was not due to the amount of processing time taken in encoding the stimulus; rather, the quality (i.e., the "semanticness") of encoding operations was shown to be the critical factor.

In recent theorizing about depth of processing, certain of the earlier ideas have been discarded (see Lockhart, Craik and Jacoby, 1976). Among these was the notion that encoding processes tended to begin at a "shallow," sensory level of analysis and move progressively towards "deeper,"

increasingly semantic levels. In fact, types of encoding operations may not lie along a continuum but may be thought of as alternative domains of processes, arranged hierarchically from less to more semantic. The basic change in thinking is that the encoding of a stimulus does not necessarily proceed from sensory to semantic domains. Rather, a stimulus encoding may be elaborated within any single domain, as indicated by the term "spread" of processing. That is, a consumer may exert substantial encoding effort at a relatively "shallow" level of processing by actively considering various physical or sensory aspects of a package or an ad, but not encoding much of the deeper semantic meaning associated with either stimulus. Similarly, one might expend relatively little effort in encoding the more structural characteristics of a package or an ad, but rather devote considerable encoding effort to analyzing and elaborating the meaning of the stimulus and its component attributes. Thus, although the notion was retained that encoding processes may proceed through several domains of operations, all possible analyses are not necessarily carried out at each domain (Lockhart et al., 1976).

The level of processing (and the degree of spread, presumably) involved in encoding any given stimulus depends upon the specific task required of the subject and the subject's degree of familiarity or past experience with the stimulus. That is, a "deep" level of semantic processing would seem to require that substantial meaning have been previously stored and organized in a form available for use in encoding. (This point is examined in greater detail later in this paper.) For familiar, frequently encountered stimuli and for simple tasks, encoding at most levels seems to occur outside conscious awareness and, in fact, seems to occur "automatically," although this may be more apparent than real (Lockhart et al., 1976).

The notions of "depth" and spread of processing have numerous theoretical implications for cognitive processing research and particularly for memory phenomena. First, the concept focuses research attention on the form and extent of initial processing during encoding as critical factors in the formation of a retrievable memory trace. Moreover, this notion essentially does away with the need for traditional theorizing regarding different memory stores (e.g., sensory, short term, intermediate, and long term memories), each containing information with different levels of durability. Rather, from a depth-of-processing view, the informational product of encoding is considered to be directly stored in memory, merely by virtue of having been encoded. However, the stored information or memory "trace" does vary in "strength," the level of which is dependent primarily upon the type and amount of initial processing the stimulus received during encoding. Finally, the depth of processing theory eliminates the need to propose differing capacities for different memory stores or to explain the mechanisms by which information is "moved" from short term to long term memroy, for example (see Craik and Jacoby, 1975, for a thorough discussion of these latter ideas).

In contrast to the appealing simplicity of the depth-of-processing notion, the measurement of encoding "depth" is more problematic. The circularity of defining encoding depth in terms of the increased memory performance is supposedly causes is, of course, not acceptable. Increased time required to encode a stimulus has been used as a surrogate indicator of increased depth, but the relationship is not invariant (Craik and Tulving, 1975). In sum, a clear and demonstrably valid measure of encoding depth has yet to be proposed (see Nelson, 1977, for several criticisms of the depth-of-processing concept).

Implications for Consumer Research

Because of the central importance of encoding processes in understanding subsequent cognitive processing phenomena, the depth-of-processing explanation has strong heuristic implications for virtually any type of information processing research. As brief examples, the following comments are restricted to four broad topics of current interest in consumer research.

Information Acquisition Research. The information display board or other mechanical devices commonly used in information acquisition research are particularly easy to control and manipulate to modify the task environment of a consumer searcher. However, as discussed above, the form of the encoded information derived from performing a search task is typically not known. More specifically, it would be valuable to know the "depth" or semantic level at which product information was being encoded. The form of encoded information might be indicated by the content of subjects' responses in freely recalling the information they remember having acquired. The depth of which certain cues are processed might be indirectly indicated by the amount of time spent with each cue as well as the "semantic-ness" of the recalled information. Alternatively, one might conduct concurrent or post-hoc protocols in an attempt to learn something regarding the degree of semantic processing involved in a sequence of cue encodings.

This recommended complication of the information acquisition paradigm by considering encoding processes and outcomes is important (even necessary) for several reasons. For one, increased insight into the processes involved in encoding product information and knowledge of the resultant form should lead to additional insights regarding consumer decision-making processes. For example, some subjects may acquire and appear to process product information by brand, by attribute, or by some combination (see Bettman and Jacoby, 1976 or Jacoby et al., 1976) because of an encoding tendency rather than due to following a particular integration strategy. As another example, why does an individual consumer select specific informational cues in a particular pattern, e.g., price first? By examining the encoding process (and possibly the judgmental processes that may accompany encoding--see discussion on memory schemata later in this paper), we may begin to explicate why particular sequences of information are selected. For instance, certain cues may be selected merely to "check" against already stored knowledge and the encoded information may not be stored and used in the decision task. Does the level of processing involved for such cues differ from that applied to cues which represent "new," not previously stored information? What effect does varying "depth" have on recall of product characteristics, or changes in cognitive structure, or on the judgment/choice outcome? For instance, do cues which are processed at a greater depth have a more potent influence on the choice outcome? These questions are but a few of those that can be heuristically derived from an explicit consideration of encoding processes. They, and others, warrant attention in future research.

Advertising Effectiveness Research. Tremendous resources are expended each year in attempts to determine the effectiveness of specific advertisements. The typical criterion measures used in these studies are ad recall or recognition, that is, measures of the strength, durability or retrievability of the memory trace for ad exposure (as stored in episodic memory--see later discussion). Because depth-of-processing theory makes specific direct predictions regarding the durability (and retrievability) of such information, it is highly relevant to research questions regarding advertising effectiveness. The basic prediction is that the "deeper" the initial processing of an ad (greater semantic encoding), the more durable and likely to be retrieved is the memory trace for the ad exposure event.

Among the issues an advertiser interested in maximizing ad recall scores might wish to study is the extent to which certain ad content, layout, pictorial images, etc. lead to or facilitate relatively "deeper" levels of initial processing by exposed consumers. The effects of personal characteristics of the receiver on processing "depth" would

also be of interest. For example, it would appear reasonable to suppose that greater semantic processing is positively influenced by individual difference factors such as ego-involvement with the stimulus (Preston, 1970) or media (Krugman, 1966), or by factors such as the degree of inherent risk perceived to be associated with the product (Bettman, 1973). More specifically, the depth of processing notion may be useful in elaborating Krugman's (1965) ideas about low involvement learning during advertising exposure. For instance, Krugman's proposition that most TV ad viewing involves very low levels of viewer involvement can be taken to mean that relatively non-semantic types of encoding operations are performed on most TV advertising stimuli. This interpretation yields predictions consistent with the low recall stores typically obtained for televised ads. Or, does "low involvement" mean that the stimulus was encoded with a relatively small "spread" of processing, i.e., a non-elaborate, but still possibly semantic encoding. Involvement "theory" might benefit from attention to information encoding processes.

Note, however, that the analysis above really concerns only the effects of depth of processing on memory for the past event of an ad exposure. One might question what real importance it is, in and of itself, that a consumer can recall having seen, read, or heard a particular ad. It may in fact be much more important from an applied perspective to know the effects of the various encoding operations on semantic memory, that is, on the organized structure of encoded knowledge associated with the advertised object. This issue is discussed more fully later in the paper.

Cognitive Response Research. Consumers' thoughts or cognitive responses elicited by an ad exposure (e.g., counter- or support arguments) are potentially important mediators of the impact of the ad on attitude (Wright, 1973, 1975) and on cognitive belief structures (Lutz and Swasy, 1977; Olson, Toy and Dover, in press). It may also be that consumers' cognitive responses, especially when measured immediately upon presentation of an ad stimulus, can be considered as protocol measures or indications of the (conscious) products of the encoding operations that were applied to the ad stimulus. If so, it may be possible to categorize the self-reported thoughts that occur when attending to an ad in terms of their processing "depth." Such an analysis would introduce an additional level of meaning and increased theoretical predictive power to cognitive response research. Cognitive responses could then be related more clearly to information processing phenomena, generally, and to encoding and memory phenomena specifically.

Cognitive Structure Research. A number of investigations in consumer research have dealt with cognitive structures, although the terminology is often different (e.g., attitude structure, Lutz, 1975; belief structure, Olson and Dover, 1976). Thus far, depth-of-processing theory has dealt primarily with effects on the strength or durability of the episodic memory trace. However, it would seem consistent with the theory that level of processing and extent of encoding "spread" should also have an impact on the cognitive structure of interrelated knowledge representations stored in semantic memory. Since this idea is elaborated in some detail later in this paper, suffice it to say that deeper levels of encoding seem likely to create more complex, more internally consistent, and more stable cognitive structures, which in turn should encourage deeper levels of processing on successive exposures to the stimulus. This idea points to the need to study the dynamic, interrelated changes in encoding processes and resultant cognitive structure over time (Olson and Dover, 1977).

SELECTED IDEAS ABOUT INFORMATION STORAGE

In this section the structure of information as stored in memory is explicitly considered, as well as the processes involved in the storage of information and in the formation of organized information structures. Processes involved in the retrieval of stored information are only briefly discussed.

Theorizing about memory structure and storage/retrieval processes has grown, particularly over the past decade or so, with the development of ideas about various kinds of memory. One "traditional" view that is currently fading from favor among cognitive researchers concerns the notion that memory is composed of discrete stores. Several such stores or types of memory have been proposed over the years since Broadbent (1958) introduced the term "short-term memory." These include sensory memory (Newell and Simon, 1972), primary memory (cf. James, 1890; Watkins, 1974) or short-term memory (Peterson and Peterson, 1958), intermediate memory, and secondary or long-term memory (Atkinson and Shiffrin, 1968). Typically, these stores are conceptualized as linked together, usually in the order just presented, and it is presumed that information is transferred from one store to the next until it either reaches permanent storage in long-term memory or is lost from the system.

These rather mechanistic notions about a system of interrelated memory stores and the processes by which they are connected have been advocated by a few consumer researchers in recent years (e.g., Jacoby and Olson, 1977; Wilkie, 1974), but criticized by Chestnut and Jacoby (1977) as being excessively cumbersome and complex as well as inconsistent with recent data. One brief example must suffice to make this point. It seems clear that in order to encode a stimulus, probably in short-term memory, some interaction with the information about the object stored in long-term memory is necessary. Thus, a structural theory of separate memory stores must be able to account for this interactive linkage in which stored information from long-term memory is retrieved and made available to the encoding operations presumably occuring in short-term memory. As complications of this nature were introduced, such models rather quickly became too large and complicated. Restle (1974), among many others (Craik and Jacoby, 1975; Jenkins, 1974), has proposed that the concept of memory stores as separate entities be eliminated. In their view, the observed behavior that led to hypothesizing discrete memory stores can be explained more parsimoniously by notions regarding depth of initial processing (Craik and Lockhart, 1972) or by differing degrees of organization of the stored information (cf. Jenkins, 1974; Restle, 1974).

Another interesting development in cognitive literature is relevant to this discussion of memory. Following the Ebbinghaus tradition, much of the past cognitive research on verbal learning has used relatively meaningless stimuli such as nonsense syllables in a direct attempt to eliminate subjects' tendencies to introduce organization and meaning into the learning task (see Cofer, 1975; Jenkins, 1974). In contrast, the newer approach, in the Bartlett (1932) tradition, studies more mundane stimuli and treats meaningfulness (usually considered in terms of semantic meaning) as a powerful influence on learning and memory, and thus as a critical variable to be examined rather than controlled. This relatively recent interest in the cognitive processes involved in encoding, storing, and retrieving more realistic stimuli (which possess numerous meaningful relationships to many other stimuli) is a refreshing and welcome advance, especially from the applied perspective of most consumer researchers, since these are the types of stimuli of major interest to us.

Several theoretical ideas grounded in this "new" approach to information storage or memory phenomena are addressed below. First, some theoretical ideas about the structure of knowledge representations in memory are examined, followed by a consideration of storage processes. The paper concludes with a brief discussion of the dynamic aspects involved in the formation of organized knowledge representations in memory over time.

What is Structure?

Researchers, particularly in consumer behavior, often discuss memory as if it were anlogous to a warehouse in which information were stored in specific locations (SM, STM, or LTM) and transferred back and forth by little forklift trucks (storage processes such as rehearsal or various retrieval processes). As mentioned above, current thinking in the cognitive literature is rejecting this notion of a pre-existing structure with fixed memory stores into which information is placed. Rather, it is becoming common to consider structure as taking form as information is encoded and organized under genral rules of cognitive processing operations (cf. Estes, 1975; Hayes-Roth, 1977; Restle, 1974).

A currently popular idea about memory structure that is consistent with this trend is Tulving's (1972) distinction between episodic and semantic memory. Episodic memory refers to one's stored knowledge of the episodes or events that have occurred in the past. In contrast, one's knowledge of rules, facts, and principles are stored in semantic memory and are thought to exist independently of knowledge regarding when this knowledge was acquired or was used in specific situations. For example, my knowledge that I purchased a loaf of whole wheat bread last Tuesday is part of my episodic memory. However, my knowledge about the attributes of whole wheat bread, appropriate usage situations, characteristics of bread in general, the various types of bread, and even more general knowledge about bread such as production processes and distribution systems comprise parts of my semantic memory. Tulving emphasized that semantic memory could be productive or generative (of other knowledge) while episodic memory was not. It must be emphasized that neither episodic nor semantic memory should be interpreted as referring to specific locations within the brain but rather concern the type of information stored in a single memory store.

In the cognitive literature, and to a lesser extent in consumer research, massive research effort has been focused on issues involving episodic memory. This emphasis is indicated by the ubiquitous recall/recognition research paradigm in which subjects indicate what stimuli (typically nonsense syllables or words) they remember experiencing at some earlier time. Similarly, the bulk of advertising research concerns the storage and retrieval from episodic memory of information about a past ad exposure. Recently, however, cognitive researchers are devoting increasing research effort to investigating the representation and structural organization of knowledge in semantic memory. As Wyer (1974) has noted, research on cognitive organization or cognitive structure is of two usually independent types: (a) studies of relatively small subsets of cognitions and the extent and determinants of their interrelationships, and (b) the determinants and influences of broader, more general aspects of cognitive structure such as cognitive complexity, differentiation, centrality (e.g., Bieri, 1961; Harvey, Hunt and Schroder, 1961; Scott, 1963, 1965). In consumer research, the bulk of effort appears directed at the latter kinds of issues, while studies of relatively "small," stimulus specific cognitive structures tend to be subsumed under attitude research. Consequently, the prime focus is seldom on describing the structure of knowledge representations for a product in semantic memory, but rather is on predicting attitude from a general measurement of such structures (e.g., Lutz, 1976; Mazis, Ahtola and Klippel, 1975). However, the recent interest in product beliefs and their interrelationships (e.g., Kuehl and Dyer, 1977; Lutz, 1975b; Olson and Dover, 1976, 1977) can be seen as early attempts to examine "smaller," organized structures of knowledge representations or cognitions.

In the cognitive literature, the traditional theoretical paradigm used to examine structural issues is "association theory" (cf. Anderson and Bower, 1973; Kintsch, 1974; Rumelhart, Lindsay and Norman, 1972). Associative models of memory structure typically assume that knowledge is represented as networks of nodes and connecting arcs, where nodes encode specific concepts and the arcs between nodes encode the relations between concepts. However, agreement among models is not high regarding the processes by which nodes and arcs are formed or accessed. Broadly speaking, learning or the acquisition of knowledge can be considered to occur in two ways. New nodes and arcs may be added to an existing cognitive structure, or the strengths (activation potential) of particular nodes or arcs may change.

This idea of memory structure is completely compatible with ideas that stimuli or concepts are represented in memory as bundles of attributes (e.g., Bower, 1967; Underwood, 1969). Of course, similar ideas about consumers' product knowledge have been held by consumer researchers for some time. Moreover, if the arcs which link nodes (cognitive representations of discriminable attributes) are considered to be operationalized as subjective judgments of belief strength, then this general view of cognitive structure is conceptually compatible with a good deal of consumer attitude research. Perhaps many attitude model researchers have been examining cognitive structure without being aware of it.

Memory Traces

It is common in the cognitive literature (Tulving and Watkins, 1975) to refer to the stored knowledge representation of an event as a memory trace, conceptualized broadly as a multidimensional collection of elements, features or attributes (Bower, 1967; Underwood, 1969; Wickens, 1970). However, neither the precise form of a memory trace nor the appropriate method for its measurement have been clearly conceptualized. Tulving and Bower (1974) reviewed and summarized 11 methods used to isolate the form of memory representations. Many of these require a subject to respond to a particular verbal "probe," question, or task which is manipulated by the experimenter. A common problem with this procedure is the difficulty in distinguishing between subject responses that are directly associated with characteristics of the memory trace and responses that are derived from stored information, but do not directly reflect that such information was in fact a part of the memory trace.

Given this and other problems, it is not possible to offer a single method for determining the elements of memory structure. Consumer researchers would be well advised to use multiple methods in any memory probing research. Tulving and Bower (1974) argue rather convincingly that our understanding may be best enhanced by investigating retrieval processes and response output under experimental manipulations of the memory probe or cue. The pattern of responses across systematic variations in retrieval cues should provide insight regarding the memory trace being probed. For instance, a consumer researcher might wish to probe the semantic structure associated with various product categories and/or specific brands within each category.

One notion that is enjoying wide general acceptance is that the "strength" of an episodic memory trace is more dependent upon the nature of the encoding processes applied to it than specific aspects of the event itself. This is essentially the depth-of-processing effect discussed above. That is, the deeper (the more semantic and elaborate) the initial encoding operations are, the more memorable the memory trace in episodic memory, thus increasing the probability of remembering the exposure/encoding situation.

As noted earlier, there appears to be a shift away from the more mechanistic associationist approaches to memory (a) to a focus on process of storage and retrieval (Tulving and

Thomson, 1973)[5] and (b) to a consideration of semantic memory structure in terms of organization of knowledge, largely defined in terms of semantic or meaningful "linkages" (Jenkins, 1974). In recognition of its strong implications for consumer research, the remainder of this paper deals with semantic memory and specifically with ideas about knowledge organization and structure.

SEMANTIC MEMORY

Although there is some disagreement (see Craik and Jacoby, 1975) as to the degree of relationship between episodic and semantic memory--e.g., are they really two essentially independent systems--the distinction is heuristic and therefore useful. This distinction does point out quite clearly that the bulk of memory research deals with episodic memory --the remembering and "forgetting" of past events and their attributes. However, it is possibly more critical, especially from an applied perspective, to examine the form and organization of semantic memory and the storage and retrieval processes involved therein. For such questions, much of the earlier cognitive literature is less relevant. One idea, however, that may be useful is that of memory schemata.

Memory Schemata

In two recent papers, Norman and Bobrow (1975; Bobrow and Norman, 1975) introduced the heuristic notion of memory schemata. Based on the idea that attention, perception, memory, and cognition are intertwined phenomena, they suggested that it should be possible to develop a single, unified conceptual explanation for information processing and cognitive structure. Given the known limitations of human cognitive processing, Norman and Bobrow proposed that memory is made up of active subunits or schemata, an idea similar to Hebb's (1949) cell assemblies or Reitman's (1965) idea that memory units have processing capability independent of central controlling mechanism. Because the central aim of cognitive processing is thought to be the formation of a meaningful interpretation of the world, the sensory information available to a person must be organized and encoded in terms of some coherent framework (Norman and Bobrow, 1975, p. 119). Schemata are the large number of such structural frames that have been learned over time as experience accumulates. A schema consists of a framework for organizing the information about a given concept into a meaningful structure. From this view, perception or encoding of a stimulus first involves the determination (activation) of the appropriate schema and then interpretation of the stimulus "in light of" that schema. Norman and Bobrow (1975) proposed that a schema or set of schemata can be activated either by incoming sensory stimulation derived from the stimulus and the situation context, by other schemata, or by the "central processing mechanism" itself. Schemata are not only thought to contain representations of knowledge but also rules of relationship among the cognitive elements and even, in well-developed schemata, evaluation or decision rules for responding to the schema concept.

---

[5]Currently popular notions in the cognitive literature include the following. Recall and recognition are complex processes of information processing that can be studied independently of storage processes. Remembering is influenced both by the stored information (e.g., strength of memory trace) and by the immediate cognitive environment of the rememberer. That is, retrieval is not just a function of trace strength, but rather some complex interaction between the stored information and information cues encoded from the retrieval environment.

Schemata and Depth of Processing

The notion of active memory schemata is easily related to depth-of-processing theory. Schemata may be considered to provide the framework of basic knowledge within which encoding operations can take place. Presumably alternative schemata are available for various levels of processing, from more sensory schemata concerned primarily with physical aspects of the stimulus, to more semantic schemata which contain the complex, abstract meanings of the stimulus. From this view, the degree of encoding "spread" at a given level of processing can be considered to be a function of the complexity of the appropriate schema as an organized structure of information and relationship rules. That is, it seems clear that a stimulus cannot be processed at a semantic level unless one has previously learned and organized one's relatively deep, semantic knowledge about the stimulus; that is, unless one has well-developed memory schema. Norman and Bobrow (1975) proposed that all incoming sensation must be accounted for and, therefore, over a series of experiences one would tend to acquire increasingly well-developed schemata capable of dealing with that stimulus at various levels and in various contexts. The latter point is critical, as the authors propose that the context of experience is as important in schema selection as is the content.

Implications

This notion of memory schemata seems quite useful in our research on consumer perceptions and behaviors. It seems reasonable that consumers "build up" active memory schemata relevant to commonly purchased products. A schema would organize the features and attributes of that product (or brand) in meaningful ways and, moreover, would contain basic rules for dealing with that product (e.g., for evaluating attributes in various situational contexts). In very highly developed product schemata, one could envision even choice rules being incorporated into the schema and essentially "automatically" activated upon presentation of the stimulus product in a purchase context.

The well-known influence of situational, context, or environmental factors on consumer evaluations or choices can be accounted for using a memory schemata approach. As one brief example, the salient attributes of wine, the evaluation associated with each attribute of wine, and the integration rule for combining attribute information in making a choice may vary dramatically across situations in which a consumer is considering buying table wine for personal everyday use vs. for a special personal-use occasion vs. as a present for another. The explanation for these differences may be that different schemata regarding wine have been learned and are activated in these different purchase contexts.

Although the concept of active memory schemata may be intuitively heuristic, measurement of schemata, particularly their content, is more problematic. One possible approach is to elicit free verbal responses to product- and situation-specific probes. For instance, consumers might be asked to ". . . tell me what comes to mind when you think about . . . buying toothpaste for yourself; . . . buying toothpaste for your children to use." Although procedures to investigate memory schemata no doubt will evolve in time, consumer researchers may wish to join in explicating this concept.

Dynamic Changes in Cognitive Structure

One issue that seems to be relatively low in salience for most cognitive researchers concerns the dynamic nature of the cognitive phenomena. For instance, I am aware of few references to the processes by which cognitive structures are formed and fewer yet regarding how cognitive processes are learned/acquired and perhaps changed over time. Perhaps because consumer behavior is so obviously a dynamic

process, consumer researchers seem more "tuned into" questions of dynamics and change. However, even a cursory review of our literature will reveal little substantive theoretical and empirical attention to dynamic changes in our phenomena beyond the common lip-service calls for more longitudinal research.

Recently, Hayes-Roth (1977) presented a rare, explicit conceptualization of the dynamic changes in cognitive structure from initial formation to a stable well-learned state. Although she did not do so, her theory about the "evolution" of cognitive structures and accompanying cognitive processes can be integrated with the major ideas described in this paper regarding depth of processing and memory schemata. Her theory, moreover, is essentially compatible with some tentative ideas proposed by Dover and Olson (1977) regarding dynamic changes in belief/attitude structures as a function of multiple exposures to information. Briefly, Hayes-Roth stated that an organized cognitive structure (perhaps made up of multiple schemata) begins with the establishment of encoded representations (nodes) of elementary knowledge about the stimulus. Basically this is the concept formation process (Dominowski, 1974). As experience increases these simple representations become stronger and associations (arcs) with other concepts/nodes are established and become stronger. This is analogous to the belief formation process described by Fishbein (1967), and an attitude theorist might operationalize these latter changes as increases in belief strength. Through repeated activations caused by multiple exposure to the stimulus, configurations or chunks of associated representations (corresponding to attributes of the stimulus, for example) develop and become stronger. This process may be considered to correspond to the development of a well-integrated memory schema of knowledge regarding the stimulus. At some point, a configuration may become so well learned that it is "unitized," after which the entire configuration acts as a single, discrete, memory representation. This idea appears similar to other ideas about cognitive organization, such as chunking (Miller, 1956; Simon, 1974). Hayes-Roth emphasized that the developmental process occurs gradually requiring a number of repeated "activations" of the evolving structure. Activation occurs simply by apprehension of the stimulus--an idea similar to the "arousal" of a memory schema. Hayes-Roth also proposed that an active unitized representation of a cognitive structure can be consciously decomposed by a subject into its prior constituent representations and sub-structures.

The idea of cognitive structure evolution or maturation has important heuristic implications for consumer research. It suggests that we should be investigating the processes by which consumers learn about products and brands and, even more basically, how people learn to consume. Consumer behaviorists should be interested in the cognitive structures or memory schemata that consumers have developed regarding shopping, buying, consuming, using and disposing of goods and services. At a less global level, knowledge of consumers' cognitive structures and schemata for frequently purchased products and services should be of great interest to applied researchers, particularly in light of currently popular thought which attributes significant impact on behavior to such learned cognitive structures. Differences in terms of information acquisition/search, encoding, and integration between consumers who possess cognitive structures at various levels of development should also be of interest. For instance, the decision process regarding discontinuous innovations for which cognitive structure is presumably neither well-developed nor highly organized should be influenced by the vague state of the existing structure and should differ in interesting ways from the decision process for more continuous, familiar innovations. I hope for an increased interest in issues regarding the dynamics of such phenomena and in the variables which influence these changes.

SUMMARY

It appears, even from the brief examples cited in this paper, that the concept of memory schemata, especially when combined with the theoretical perspectives of an evolving cognitive structure and varying depth and spreads of encoding processing, may eventually be combined into a coherent, compelling, and relatively parsimonious model (if not a theory) of cognitive processing. For the present, however, the theories, models and ideas presented in this paper are primarily meant to be heuristic prods to the reader's thinking about consumer information processing and related cognitive structural phenomena. One of the most useful aspects of theory is the generative power it provides for considering new research questions or new approaches to or explanations for old issues. Much of the current theorizing in the cognitive literature can provide this heuristic, generative perspective. Moreover, it appears that new, more encompassing, and in many ways, simpler theories of information processing and cognitive structures are imminent and that some of the ideas discussed here will be important in such developments. Therefore, these theories are important beyond their heuristic quality for consumer researchers. The interested reader is encouraged not to rely on this broad and highly selected overview but, rather, to read the original literature and develop his or her own interpretations and implications. Consumer behavior phenomena are excellent vehicles for theoretical tests and development of applications of these ideas and the interaction cannot help but advance our understanding of consumer behavior.

REFERENCES

Ahtola, Olli T. "The Vector Model of Preferences: An Alternative to the Fishbein Model," Journal of Marketing Research, 12 (February 1975), 52-9.

Anderson, John R. and Gordon H. Bower. Human Associative Memory. Washington, D.C.: Winston, 1973.

Atkinson, Richard C. and R. M. Shiffrin. "Human Memory: A Proposed System and Its Control Processes," in K. W. Spence and J. T. Spence, eds., The Psychology of Learning and Motivation: Advances in Research and Theory: Vol. II. New York: Academic Press, 1968.

Bartlett, F. E. Remembering. Cambridge, England: Cambridge University Press, 1932.

Bettman, James R. "Information Processing Models of Consumer Behavior," Journal of Marketing Research, 7 (August 1970), 370-6.

Bettman, James R. "The Structure of Consumer Choice Processes," Journal of Marketing Research, 8 (November 1971), 465-71.

Bettman, James R. "Perceived Risk and Its Components: A Model and Empirical Test," Journal of Marketing Research, 10 (May 1973), 184-90.

Bettman, James R. "Decision Net Models of Buyer Information Processing and Choice: Findings, Problems, and Prospects," in G. David Hughes and Michael L. Ray, eds., Buyer/Consumer Information Processing. Chapel Hill, N.C.: University of North Carolina Press, 1974.

Bettman, James R. An Information Processing Theory of Consumer Choice. Reading, Mass.: Addison-Wesley, in press.

Bettman, James R., Noel Capon and Richard J. Lutz. "Cognitive Algebra in Multi-Attribute Attitude Models," Journal of Marketing Research, 12 (May 1975), 151-64.

Bettman, James R. and Jacob Jacoby. "Patterns of Processing in Consumer Information Acquisition," in Beverlee B. Anderson, ed., Advances in Consumer Research: Vol. III. Cincinnati: Association for Consumer Research, 1976, 315-20.

Bieri, James. "Complexity-Simplicity as a Personality Variable in Cognitive Preferential Behavior," in Donald W. Fiske and Salvatore R. Maddi, eds., Functions of Varied Experience. Homewood, Il.: Dorsey, 1961.

Bither, Stewart W. and Gerardo Ungson. "Consumer Information Processing Research: An Evaluative Review," Paper No. 28, Working Series in Marketing Research, College of Business Administration, Pennsylvania State University, 1975.

Bobrow, Daniel G. and Donald A. Norman. "Some Principles of Memory Schemata," in D. G. Bobrow and A. M. Collins, eds., Representation and Understanding: Studies in Cognitive Science. New York: Academic Press, 1975.

Bower, Gordon H. "A Multicomponent Theory of the Memory Trace," in K. W. Spence and V. T. Spence, eds., The Psychology of Learning and Motivation: Advances in Research and Theory: Vol. I. New York: Academic Press, 1967, 229-325.

Bower, Gordon H. "Cognitive Psychology: An Introduction," in William K. Estes, ed., Handbook of Learning and Cognitive Processes: Vol. I. Hillsdale, N.J.: Lawrence Erlbaum, 1975.

Broadbent, Donald E. Perception and Communication. New York: Pergamon Press, 1958.

Buschke, Herman. "Short-Term Retention, Learning, and Retrieval from Long-Term Memory," in Diana Deutsch and J. Anthony Deutsch, eds., Short-Term Memory. New York: Academic Press, 1975.

Buschke, Herman. "Two Dimensional Recall: Immediate Identification of Clusters in Episodic and Semantic Memory," Journal of Verbal Learning and Verbal Behavior, Vol. 16 (April 1977), 201-15.

Chaffee, Steven H. and Jack M. McLeod. "Consumer Decisions and Information Use," in Scott Ward and Thomas S. Robertson, eds., Consumer Behavior: Theoretical Sources. Englewood Cliffs, N.J.: Prentice-Hall, 1973.

Chestnut, Robert W. and Jacob Jacoby. "Consumer Information Processing: Emerging Theory and Findings," in Arch G. Woodside, Jagdish N. Sheth and Peter D. Bennett, eds., Consumer and Industrial Buying Behavior. Elsevier North-Holland, 1977.

Cofer, Charles N. "An Historical Perspective," in Charles N. Cofer, eds., The Structure of Human Memory. San Francisco: W. H. Freeman, 1975.

Craik, Fergus I. M. and Larry Jacoby. "A Process View of Short-Term Retention," in Frank Restle, R. M. Schiffrin, N. J. Castellan, H. R. Lindman and D. B. Pisoni, eds., Cognitive Theory: Vol. I. Hillsdale, N.J.: Lawrence Erlbaum, 1975.

Craik, Fergus I. M. and Robert S. Lockhart. "Levels of Processing: A Framework for Memory Research," Journal of Verbal Learning and Verbal Behavior, 11 (December 1972), 671-84.

Craik, Fergus I. M. and Endel Tulving. "Depth of Processing and the Retention of Words in Episodic Memory," Journal of Experimental Psychology: General, Vol. 104 (September 1975) 268-94.

Dominowski, Roger L. "How Do People Discover Concepts?", in Robert L. Solso, ed., Theories in Cognitive Psychology: the Loyola Symposium. Potomac, Md.: Lawrence Erlbaum, 1974.

Dover, Philip A. and Jerry C. Olson. "Dynamic Changes in an Expectancy-Value Attitude Model as a Function of Multiple Exposures to Product Information," in Barnett A. Greenberg and Danny N. Bellenger, eds., Contemporary Marketing Thought, 1977 Educators Proceedings. Chicago: American Marketing Association, 1977, 455-60.

Estes, William K. "An Associative Basis for Coding and Organization in Memory," in A. W. Melton and E. Martin, eds., Coding Processes in Human Memory. Washington, D.C.: Winston, 1972.

Estes, William K. "Structural Aspects of Associative Models for Memory," in Charles N. Cofer, eds., The Structure of Human Memory. San Francisco: W. H. Freeman, 1975.

Fishbein, Martin. "A Consideration of Beliefs and Their Role in Attitude Measurement," in Martin Fishbein, ed., Readings in Attitude Theory and Measurement. New York: Wiley, 1967.

Frijda, Nico H. "Things to Remember," in Alan Kennedy and Alan Wilkes, eds., Studies in Long Term Memory. London, Wiley, 1975.

Geistfeld, Loren V., George B. Sproles and Suzanne B. Badenhop. "The Concept and Measurement of a Hierarchy of Product Characteristics," in William D. Perrault, Jr., ed., Advances in Consumer Research: Vol. IV. Atlanta Association for Consumer Research, 1977, 302-7.

Haines, George H. "Process Models of Consumer Decision Making," in G. David Hughes and Michael L. Ray, eds., Buyer/Consumer Information Processing. Chapel Hill, N.C.: University of North Carolina Press, 1974.

Harvey, O. J., David E. Hunt and Harold M. Schroder. Conceptual Systems and Personality Organization. New York: Wiley, 1961.

Hayes-Roth, Barbara. "Evolution of Cognitive Structures and Processes," Psychological Review, 84 (May 1977), 260-78.

Hebb, Donald O. The Organization of Behavior. New York: Wiley, 1949.

Hyde, Thomas S. "Different Effects of Effort and Type of Orienting Task on Recall and Organization of Highly Associated Words," Journal of Experimental Psychology, 97 (January 1973), 111-13.

Hyde, Thomas S. and James J. Jenkins. "Differential Effects of Incidental Tasks on the Organization of Recall on a List of Highly Associated Words." Journal of Experimental Psychology, 82 (December 1969), 472-81.

Hyde, Thomas S. and James J. Jenkins. "Recall for Words as a Function of Semantic, Graphic and Syntactic Orienting Tasks," Journal of Verbal Learning and Verbal Behavior, 12 (October 1973), 471-80.

Jacoby, Jacob. "Consumer Reactions to Information Displays: Packaging and Advertising," in Salvatore F. Divita, ed., Advertising and the Public Interest. Chicago: American Marketing Association, 1974, 101-18.

Jacoby, Jacob. Perspectives on a Consumer Information Processing Program," Communication Research, 2 (July 1975), 203-15.

Jacoby, Jacob, Robert W. Chestnut, Karl C. Weigl, and William Fisher. "Pre-purchase Information Acquisition: Description of a Process Methodology, Research Paradigm, and Pilot Investigation," in Beverlee B. Anderson, ed., Advances in Consumer Research: Vol. III. Cincinnati: Association for Consumer Research, 1976, 306-14.

Jacoby, Jaocb and Jerry C. Olson. "Consumer Reaction to Price: An Attitudinal, Information Processing Perspective," in Yoram Wind and Marshall Greenberg, eds., Moving Ahead with Attitude Research. Chicago: American Marketing Association, 1977, in press.

Jacoby, Jacob, Jerry C. Olson and Rafael A. Haddock. "Price, Brand Name, and Product Composition Characteristics as Determinants of Perceived Quality," Journal of Applied Psychology, 55 (December 1971), 570-9.

Jacoby, Jacob, Donald E. Speller, and Carol A. Kohn-Berning. "Brand Choice Behavior as a Function of Information Load: Replication and Extension," Journal of Consumer Research, 1 (June 1974), 33-42.

Jacoby, Jacob, George J. Szybillo and Jacqueline Busato-Schach. "Information Acquisition Behavior in Brand Choice Situations," Journal of Consumer Research, 3 (March 1977), 209-16.

James, William. Principles of Psychology. New York: Holt, 1890.

Jenkins, James J. "Remember That Old Theory of Memory? Well, Forget It!", American Psychologist, (November 1974), 785-95.

Johnson, Neal F. "Organization and the Concept of a Memory Code," in A. W. Melton and E. Martin, eds., Coding Processes in Human Memory. Washington, D.C.: Winston, 1972.

Kintsch, Walter. The Representation of Meaning in Memory. Potomac, Md.: Lawrence Erlbaum, 1974.

Krugman, Herbert E. "The Impact of Television Advertising: Learning Without Involvement," Public Opinion Quarterly, 29 (Fall 1965), 349-56.

Krugman, Herbert E. "The Measurement of Advertising Involvement," Public Opinion Quarterly, 30 (Winter 1966-67), 383-96.

Kuehl, Philip G. and Robert F. Dyer. "Applications of the 'Normative Belief' Technique for Measuring the Effectiveness of Deceptive and Corrective Advertisements," in William D. Perrault, Jr., ed., Advances in Consumer Research: Vol. IV. Atlanta: Association for Consumer Research, 1977, 204-12.

Kuipers, Benjamin J. "A Frame for Frames: Representing Knowledge for Recognition," in D. G. Bobrow and A. Collins (eds.), Representation and Understanding: Studies in Cognitive Science. New York: Academic Press, 1975.

Lockhart, Robert S., Fergus I. M. Craik and Larry Jacoby. "Depth of Processing, Recognition and Recall," in John Brown, ed., Recall and Recognition. London, Wiley, 1976.

Lutz, Richard J. "Changing Brand Attitudes Through Modification of Cognitive Structure," Journal of Consumer Research, 1 (March 1975), 49-59. (a)

Lutz, Richard J. "First-Order and Second-Order Cognitive Effects in Attitude Change," Communication Research, 2 (July 1975), 289-99. (b)

Lutz, Richard J. "An Experimental Investigation of Causal Relations Among Cognitions Affect and Behavioral Intention," Journal of Consumer Research, 3 (March 1977), 197-208.

Lutz, Richard J. and John L. Swasy. "Integrating Cognitive Structure and Cognitive Response Approaches to Monitoring Communications Effects," in William D. Perrault, Jr., ed., Advances in Consumer Research: Vol. IV. Atlanta: Association for Consumer Research, 1977, 363-71.

Mahoney, Michael J. "Reflections on the Cognitive-Learning Trend in Psychotherapy," American Psychologist, (January 1977), 5-12.

Mazis, Michael B., Olli T. Ahtola, and Eugene R. Klippel. "A Comparison of Four Multi-Attribute Models in the Prediction of Consumer Attitudes," Journal of Consumer Research, 2 (June 1975), 38-52.

McGuire, William J. "Some Internal Psychological Factors Influencing Consumer Choice," Journal of Consumer Research, 2 (March 1976), 302-19.

Miller, George A. "The Magic Number Seven, Plus or Minus Two: Some Limits on Our Capacity for Processing Information," Psychological Review, 63 (March 1956), 81-97.

Minsky, M. "A Framework for Representing Knowledge," in P. H. Winston, ed., The Psychology of Computer Vision. New York: McGraw-Hill, 1975.

Mitchell, Andrew A. and Jerry C. Olson. "Cognitive Effects of Advertising Repetition," in William D. Perrault, Jr., ed., Advances in Consumer Research: Vol. IV. Atlanta: Association for Consumer Research, 1977, 213-20.

Murdock, Bennett B., Jr. Human Memory: Theory and Data. Hillsdale, N.J.: Lawrence Erlbaum, 1974.

Nelson, Phillip. "Information and Consumer Behavior," Journal of Political Economy, 78 (March/April 1970), 311-29.

Nelson, Phillip. "Advertising as Information," Journal of Political Economy, 82 (July/August 1974), 729-54.

Nelson, Thomas O. "Repetition and Depth of Processing," Journal of Verbal Learning and Verbal Behavior, 16 (1977), 151-71.

Newell, Allen and Herbert A. Simon. Human Problem Solving. Englewood Cliffs, N.J.: Prentice-Hall, 1972.

Norman, Donald A. and Daniel G. Bobrow. "On the Role of Active Memory Processes in Perception and Cognition," in Charles N. Cofer, ed., The Structure of Human Memory. San Francisco: W. H. Freeman, 1975.

Olson, Jerry C. "Price as an Informational Cue: Effects on Product Evaluations," in Arch G. Woodside, Jagdish N. Sheth, and Peter D. Bennett, eds., Consumer and Industrial Buying Behavior. New York: Elsevier North-Holland, 1977, 267-86.

Olson, Jerry C. and Philip A. Dover. "Attitude Maturation: Changes in Underlying Belief Structures over Time," in H. Keith Hunt, ed., Advances in Consumer Research: Vol. V. Association for Consumer Research, 1977, in press.

Olson, Jerry C. and Philip A. Dover. "Cognitive Effects of Deceptive Advertising," Journal of Marketing Research, in press.

Olson, Jerry C. and Jacob Jacoby. "Cue Utilization in the Quality Perception Process," in M. Venkatesan, ed., Proceedings, Third Annual Conference. Iowa City, Iowa: Association for Consumer Research, 1972, 167-79.

Olson, Jerry C. and Andrew A. Mitchell. "The Process of Attitude Acquisition: The Value of a Developmental Approach to Consumer Attitude Research," in Mary J. Schlinger, ed., Advances in Consumer Research: Vol. II. Chicago: Association for Consumer Research, 1975, 249-64.

Olson, Jerry C., Daniel R. Toy and Philip A. Dover. "Mediating Effects of Cognitive Response to Advertising on Cognitive Structure," in H. Keith Hunt, ed., Advances in Consumer Research: Vol. V. Association for Consumer Research, 1977, in press.

Paivio, Allan. Imagery and Verbal Processes. New York: Holt, Rinehart and Winston, 1971.

Paivio, Allan. "Coding Distinctions and Repetition Effects in Memory," in Gordon H. Bower, ed., The Psychology of Learning and Motivation: Advances in Research and Theory: Vol. 9. New York: Academic Press, 1975.

Paivio, Allan. "Imagery in Recall and Recognition," in John Brown, ed., Recall and Recognition. London: Wiley, 1976.

Payne, John W. "Heuristic Search Processes in Decision Making," in Beverlee B. Anderson, ed., Advances in Consumer Research: Vol. III. Cincinnati: Association for Consumer Research, 1976, 321-7.

Peterson, L. R. and M. J. Peterson. "Short-term Retention of Individual Verbal Items," Journal of Experimental Psychology, 58 (September 1959), 193-98.

Peterson, Robert A. "The Price-Perceived Quality Relationship: Experimental Evidence," Journal of Marketing Research, 7 (November 1970), 525-8.

Postman, L. "Verbal Learning and Memory," in M. R. Rosenzweig and L. W. Porter, eds., Annual Review of Psychology, Vol. 26. Palo Alto, Calif.: Annual Reviews, Inc., 1975.

Preston, Ivan L. "A Reinterpretation of the Meaning of Involvement in Krugman's Models of Advertising Communication," Journalism Quarterly, 47 (Summer 1970), 287-95.

Pylyshyn, Zenon W. "What the Mind's Eye Tells the Mind's Brain: A Critique of Mental Imagery, Psychological Bulletin, 80 (July 1973), 1-24.

Reitman, Walter R. Cognition and Thought. New York: Wiley, 1965.

Reitman, Walter. "What Does It Take To Remember?", in Donald A. Norman, ed., Models of Human Memory. New York: Academic Press, 1970.

Restle, Frank. "Critique of Pure Memory," in Robert L. Solso, ed., Theories in Cognitive Psychology: The Loyola Symposium. Potomac, Md.: Lawrence Erlbaum, 1974.

Rosch, Elanor. "Cognitive Reference Points," Cognitive Psychology, 7 (October 1975), 532-47.

Rossiter, John R. "Visual and Verbal Memory in Children's Product Information Utilization," in Beverlee B. Anderson, ed., Advances in Consumer Research: Vol. III. Association for Consumer Research, 1976, 523-7.

Rumelhart, D. E., P. H. Lindsay and Donald A. Norman. "A Process Model for Long-Term Memory," in Endel Tulving and W. Donaldson, eds., Organization of Memory, New York: Academic Press, 1972.

Russo, J. Edward and Larry D. Rosen. "An Eye Fixation Analysis of Multi-Alternative Choice," Memory and Cognition, 3 (May 1975), 267-76.

Sawyer, Alan G. "Repetition and Affect: Recent Empirical and Theoretical Developments," in Arch G. Woodside, Jagdish N. Sheth and Peter D. Bennett, eds., Consumer and Industrial Buying Behavior. New York: Elsevier North-Holland, 1977, 229-42.

Schulman, Arthur I. "Encoding Processes and the Memorability of Events," in Alan Kennedy and Alan Wilkes, eds., Studies in Long-Term Memory. London: Wiley, 1975.

Scott, William A. "Conceptualizing and Measuring Structural Properties of Cognition," in O. J. Harvey, ed., Motivation and Social Interaction. New York: Ronald Press, 1963.

Scott, William A. "Psychological and Social Correlates of International Images," in Herbert C. Kelman, ed., International Behavior. New York: Holt, Rinehart and Winston, 1965.

Sheehan, P. W. "The Role of Imagery in Incidental Learning," British Journal of Psychology, 62 (May 1971), 235-44.

Simon, Herbert A. "How Big Is a Chunk?" Science, 183 (February 1974), 482-8.

Tulving, Endel. "Episodic and Semantic Memory," in Endel Tulving and W. Donaldson, eds., Organization of Memory. New York: Academic Press, 1972.

Tulving, Endel and Gordon H. Bower. "The Logic of Memory Representations," in Gordon H. Bower, ed., The Psychology of Learning and Motivation: Advances in Research and, Vol. 8. New York: Academic Press, 1974.

Tulving, Endel and Donald M. Thomson. "Encoding Specificity and Retrieval Processes in Episodic Memory," Psychological Review, 80 (September 1973), 352-73.

Tulving, Endel and Michael J. Watkins. "Structure of Memory Traces," Psychological Review, 82 (July 1975), 261-75.

Underwood, Benton J. "Attributes of Memory," Psychological Review, 76 (November 1969), 559-73.

Walsh, David A. and James J. Jenkins. "Effects of Orienting Tasks on Free-Recall in Incidental Learning: 'Difficulty,' 'Effort,' and 'Process' Explanations," Journal of Verbal Learning and Verbal Behavior, 12 (October 1973), 481-88.

Watkins, Michael J. "When is Recall Spectacularly Higher than Recognition?", Journal of Experimental Psychology, 102 (January 1974), 161-63.

Wickens, Delos D. "Encoding Categories of Words: An Empirical Approach to Meaning," Psychological Review, 77 (January 1970), 1-15.

Wickens, Delos D. "Characteristics of Word Encoding," in A. W. Melton and E. Martin, eds., Coding Processes in Human Memory. Washington, D.C.: Winston, 1972.

Wilkie, William L. "Assessment of Consumer Information Processing Research in Relation to Public Policy Needs." Draft Report to the National Science Foundation (Grant No. GI-42037), June, 1974.

Wilkie, William L. Public policy and product information: Summary findings from consumer research. (NSF report, Grant No. GI-42037). Washington, D.C.: U. S. Government Printing Office, 1975.

Woodside, Arch G. "Relation of Price to Perception of Quality of New Products," Journal of Applied Psychology, 59 (February 1974), 116-8.

Wright, Peter L. "Consumer Judgment Strategies: Beyond the Compensatory Assumption," in M. Venkatesan, ed., Proceedings, Third Annual Conference. Association for Consumer Research, 1972.

Wright, Peter L. "The Cognitive Processes Mediating Acceptance to Advertising," Journal of Marketing Research, 10 (February 1973), 53-62.

Wright, Peter. "Consumer Choice Strategies: Simplifying vs. Optimizing," Journal of Marketing Research, 12 (February 1975), 60-7. (a)

Wright, Peter. "Factors Affecting Cognitive Response to Advertising," Journal of Consumer Research, 2 (June 1975), 1-9. (b)

Wyer, Robert S. "Category Ratings as 'Subjective Expected Values': Implications for Attitude Formation and Change," Psychological Review, 80 (November 1973), 446-67.

Wyer, Robert S., Jr. Cognitive Organization and Change: An Information-Processing Approach. Potomac, Md.: Lawrence Erlbaum, 1974.

EXTRACTING INFORMATION FROM MASS MEDIA ADVERTISEMENTS

Peter Wright, Stanford University

The purpose of this paper is to briefly review what behavioral scientists know about how audiences extract information from mass media advertising. The empirical evidence on this permits only highly qualified conclusions at this point in time, however, the reasons why behavioral scientists have not made more progress on this issue may be of as much interest as a recitation of findings.

This paper will also show, wherever possible, instances where behavior science may prove helpful to economists to aid them in understanding the transmission of information between buyers and sellers in markets. Economists rarely have to wrestle with translating hypothetical internal state variables (e.g., utility; the perceived value of new information; the change that occurs in prior beliefs) into operational measures or with matching a given complex experimental environment in which causal effects on someone's beliefs are documented with some specific complex real-world environment to which specific predictions about comparable effects can reasonably be made. As economists begin to worry over public policy issues which involve intervention in the information-supply available to consumers, the sticky problems of measurement and situational context that occupy much of a behavioral researcher's time will become increasingly salient to economists too.

Constraints on Knowledge of How Audiences Respond to Mass-Media Advertising

Why are only limited generalizations available about how audiences derive new information from a mass media advertisement? One reason is that the parameters of many of the experimental message reception environments in psychologists' or marketing researchers' experiments have been set to encourage active responses by subjects. The list is familiar: The subject is forewarned about the topic of the upcoming message. He is warned, explicitly or implicitly, to expect some sort of post-exposure test. He is force-exposed to an isolated message one time, and he then answers more-or-less directive questions about his mental world. Experiments with the opposite set of characteristics -- no forewarnings about topic or testing, exposure in a clustered situation where stimuli other than the message compete for and sometimes demand one's attention, exposure to a series of terse multi-media messages (as on television) followed by a period featuring new distractions and no necessary incentive to engage in contemplation about what one just heard or read -- are unfortunately quite rare. So the sampling of message reception environments in persuasion process research has been skewed. Further, in many cases seemingly interesting aspects of an experimental setting are not monitored, such as a subject's topical interest, the intensity of distractors in the immediate environment, etc. Or those situational parameters which are held constant throughout an experiment are not chosen with another generic real-world message-reception setting in mind, especially not a mass-media message reception setting.

A second problem is that to relate experimental findings to real-world message reception settings, one must know what the real-world setting of interest is like. In setting public policy, this means "typical" real-world mass media message-reception settings. But if behavioral scientists know more about how to characterize the magazine-reading or television-watching environments of

interest than do economists, it is primarily because they are more aware of which parameters might be important influences on behavior and hence worth trying to describe. Characterizations of "typical" settings are not based on empirical studies that describe the frequency with which audiences find themselves in generic types of advertising-reception settings, because descriptive research like this is done only rarely. In a sense, this is an eminently reasonable allocation of scarce research resources; until one has a good idea about the factors that strongly influence behavior it is wasteful to try describing behavioral settings, since one's description may well focus on irrelevant parameters and ignore some key ones. However, this presents a problem when a behavioral scientist tries to discuss public policy interventions (or any interventions) that will ultimately unfold in a melange of message-reception settings (e.g., the television-watching settings of the adult population of the country). What is the distribution of these settings like on theoretically important variables? In what proportion of the magazine-reading or television-watching episodes that occur are audience members acutely, moderately, and trivially motivated to bother trying to decode an advertisement's assertions and to respond? In what proportion of television-watching settings is an audience member slightly, moderately, or almost totally distracted from receiving an advertising message by the extraneous sights or sounds nearby? In what proportion of television advertisements is a combination of audio-text, moving pictures, and superimposed print concurrently used for most of the transmission period? Because no one documents these things, behavioral scientists must draw on personal experiences honed by research-induced sensitivity to the important situational factors in the settings they personally observe in characterizing "typical" mass-media advertising reception settings.

Aside from this problem of going from research to theory to real-world settings, there is the problem of defining and measuring someone's "state of information." Assuming that information is defined in terms of someone's subjective beliefs, what types of subjective beliefs are of interest? In executing a decision-making strategy, different categories of beliefs become relevant to a consumer. One task that has occupied behavioral theorists is building taxonomies of beliefs, as a basis for research on the differential responsiveness of different types of beliefs to different types of message transmissions or on the way that a change in one type of belief causes change in another. These taxonomical schemes, often labeled "cognitive structure theories," describe how people may partition information stored in memory (e.g., Azjen and Fishbein [1]). These may stimulate economists toward more precision in defining the "information" that is the object of their own theorizing. Their relevance to the question of responses to mass-media advertising is suggested by a simple decomposition of a consumer's decision process into hypothetical stages. A person (1) defines the target number of options he can buy, (2) defines the candidates he will review, (3) defines the cues on which he will try to make discriminations, (4) defines the comparison operations and final stopping rule he will apply, (5) samples his beliefs about the attributes that he associates with an option, the outcomes he associates with those attributes, and/or the value he associates with those outcomes, and outputs a choice. Let us call the first four activities "problem framing" and the activity in which someone executes a choice procedure that is parameterized by his "information" about option-attribute, attribute-outcome, and outcome-value links "preference determination". Without becoming too theoretical, we are quickly confronted with a plethora of subjective beliefs that can enter and bias a consumer's decision-making. Now in talking about providing information, which types of information do we mean?

Approaches to the Question of How People Extract Information from Media Advertising

Behavioral researchers have tended to focus on people's beliefs about option-attribute, attribute-outcome, or outcome-value links, or on global beliefs about option-value links, called attitudes. Most of the theorizing and virtually all the empirical research is on how messages bias beliefs. This means, of course, that little is known about how mass-media messages supply information relevant to a consumer's problem-framing activities. To the extent economists decide that it is information about the candidates to consider, the cues to consider, and the choice strategy to apply that their own theorizing of public policy concerns makes important, they face an opportunity to influence behavioral research by their own ideas about the supply of and demand for problem-framing information. To the extent economists decide that it is preference-determination type of information that their theorizing and public policy concern highlights, they may find interesting empirical research that has already been done.

One can discern in psychological theories at least four versions of how ads bias one's beliefs about a product's properties or one's global evaluation of it.

(1) Beliefs about properties are revised, due to ad-stimulated implicative reasoning.

The ad explicitly describes the advertiser's beliefs about his product's, perhaps with supportive evidence from empirical tests, means-ends logic, or other people's experiences/beliefs. The audience member more-or-less critically tests this mixture of opinions, logic, and data against his own prior beliefs. His cognitive activity of this sort culminates in a revision of some of his beliefs about the product's properties. If one presents him with belief scales on which he can describe the current state of his beliefs, his ad-stimulated responses will show up as belief-scale changes.

(2) Beliefs are reconciled with each other via conscious cognitive reasoning or via consistency-maintenance mechanisms.

The argument is that sometimes an audience member who works through to a belief revision about a product property discussed in the ad, ala Version 1, "keeps on pluggin" and accomplishes a whole host of other belief revisions too. These are of the form: "if I change my mind about X, that implies I should also change my mind about Y". One scenario depicts an audience member who sees causal correlations between different product category dimensions, e.g., "low price implies low quality", "bad taste implies strong medicinal value power", "cleansing power implies lots of suds". The audience member keeps on reasoning once one ad-stimulated belief revision occurs to correct other causally related beliefs. Another scenario depicts these similar "second order" belief adjustments occurring somewhat mechanistically, impelled by the person's need to maintain affective balance among his beliefs.

(3) Ads stimulate belief reintegrations via conscious cognitive reasoning or consistency-maintenance mechanisms, that result in changes in global attitudes.

This view also depicts the audience member performing implicative reasoning. Any ad-stimulated belief revisions are factored into a new calculation of the advertised product's global evaluation. An alternate view is that this working-through from belief revision to evaluation/ impression/attitude revision is accomplished more mechanistically, as the fallout from the consistency-restoration drive.

(4) Evaluation revision, "mere exposure" version.

This idea is that repeated exposures to the brand name may lead to a change in one's global evaluation of the brand. No effects of the ad on beliefs about the brand's properties are postulated. Other hypotheses about ads exerting effects on one's global feeling toward a brand without causing any effect on one's subjective information about the brand's properties postulate such things as the audience member letting his affective response to the ad's creative execution bias his global impression of the brand itself. Note that these notions vary in how much cognitive work they envision an audience member accomplishing before the ad completely loses its value as a stimulus and the audience member turns his thoughts to other things.

To document the effect that exposure to a message has on someone's subjective beliefs (i.e., his product-related attribute-outcome-value associations) behavioral researchers have relied heavily on soliciting his endorsements of directive statements that describe possible beliefs he might "hold" at the time. Much can be learned from studies of this type about how messages transmitted in one form or another might affect belief revisions should an audience member have an incentive to worry about the types of beliefs or the belief topics on which the researcher gets an endorsement.

An alternative theoretical perspective for gaining insight about mass media audience behavior involves examining spontaneous audience belief rehearsals (i.e., conscious thinking) to advertisements. Under this perspective, the information one gains from inspecting an advocacy message is primarily the content of one's own spontaneous thoughts that the inspection prompts. There are signs that the direction that future research on persuasion will take is to emphasize spontaneous message-induced belief rehearsals more so than has historically been true. The issues that arise in theorizing about what inspires or facilitates spontaneous audience efforts to generate information from an advocate's message are closely related to information-value theorizing by economists.

The Cognitive-Response Model of Audience Information-Extraction Activity

The "cognitive response" school of thought argues that conscious ad-stimulated thinking is the key response. Cognitive responses (thoughts) are elicited by exposure to an ad. These thoughts are the fodder on which any revisions in prior beliefs, or global expressions of product evaluation, or choice probabilities are based. The ad has an effect only if it elicits conscious thoughts. Hence such responses should be measured directly, but not directively.

Inducing someone to "think" a thought amounts to inducing him to "practice" a cognitive response. Any instance when he consciously thinks a particular product-related or choice problem-related thought represents one rehearsal. Covert subvocal rehearsals of one's thoughts determine in large part which thoughts come naturally to mind in future deliberations, in much the same way that overt practice of motor responses increases one's tendency to display the same response later. Briefly, the idea is that the specific thoughts a person has about problem-framing or preference determination in a given product-choice episode will substantially determine which product is chosen. And the specific thoughts only occur probabilistically, i.e., a person does not necessarily sample the same thoughts on different occasions of pre-choice deliberations in a product category, even holding his exposure to new information constant. In this view, a person's subjective beliefs are merely those associations from his repertoire of associations that become conscious in a given deliberation episode. Among other things, the probability that a given thought occurs in a given deliberation episode is directly related to how frequently the person had rehearsed ("thought") that same idea on prior occasions. Hence, the way an ad biases the outcome of future deliberations is merely by stimulating an audience member to consciously rehearse a response he otherwise would have no reason to rehearse at that time without the ad's presence.

This viewpoint would be compatible with the models that depict an audience member actively generating thoughts in reaction to an ad that in turn trigger other thoughts and that culminate in second-order belief reconciliations or revisions of global evaluations. However, it is also compatible and more appealing if one assumes that in many situations no such elaborate thinking is inspired by an ad exposure. The audience member outputs only a few simple responses and makes no further effort to figure out whether any inconsistencies with prior beliefs are implied, or whether his global impression should change, or anything. Indeed, beyond the thoughts triggered by the ad's presence, he does not bother with added cognitive activity about the product or choice problem until a future event, like the need to express an opinion to someone or the need to deliberate before choice, prompts him.

Clearly, the power of an ad exposure to bias the person's future choices depends on the incremental effect of this episode of thought on the relative rehearsal records of the possible problem framing or preference determination thoughts in his repertoire (all those he has thought on some occasion in the past). So one ad-induced rehearsal of a thought may or may not significantly increase the probability that thought will recur when next the person mulls over the product-choice problem, depending on how actively and often he thinks other thoughts related to the problem in the period near in time to the pre-choice deliberations. (The length of the relevant period over which thought rehearsal records are meaningful is not, of course, known.) Campaigns that can induce self-initiated re-thinkings (belatedly) or that induce self-initiated repetitions of ad assertions, as by singing a jingle, should have more effect.

The Findings

A review of the several dozen experiments where audience thoughts were elicited and analysed suggests that factors which theoretically affect someone's response opportunity can significantly affect his generation of ad-stimulated thoughts. Presumably, increases in response opportunity may be related to decreases in an audience member's expected processing costs vis-a-vis the advertisement. Examples of the variables manipulated in these experiments include whether the mode of the text is audio or print (Wright [13], [14], the intensity of the potential distractors transmitted concurrently to the ad's text or the type of cognitive activity the audience member directs at the distractor (Osterhouse and Brock [7]; Insko, et al. [3]; Keating and Brock [5]; Petty et al. [8]), and the appeal of and the scheduling of the other media transmissions that bracket (lead into and follow) the ad's text (Krugman [6], Roberts and Maccoby [11]). There is also one indication that someone who anticipates attending to and responding to upcoming stimuli (e.g., whatever editorial or programming matter he will find on upcoming pages or in the next radio or TV segment) may tend to curtail responses to the current ad (Cullen [2]), although

the author makes this interpretation post-hoc. Of course there are also experiments where variations in a factor that might affect response opportunity have not seemed to affect cognitive response data (e.g., Ray, Ward, and Lesser [9]; Rothschild [12]; Ray and Webb [10]). In those cases, the other parameters of the ad-reception environment were set to tax fairly heavily someone's response opportunity, perhaps limiting the effect of such things as the number of repeats of the ad in the transmission segment (Rothschild [12]), the level of background conversation (Ray et al. [9]) or the number of directly adjacent ads in the program break (Ray and Webb [10]).

In summary, there is some evidence from the experiments where immediate audience thought samples were elicited that things like audio texts, concurrent ad-related or background distractors, bracketing transmissions, and perhaps anticipated cognitive responses to an upcoming stimulus significantly inhibit audience response opportunity. In these experiments, usually one response inhibitor was varied while others were kept at trivial-to-moderate levels. The combination of several of these response inhibitors should, it seems, most severely inhibit audience response opportunities. Television and to a lesser extent radio create response environments which inherently combine several of these inhibitors. And the way advertisers often use these media (fast-paced, multi-stimulus ads that tailgate into each other) contributes to the effect. The extent of non-media related distractions broadcast media audiences most contend with is not really known, and no doubt varies situationally. But this may add to the inhibiting effect in some situations.

We also have available a number of studies where a factor was manipulated that theoretically should relate to the audience member's acute motivation to respond to the ad. Increased motivation to respond presumably may relate to increases in the audience-member's expected gains from processing an advertisement. My reviews of these effects indicated that they have been weaker and less unpredictable than the effects due to the manipulations of opportunity-related factors (Wright [15], [16]). Examples of manipulations that should have heightened response motivation include leading some women to expect the ad is relevant to an imminent decision (Wright [13], [14]), instructing some subjects to attend to the ad and some elsewhere (Krugman [6]; Ray et al. [9]; Insko et al. [3]), instructing some subjects that the ad's assertions or its source are incompetent (Osterhouse and Brock [7]); making the message more threatening (Janis and Terwilliger [4]) or varying the ad's topic from an apparently trivial one to an apparently more important one (Krugman [6]; Rothschild [12]). These manipulations have not affected thought outputs very much, even when they seemed like quite strong manipulations of the underlying variable. Perhaps heightened acute response motivation may not compensate too much for the inhibiting effects of things like audio texts, distractors, etc. Of course it may be that the attempts to manipulate acute motivation were really not successful.

Empirical evidence about the moderating effects of the personal cognitive skills of the audience member of the audience member's prior stock of ideas about the product is still very scanty, and will not be reviewed here. We may speculate that if the college student populations managed only limited thinking under facilitative conditions in some past studies, segments in a mass media audience who have less cognitive agility will suffer even more from the loss of response opportunity.

SUMMARY AND SPECULATIONS

The perspective adopted in this discussion was that the

"information" an audience member derives from inspecting a media ad takes the form of a subjective belief. He "learns" his own ad-stimulated responses. Further, a person's "current beliefs" are simply whatever sampling of prior thoughts about a topic he calls to mind on a given occasion. So ad exposure can bias the rehearsal records for different beliefs by increasing the number and/or the recency of prior rehearsals of a given belief.

Basically, economists' theorizing about the value of information has borrowed the principle of marginal analysis from the economic model of utility maximization. This emphasizes the comparison of expected costs and expected gains, with the discovery that the two are equal being seen as a signal that one's investment of resources is optimal. Applied to information, the costs of concern would be those associated with the cognitive strain one expects from further processing operations or the expected opportunity costs from forfeiting the chance to devote scarce cognitive capacity to other problem-solving or intrinsically enjoyable cognitive work. The gains presumably have to do with the perceived usefulness to one's foreseeable problems of the information one thinks can be extracted from environmental data one expects to or does encounter.

As is evident from the brief review of behavioral research on audience thought processes, psychologists often seem to implicitly assume that processing costs and perceived information gains are being considered when someone analyses whether or not to continue attending to message or how much effort he should expend doing the "thinking" that extracts information from the stimulus message. Psychologists' tendencies are to worry about how people map processing cost estimations jointly into environmental phenomena and processing acts, recognizing that processing operations may differ (or appear to differ) in the strain they will impose under different conditions. Hence, one can follow the evolution of research on message-stimulated cognitive responses and see the transition from theorizing about environmental effects on general thinking activities to the effects on specific types of activities. Are certain types of audience-produced information more strainful to produce under certain processing conditions? Are certain types of audience-produced information likely to facilitate future judgments moreso than others, as predicted by some normative model, and are these differences accurately recognized in an audience member's intuitive value-of-information computations? These are the questions psychological research on mass-media communication is confronting now. Economists wishing to complicate their own theorizing about information valuation may perhaps do so by keeping abreast of evolving psychological research in this area and adding to it the rigorous normative theorizing economists do so well.

REFERENCES

1. Ajzen, I., and Fishbein, M., Belief, Attitude, Intention, and Behavior. Reading, Massachusetts: Addison Wesley, 1975.

2. Cullen, D., unpublished manuscript, cited in A.G. Greenwald, "Cognitive learning, cognitive response to persuasion, and attitude change." In A.G. Greenwald, T.C. Brock, and T.M. Ostrom [Eds.], Psychological Foundations of Attitudes. New York: Academic Press, 1968.

3. Insko, C.A., Turnbull, W., and Yandell, B., "Facilitative and inhibiting effects of distraction on attitude change," Sociometry, 1974, 37, 508-528.

4. Janis, I.L. and Terwilliger, R.F., "An experimental study of psychological resistance to fear arousing communications," Journal of Abnormal and Social Psychology, 1974, 10, 301-309.

5. Keating, J.P. and Brock, T.C., "Acceptance of persuasion and the inhibition of counterargumentation under various distraction tasks," Journal of Experimental Social Psychology, 1974, 10, 301-309.

6. Krugman, H.E., "The measurement of advertising involvement," Public Opinion Quarterly, 1967, 30, 583-596.

7. Osterhouse, R.A., and Brock, T.C., "Distraction increases yielding to propaganda by inhibiting counterarguing," Journal of Personality and Social Psychology, 1970, 15, 344-358.

8. Petty, R.E., Wells, G.L., and Brock, T.C., "Distraction can enhance or reduce yielding to propaganda: Thought disruption versus effort justification," Journal of Personality and Social Psychology, 1976, (in press).

9. Ray, M.L., Ward, S. and Lesser, G., "Experimentation to improve pretesting of drug abuse education and information campaigns," unpublished NIMH Report, 1973.

10. Ray, M.L., and Webb, P., "Experimental research on the effects of TV clutter: Dealing with a difficult media environment," Marketing Science Institute Working Paper 102, 1976.

11. Roberts, D., and Maccoby, N., "Information processing and persuasion; counterarguing behavior." In New Models for Communications Research. Beverly Hills, California: Sage Publishing, 1973.

12. Rothschild, Michael L., "The effects of political advertising on the voting behavior of a low involvement electorate," unpublished Ph.D. dissertation, 1975, Stanford University.

13. Wright, P., "Analysing media effects on advertising responses," Public Opinion Quarterly, 1974 (a), 38, 192-205.

14. Wright, P., "Factors affecting cognitive resistance to advertising," Journal of Consumer Research, 1975, 12, 60-67 (b).

15. Wright, P., "Cognitive Responses to Mass Media Advocacy and Cognitive Choice Processes", in R. Petty, T. Ostrom and T. Brock [Eds], Cognitive Responses in Persuasion. New York: McGraw-Hill, 1977a, in press.

16. Wright, P., "Research on ad-stimulated thought processes: A Review," Faculty Working Paper, Graduate School of Business, Stanford University, 1977b.

COMMENTS ON BEHAVIORAL AND ECONOMIC APPROACHES TO STUDYING MARKET BEHAVIOR[1]

J. Edward Russo, University of Chicago Graduate School of Business

In the spirit of this conference, one goal of this paper is to identify several conceptual bridges that span the border between economics and behavioral science. The optimization principle is an important common paradigm for theory construction although the individual theories it generates often seem unrelated. An appreciation of shared paradigms for theory generation should increase the accessibility of economic theories to behavioral scientists and vice versa.

A second goal is to comment on the chapters by Bettman, Olson and Wright. Their papers illustrate a new research orientation, the information processing approach. This theoretical viewpoint is growing in importance and will guide the direction of much of consumer research in the near future.

A final goal is the recommendation of a research tactic that could improve both economic and behavioral studies of market behavior. Rather than confine our investigations to existing market environments, we should consider possible alternative environments. Results from analytical and experimental studies of additional environments will both broaden the range of phenomena that inform our theories of market behavior and also enhance the value of resulting policy recommendations.

This chapter is organized around three essential components of any research paradigm, whether in economics or behavioral science. These components are: (1) theory construction, (2) methodology, and (3) research goals.

THEORY CONSTRUCTION

A basis of theory construction that is shared by both economics and behavioral science is the optimization principle. The fundamental idea of optimization is that agents never choose an action that they know is not in their own best interest. The popularity of this principle has been assured by its intuitive appeal and wide applicability. Its application requires only that agents receive feedback, reward or punishment, from their chosen action.

In economics, optimization is associated with the notion of rationality. In behavioral science, optimization translates into the concept of successful adaptation to the environment. Historically, the roots of the rationality viewpoint lie in the concept of Natural Law peculiar to 17th and 18th century science. Just as inanimate objects conformed to the Natural Laws of physics that insured a harmonious universe, so human behavior was viewed as guided by laws that guaranteed proper "moral" functioning. In the language of contemporary economics, agents are viewed as maximizing their utility under various constraints. Naturally, the most prominent of these constraints are economic, such as income and prices, but the complete framework also includes behavioral constraints such as the cost of information gathering and computation.

In contrast, the notion of adaptation has its roots in 19th century Darwinism. Behavioral scientists have transposed the traditional view, a species' adapting to its natural environment over generations through genetic altera-

tion, to an individual organism's adapting to a man-made "task environment" through a relatively rapid learning process. Though this transposition of Darwin may seem too literal, the concept of adaptation has, over the last fifteen years, replaced learning as the closest thing to a unifying paradigm in behavioral science [25].

The identification of rationality with economics and adaptation with behavioral science is not intended to be exclusive. The notion of adaptation predates Darwin, and appears in economics at least as early as Malthus. Similarly, the idea of rational behavior occurs throughout psychology from human engineering to psychopathology. The common thread is the optimality principle, which inspires both the rationality and adaptation viewpoints. This principle, though different in appearance, is similar in substance across the two disciplines. Furthermore, one version of this principle, a cost-benefit analysis, forms an important conceptual link between economics and the behavioral sciences. Cost-benefit analysis is particularly appropriate to the focus of this conference, the role of information in market and consumer behavior.

Failures of Optimization-Based Theories

The optimization principle has provided the foundation for numerous theories, both in economics and behavioral science. These individual theories have not always successfully accounted for human behavior. Of course, the problem may not lie with the optimization principle but rather with the particular instantiation. Indeed, there seems to be little doubt that people sincerely attempt to behave in their own best interests.[2] Why then do we observe consistent discrepancies between a normative model and human behavior?

I want to suggest three reasons for these discrepancies.
1. Capturing human complexity. The optimal model does not adequately reflect complexities of the environment that people incorporate into their behavior.
2. Personal knowledge limitations. The subjective perception of the task does not correspond to the optimal model of that same task.
3. Information processing costs. When the cost of mental effort is considered, a different version of the optimal processing strategy can emerge.

The last of these reasons pertains directly to cost-benefit analyses, which will be discussed shortly. But an appreciation of the first two causes of normative-descriptive differences is also worthwhile.

Capturing Human Complexity

The richness of knowledge that people bring to complex tasks often exceeds researchers' modelling ability. A well-publicized illustration is the present inability to construct a computer-implemented chess algorithm that can beat a chess master.

[1] This chapter has benefited from discussions with Roger Kormendi and Charles Plott. Their contributions are gratefully acknowledged. Support was provided by NSF Grant APR76-81806.

[2] The presumption of striving for optimality is well illustrated by the following apocryphal dialog. A visitor to a behavioral laboratory has been closely observing subjects performing a task. Asking the lab director for his/her explanation of the observed behavior, the visitor inquires, "What exactly are your subjects doing?" "They're doing the best they can" is the only reply.

A more pertinent example, however, is the expected utility (EU) model for risky decisions. This normative model is a classic example of the application of the optimization principle to a specific economic task (although its roots extend to the 17th century, predating formal economics). In the last thirty years, the EU model has been subjected to numerous experimental tests by psychologists, usually in gambling situations. For very simple gambles the EU model, or the SEU model which admits subjective probabilities, adequately accounts for behavior [11, 52]. When experimental subjects gambled for 1, 2, 3 or 4 packs of cigarettes with probability levels of .2, .4, .6 or .8, Tversky [52] observed good, though less than perfect, descriptive validity of the SEU model.

The expectation rule, however, may not adequately characterize optimality in more logically complex environments. (Logical complexities imply a disagreement over the optimal course of action. This is different from the computational confusion caused by combinatorial complexities such as multiple outcomes and compound lotteries.)

An important logical complexity is the conflict between maximizing expectation and minimizing risk. The importance of the concept of risk was illustrated by Allais [2] and Ellsberg [14] in their counterexamples to EU theory. In spite of continued examination of the problem by economists, e.g. [3], and behavioral analyses by psychologists [10], the issue of whether optimal behavior with respect to risk is successfully incorporated within the EU model is not resolved [29].

A major contribution to this resolution has been made by Slovic and Tversky [50] and Kahneman and Tversky [21]. The former demonstrated the empirical validity of Allais's and Ellsberg's counterexamples, even under conditions most favorable to EU theory. Kahneman and Tversky then succeeded in constructing an alternative to the EU model that incorporates several behavioral phenomena yet preserves the notion of optimization. Tversky [54] has claimed that the heart of the problems encountered by EU theory is that the concept of utility was made to bear too heavy a conceptual burden. Utility should represent the value of alternatives; it cannot simultaneously represent the risk that may be associated with those same alternatives when embedded in a wide variety of probabilistic situations.

To summarize, one cause of discrepancies between normative models and observed behavior is that the models themselves may be inadequate. The EU model cannot satisfactorily represent certain risky choice situations (although not everyone would agree with this assertion). Such shortcomings of optimal models do not imply a failure of the optimization principle. Rather, the fault lies in the specific representation of the environment to which the optimization principle is applied.

Personal Knowledge Limitations

Although sometimes the normative model is at fault, more often people cannot match the model's performance. Either their subjective perception of the task environment is inferior to the view represented in the normative model or computational limitations lead to suboptimal performance. Computational problems are postponed until the next section. Here we consider knowledge limitations, i.e., when the subjective understanding of the situation differs from the representation of the optimal model.

Consider dynamic probabilistic decision environments where people often diverge markedly from the optimal Bayesian model [49, 55]. In a typical situation, samples are drawn (with replacement) from a bag that contains either 70 Red and 30 Blue chips or 30 Red and 70 Blue chips. A correct guess might be rewarded by a $2 payment, with no loss for being wrong; and samples might cost 1¢ each. The task for the experimental subjects is to decide when they have purchased just enough samples. The normative Bayesian model specifies the optimal decision criterion solely in terms of $|N_R - N_B|$, the difference between the frequencies of red chips (N_R) and blue chips (N_B) in the observed sample [12]. For the parameters given above the optimal point at which sampling should cease is $|N_R - N_B| = 5$.

Experimental subjects, however, don't employ anything like this strategy.[3] Instead, they seem to use the representativeness heuristic described by Kahneman and Tversky [20]. The subjectively relevant statistic is not $|N_R - N_B|$ but $N_R/(N_R + N_B)$, the relative frequency of red chips. Subjects are most confident of their decisions when $N_R/(N_R + N_B) = .70$, i.e., when the observed sample is most representative of the population.

This type of suboptimality is not easily removed. It is generally assumed that the optimization principle incorporates a kind of self-educating mechanism. Whenever the environment provides feedback, people will approach optimal performance as they gain experience or as the stakes are raised. Unfortunately, this is not always the case. As long as the representativeness heuristic is used there will be a suboptimal upper bound on performance. To attain optimality, the optimal strategy (or some equivalent) must be discovered. If this strategy is counterintuitive, as in the present example,[4] its discovery is a formidable intellectual task.

Consider a gambling experiment by Lichtenstein and Slovic [26] which exposed an inconsistent weighting of probability and payoff that depended on how people were asked to evaluate the gambles. When choosing between a pair of gambles with equal EV, the experimental subjects considered probability and payoff to be about equally important. But when judging the certainty (cash) equivalent for the same gambles, the payoff was significantly overweighted. As with most such experimental demonstrations, college students were used as subjects and the stakes were low. To test the robustness of the observed inconsistency Lichtenstein and Slovic [27] repeated the study in Las Vegas using professional gamblers who played with their own money for much higher stakes. The Las Vegas gamblers exhibited the same inconsistency as college students.

This phenomenon was analyzed with respect to the economic theory of preference by Grether and Plott [18]. These two economists considered alternative explanations consistent with preference theory, conducted the critical experimental tests, and reconfirmed Slovic and Lichtenstein's original findings (somewhat to their dismay[5]). Their paper is highly recommended as testimony to the persistence of suboptimality induced by personal knowledge limitations.

---

[3] This and subsequent assertions about behavior in this task environment are based on an unpublished experiment that I performed in collaboration with Ward Edwards and Cameron Peterson.

[4] The optimal Bayesian strategy implies equal diagnostic value for a sample of 4 red and 0 blue chips as for a sample of 1004 red and 1000 blue chips. This complete independence of sample size is counterintuitive even to persons with statistical training.

[5] In their conclusion, Grether and Plott [18] state, "Needless to say the results we obtained were not those expected when we initiated this study. Our design controlled for all the economic theoretic explanations of the phenomenon which we could find. The preference reversal phenomenon which is inconsistent with the traditional statement of preference theory remains."

The expense of conducting experiments for large cash rewards using experienced subjects prohibits more demonstrations like the one in Las Vegas. Nonetheless, it is generally recognized in behavioral studies that knowledge limitations are seldom overcome through greater experience or larger rewards alone. Often considerable effort must be made to educate decision makers about the optimal representation of the task environment.

Information Processing Costs

Both economics and behavioral science have shown an increasing recognition of information acquisition and processing costs. The last ten years of research literature in economics reflects an accelerating concern with incorporating such costs into economic models. Similarly the information processing paradigm has recently come to dominate research in psychology [45]. Nonetheless, failure to incorporate information processing costs into normative models is probably the most common source of the descriptive inaccuracy of these models. Because these costs are an especially important factor in market behavior, the consequences of ignoring them are considered and illustrated below.

The heart of the problem is the failure to fully appreciate the conflict between information processing costs and decision accuracy. Consider the following example. The reader is asked to participate in this example by performing the decision task just as if the lotteries were actually available. The time required is brief, and the lesson valuable. One condition: no computational aids like pencil and paper are permitted.

Consider the pair of simple gambles shown below. The probability of winning the designated amount is shown; nothing can be lost. The task is to choose the more attractive gamble.[6]

.27	.59
$8.50	$3.80 (a)

To facilitate the development of a stable strategy, subjects are required to perform more than one such choice, often many of them. Because it is important to the present demonstration, four more pairs of gambles are presented and the reader is asked to choose the higher EV gamble in each case. The correct answers are given below.[7]

.85	.41		.48	.39
$3.60	$7.60 (b)		$3.40	$4.30 (c)

.71	.53		.94	.83
$6.90	$9.10 (d)		$6.20	$7.10 (e)

The most obvious decision strategy is straightforward calculation of the EV of each gamble in a pair. The trouble with this multiplication strategy is that the computation cost is high. People typically need three to four minutes when first using this strategy. (The mean time drops to less than two minutes with an hour of practice and to less than one minute with several hours of practice.) Consider the value of this time compared to a pure guessing strategy that can be executed in a few seconds. The multiplicative strategy produces an EV gain of about .6¢ per decision, assuming perfect accuracy. At 3.5 minutes per decision this is equivalent to paying oneself a wage rate of 5¢/hr.[8]

Since the multiplicative strategy is unreasonably effortful, what strategies do people use to choose among gambles like those above? The strategies of ten experimental subjects were investigated by recording eye fixation sequences and verbal reports [41]. The data reveal almost zero use of the multiplicative strategy. Instead, subjects tended to rely on attribute differences, i.e., on the differences between the two probabilities and between the two payoffs. In almost all cases it could not be concluded precisely how the pairwise choice was based upon these two differences. However, it was clear that attribute differences were almost always computed and that the multiplication dictated by the EV rule was rarely performed.

The finding described above is not singular. In his chapter Bettman describes an experiment that demonstrates how the strategy chosen to acquire product information will adapt to the presentation format of that information [6]. Independent of their predispositions, subjects tended to choose an acquisition strategy that minimized effort. In a choice among six used cars, Russo and Rosen [43] reported a pair comparison strategy in which the pairs were selected to minimize effort rather than to maximize choice accuracy. For example, one alternative in a pair comparison was usually carried over to the next comparison, thereby preserving some of the contents of short-term memory.

The desire to minimize information processing costs can, in the extreme, have a disastrous effect on choice accuracy. In a second experiment Russo and Dosher [41] demonstrate the adoption of the "majority of confirming dimensions" heuristic. The heuristic is a simplification of the additive difference rule for multiattribute binary choices [53]. Instead of computing the magnitude of the difference between the two alternatives on each attribute, only the direction of each attribute is discerned. The alternative with more attributes in its favor becomes the tentative choice. Although this majority choice is then revised to take into account the magnitude of the attribute differences, this adjustment is usually incomplete, and a bias toward the majority alternative remains. For the half of the choices when the majority alternative was not correct, the eleven experimental subjects chose this incorrect alternative 61% of the time, an error rate significantly below chance. I know of only one other report in the experimental choice literature of below chance performance [53]. The trade-off between processing effort and choice accuracy implies that different strategies are not just different paths to the same goal (an accurate choice). The less effortful strategies don't reach this goal at all a higher proportion of the time.

A real-world demonstration of the damage of information processing difficulty to choice accuracy exists in consumer behavior. Shoppers were sent to typical supermarkets and asked to find items with the lowest unit prices. In those stores, only total prices were posted. In five independent replications of this experiment the error rate ranged between 43% and 54% [42]. In all cases the shoppers, many of whom had college degrees, were highly motivated and were under no external time constraints.

---

[6]Occasionally it helps to expand the instructions to "more attractive in the long run," referring to repeated plays of the same gamble. But most college students who have served as subjects in experimental versions of this task are aware they should choose the gamble with the larger EV.

[7]The five gambles with the higher EV are left, right, right, left and right.

---

[8]This estimate assumes that there is no "psychological" reward associated with getting the correct answer. It is difficult to eliminate such psychic transactions, but the satisfaction of being correct cannot be very great for such a strenuous, noncreative task as mental multiplication performed repeatedly. In addition, subjects perform the task in computer-controlled isolation, with minimal social reinforcement from the experimenter.

The error rates are well explained by the magnitude of the information processing costs in this task. Gatewood and Perloff [17] compared the situation without unit prices to one when those calculations had already been performed and posted. Their experimental subjects took eight times longer to find the lowest unit priced item when they had to compute unit prices themselves. See Wright [57] for a further discussion.

The decision to purchase insurance provides another example of the negative effect of the desire to minimize information processing costs [48]. When the probability of loss falls below some threshold, people apparently approximate it to zero. This leads to the decision not to purchase insurance against low-probability, high-loss events.

Cost-Benefit Analysis

The preceding assertions and examples are reconciled with the optimization principle via the framework of a cost-benefit analysis. When people adapt to decision environments they select a strategy that will minimize total cost, i.e. the cost of errors and the cost of effort. Cost-benefit analysis has an intuitive appeal almost as great as that of the optimization principle itself. At this intuitive level it has a long history of acceptance in both economics and psychology. The difficulties with cost-benefit analysis have occurred either when optimal theories were expanded to include the effect of transaction costs or when applications have required the accurate measurement of these costs.

The record of substantive use of cost-benefit analysis is significantly better in economics than in psychology. Information costs have been intensively modelled, especially recently but extending back at least to the work of Stigler [51]. Applications involving the complete measurement of costs and benefits have been less frequent, occurring mainly in public economics. This concentration is more a reflection of measurement problems, both theoretical and practical, than of any failure to accept the concept of a cost-benefit analysis. In psychology, only a few cost-benefit analyses can be found, mainly in cognitive processes [36, 38] and in evaluation research [13, 15]. The early time and motion studies of industrial engineering should also be acknowledged [4]. By and large, however, the record is neither as good as that of economics nor as hopeful of improvement. Because I believe behavioral cost-benefit analyses are critical to the development of theories of market behavior, the problem in psychology is considered further.

The new breed of information processing psychologists has chosen to focus on processing limitations rather than on processing costs. These limitations are viewed as fixed constraints rather than as resources to be allocated. The classic example is the limit of five to seven items that can be retained in short-term memory. The trade-off between processing costs and task accuracy demonstrated above has been avoided by assuming that motivation levels are always high enough to assure asymptotic performance. In other words, "motivation" is so high that optimal adaptation means only the minimization of errors, and not the minimization of processing costs as well. (This ignoring of "operational costs" may be an unfortunate holdover from the original metaphor for adaptation, biological evolution. There the "costs" of adaptation are invisibly borne by the mutating species over a very long period of time.)

Although cost-benefit analysis has not been as generally accepted in psychology as in economics, there are two reasons to expect this to change in the near future. First, the cost-benefit framework is beginning to appear in basic research into detailed cognitive processes. For example, Posner and his associates have applied this framework to the allocation of visual attention [36, 37]. Second, the

growing focus on the effect of information on market behavior will eventually necessitate an explicit recognition of information processing costs. For example, reorganizing unit prices into a single list has been shown to triple the impact of this form of price information on actual purchases [37]. Similarly, providing energy consumption information in terms of a percentage change from the previous year can reduce residential energy use by 3% [39]. Both of these changes in purchase patterns were accomplished almost exclusively by reducing the cost of information processing.

The optimization principle per se was not discussed in any of the three papers in this session. However, Bettman explicitly considers the costs and benefits of information search. He also points out the naivete of presuming that consumers consciously "assess the marginal revenue of various advertisements." It is natural to ask why we didn't see more use of the optimization principle in these three papers. Olson's paper reflects the current situation in psychology, namely little use of the optimization principle in general and cost-benefit analysis in particular. Wright's paper is devoted exclusively to one market activity, advertising. This topic raises the question of whether all market behavior is goal-directed and therefore amenable to optimization-based analyses. Phrased differently, the question becomes: is there nonrational consumer behavior?

Nonrational Behavior

In the following discussion nonrational behavior refers to behavior that is not consciously rational or is not deliberately goal-directed. This usage should not be confused with philosophical analyses of irrationality that involve epistemological questions and such distinctions as irrational ends versus irrational strategies given rational ends [5]. The behavioral view is captured in the difference between top-down (or goal-driven) and bottom-up (or data-driven) processing [33]. Any conscious execution of a goal-oriented strategy is top-down processing. The focus of the present discussion, however, is the large part of our cognitive activity, including market-related activity, that is data- or stimulus-driven.

Bottom-up cognitive activity is nonrational in the sense that it is not consciously purposive or goal-directed. Consider the classic psychiatric use of free association. Patients are instructed to respond to a cue word with the first word to come into their minds. These instructions are designed to prevent goal-directed strategies for censorship from concealing natural, possibly unattractive, associations. For example, first responses to the word "black," such as negro, often reveal racial associations that are censored in most social situations.

The perception of advertisements is an example of nonrational data-driven behavior. Most advertisements are perceived under so-called low involvement conditions. Consider a television advertisement about dentures seen by a viewer with natural teeth. This person has no interest in the advertised good and no deliberate effort is made to apprehend the advertisement's message [16]. Yet casual observation will reveal that this same low involved viewer is fully attending to the television during the advertisement. Explaining this high attention but low involvement phenomenon at a micro level does not involve the optimization principle or a cost-benefit analysis. One can rephrase low involvement perception in this framework (e.g., by citing the entertainment value of the advertisement), but such a conceptualization seems forced and is not particularly useful.

Conclusion

The optimization paradigm is shared by economics and behavioral science, although its role is more central in the former. The resistance of psychologists to a more optimization-oriented view stems from the consistent discrepancies between normative theories and observed behavior.[9] When these discrepancies occur because of subjective knowledge limitations psychologists focus on these limitations, accepting the problems of idiosyncratic perceptions of reality. In contrast, the phenomena of economics are more aggregate in nature, and there is less interest in individual limitations and their consequences. The area of information transaction costs, especially in the marketplace, is one where economists and psychologists can comfortably share the framework of a cost-benefit analysis. I am hopeful that important work in market behavior will emerge from both disciplines, either independently or jointly.

The Concept of Information

Central to this conference is the concept of information. If economists and behavioral scientists are to communicate effectively it is essential that they share the same definition of information. Olson forcefully presents the current behavioral view, that the information in a message can only be defined in terms of the personal interpretation of the recipient. This contrasts with the Shannon-Weaver measure of information, $-\sum_i p_i \log p_i$, where p_i is the prior probability of receiving the ith message.

Let me state now that I believe that Olson is correct. The same message can mean different things to different people, including market messages that are apparently factual. For example, the announcement that bed sheets are percale not muslin is informative only if the meanings of percale and muslin are already known. An advertisement claiming that a breakfast cereal is "natural" may be interpreted as "healthy for me" by the credulous, as misleading puffery by the cynical, or as a claim requiring verification by the consumerist.

The trouble with the Shannon-Weaver measure is that it focuses entirely on the stimulus, i.e., on the message. It ignores differences in the human receiver, assuming tacitly that all persons will uniformly comprehend the received message. Attempts to use the Shannon-Weaver measure to explain human information processing have been largely unsuccessful [8]. Its use is restricted to message sets that are carefully circumscribed and highly structured. Of course, the measure does offer the advantages of objectivity and numerical precision. However, any meaningful conceptualization of information must include a subjective component based on the existing knowledge and dispositions of the message's recipient.

To summarize, information must be defined in terms of the subjective complexity of the receiver's internal representation of the message. Information is not simply a property of the message, but also of the individual recipient. Let me suggest a simple procedure for coping with the temptation to oversimplify the concept of information. Substitute the word knowledge. Thinking of the information conveyed in a marketing message as the knowledge conveyed can help avoid the problem of associating information solely with the message/stimulus.

METHODOLOGIES

The gap between economics and behavioral science is probably widest in the area of methodology. This differ-

[9]Abelson [1] has noted that a further difficulty psychologists have with the concept of rationality is that it seems "too prescriptive." Psychologists are wary of the ease of confusing personal values with scientific beliefs. Abelson thoroughly considers this and other difficulties, and his paper is recommended.

ence between the two disciplines is manifest in the papers delivered at this conference. Although much could be said about each of the available methodologies, the present discussion is restricted to a contrast between the preferred methodologies of economics and behavioral science and to some comments on the papers by Bettman, Olson and Wright.

Empirical Versus Experimental

To simplify the discussion, all methodologies will be classified into three categories:
1. observational records, such as market shares and advertising expenditures;
2. questionnaire surveys, including all verbal report data; and
3. controlled experiments, whether conducted in a laboratory or in the field.

The list is roughly ordered from empirical to experimental and from aggregate to individual.

The central thesis of this discussion is that an effective study of market behavior will require more controlled experimentation, especially field experiments. Economic analyses of market behavior have relied primarily on observational records. This is especially true of econometric models for predicting aggregate behaviors like future sales from advertising expenditures [7, 9]. In contrast, behavioral studies of market phenomena are typically questionnaire surveys and controlled experiments. The studies discussed by Bettman, Olson and Wright are almost exclusively of this type.

Needed Behavioral Methodology

I want to encourage behavioral researchers of market phenomena to expand their methodological repertoire in two directions, field experimentation and process tracing.

Field experimentation is best viewed as the culmination of a research process. This process begins with a questionnaire-type study that qualitatively establishes the range of shopper reactions to a potential market manipulation. The next phase is controlled experimentation in the laboratory to identify the relevant variables and to estimate the relative strengths of the possible treatments. Finally, an experiment in the field provides realistic estimates of the effect of manipulation, and also its cost. This last information offers both validity to researchers and relevancy to policy makers. This three-stage process is familiar to industry practitioners. To cite just one example, the marketing of new products tends to follow this procedure (although the laboratory stage is sometimes omitted).

Behavioral researchers seldom go as far as the stage of field experimentation. Indeed, far too many behavioral studies rely exclusively on questionnaire methods, not even observing the relevant nonverbal behavior in the laboratory. Economists, though shy of the laboratory, have been less reluctant to engage in large-scale field experiments, like the New Jersey negative income tax study [23, 34]. Behavioral researchers should consider adopting the approach of economists and marketing practitioners in this regard.

The second direction for the expansion of behavioral methodology is process analysis. This approach involves a dynamic view of consumer behavior, in contrast to the more familiar static methods.

Static Versus Dynamic Analyses of Consumer Behavior

The traditional analyses of observed behavior have attempted to relate the output of a behaving system to its input. This static approach makes no attempt to observe the inner workings of the behaving system. The resulting models are "as if" models with no pretensions of process veridicality. A prototypical example is the use of observed choices to infer decision rules. Bettman accurately surveys this literature in the area of consumer decisions.

Dynamic analyses refer to theories that describe the time course of behavior. They have arisen in cognitive psychology as part of the information processing paradigm, and are especially associated with Newell and Simon's studies of problem solving, e.g. [30]. To model the dynamics of behavior, data that reveal the actual cognitive processes are needed. The most common process tracing data are verbal protocols, subjects' "thinking aloud" verbalizations of their thoughts as they are performing some task. The formal analysis of these data was pioneered by Newell and Simon. Another method is to record the sequence of eye fixations exhibited during a cognitive process [40].

Dynamic analyses have recently been introduced into the study of consumer behavior, especially consumer decision making. Bettman surveys the emerging literature, including some of his own experimental work. I believe that dynamic analyses offer major advantages for research advancement over input-output analysis. An example may help make this point. That data are taken from my own research, as yet unpublished.

A combination of eye fixations and verbal protocols were used to trace several shopping decisions for 47 consumers. The data reveal a three-stage process: an initial overview, followed by a detailed comparison of products, terminating in a confirmation of the tentative choice. Not every stage occurs for each purchase decision, especially if the shopper needs only to locate the habitually purchased brand/size. A hypothetical but quite representative sequence of eye fixations is shown in Figure 1.

FIGURE 1

REPRESENTATIVE HYPOTHETICAL SEQUENCE OF EYE
FIXATIONS FROM A CONSUMER CHOICE TASK

Seneca with Cinnamon 15 oz. 39¢ (29)	Mott's Natural Style 20 oz. 55¢ (28)	S&W Gravenstein 8.5 oz. 27¢	Town House Gravenstein 8.5 oz. 22¢ 2
S&W Gravenstein 15 oz. 43¢ 7, 9, 17	Country Pure unsweetened 14 oz. 43¢ 8, 19, (27)	Town House Gravenstein 15 oz. 39¢ 10, 15	Town House Gravenstein 25 oz. 52¢ 1, 11, 23
S&W Gravenstein 25 oz. 70¢ 6, 18	Mott's 25 oz. 56¢ (26)	Country Pure unsweetened 23 oz. 54¢ 21	Town House Gravenstein 35 oz. 69¢ 12
Seneca 46 oz. 97¢ 5	Apple Time 49 oz. $1.04 4	Mott's 35 oz. 75¢[a] 25 3, 14, 16, 20, 22	Town House Gravenstein 50 oz. 99¢ 13, 24

[a]This is the brand/size usually purchased and the one chosen during this decision.

The fixations shown in parentheses, 26 to 29, were generated after the chosen product was announced and the shopper was turning away from the display. This post-decision checking occurred in over half of the purchase decisions.

The comparison stage is the most important and the longest, accounting for an average of 70% of the decision time. In the example the comparison stage extends from Fixations 7 to 22. This stage is composed mainly of pair comparisons, a result also found in nonconsumer decisions

[43]. Furthermore, those pair comparisons tend to be anchored on the brand/size habitually purchased whenever there is one. The overview and confirmation stages account for the remaining time, with the former usually longer.

Putting these data together provides the following picture of the consumer choice process. Consumers initially examine the display and often eliminate entire groups of brands or sizes while searching for their usual brand/size and likely alternatives to it. The usual choice is directly compared to one or more possible competitors until a tentative decision is made. That decision is briefly checked by scanning the product display for the last time. This description of the consumer choice process is much more detailed than could have been obtained from an input-output analysis. It has important implications for the provision of product information by either sellers or public policy makers.

The only major criticism I have of Olson's paper is that in his discussion of encoding and memory he ignores dynamic analyses, e.g. [44]. These analyses are infrequent, but important. Olson partly covers this topic in his presentation of episodic memory, but the full importance of dynamic analyses is not appreciated.

Needed Economics Methodology

From a methodological perspective, economists' studies of market behavior are narrowly restricted in scope. Empirical work is based almost exclusively on observational records. Exceptions are some questionnaire surveys, notably the tradition established by Katona [22], and a few major field experiments like the negative income tax study cited earlier. Recently a line of laboratory-based experimental work has been initiated by economists investigating decision making [28]. This work, though encouraging, is uncommon.

The predominant focus on aggregate phenomena explains, to a large extent, the reliance on observational records. Many economists feel that individual behavior is the trees while aggregate behavior is the forest whose shape they must not lose sight of. Although this is usually good advice, sometimes it is not. For example, questionnaire surveys based on only hundreds of subjects are such good predictors of market behavior that they are the most frequently used method in market research. Many microeconomic theories, such as decision and utility theory, can be adequately tested on even fewer individuals.

I suggest that there is a growing place in economics for controlled experimentation. I foresee an enlarged emphasis on process-based explanations which will require more detailed empirical observations. For example, theories for predicting aggregate phenomena like market shares are being elaborated to predict brand switching rates. These switching rates are affected by market information like advertising and price changes. The pursuit of these effects on market share will require the observation of individual consumers in a controlled experimental framework. The need for this methodological expansion is particularly strong in the areas where economics borders the behavioral sciences. The focus of this conference, market behavior, is certainly one such area. Now this is not to say that every economist should become an experimental researcher, any more than one needs a Ph.D. in statistics to perform a regression analysis. But a functional acquaintance with experimental methodology will facilitate communication, or even cooperative research, with the behavioral science community.

Validity of Wright's Cognitive Response Technique

A major methodological problem for consumer behavior is the validity of verbal reports. These data are often inconsistent with observations of the behavior they are supposed to describe or predict [56]. Bettman acknowledges this problem and cites Newman and Lockeman's study [31] as an example in consumer research. In this experiment subjects' descriptions of information searched while buying shoes differed markedly from the search revealed by unobtrusive observation.

Unfortunately the methodology used by Wright relies exclusively on verbal reports. Subjects in Wright's experiments view advertisements. After each one they are asked to recall and write out all thoughts that occurred as they viewed the ad. They are given exactly three minutes for this recall task.

A major problem with this technique is the absence of a validity check on the responses. How can the experimenter distinguish between genuine recall of past cognitive activity and three minutes of realistic fiction? The danger is especially great for retrospective verbal protocol [32]. Furthermore, recalling cognitive details from memory is difficult enough for tasks with a logical episodic structure that can aid memory. But such recall is even more difficult for a task as unstructured as the viewing of advertisements. Since experimental subjects are required to write for three minutes even if they cannot recall this much cognitive activity, they must surely be tempted to generate spurious retrospections.

A second major problem originates in the associative nature of human thought processes. There is a continuous generation of associations to any active concept. Thus, as valid cognitive responses are recalled and written, new associations are occurring. Since writing a complete thought requires considerable time, many newly activated associations become available for confusion with the valid previous ones. Note that this potential source of invalidity could be reduced if subjects in Wright's experiments could report their cognitive responses orally. Because speaking is much faster than writing, there would be less time for the confusing spread of new associations. [10]

A final criticism of Wright's technique is that it relies exclusively on conscious cognitive responses. I have argued elsewhere that much of the power of advertising lies in infraconscious associations [16]. Thus, the cognitive response technique may be missing much of the full cognitive activity stimulated by an advertisement. The missed infraconscious activity is probably more important for understanding advertising than for any other common mental activity (with the possible exception of dreams). The persuasive power of advertising relies crucially on this infraconscious activity.

A major attraction of Wright's technique is its cost effectiveness. And it must be recognized that because of its use much more is now known about our reactions to advertising messages. Nonetheless, we should not rely on Wright's technique as exclusively as we have, especially because other methods are available, e.g. [16].

RESEARCH GOALS

Scientific Versus Applied Goals

There is a traditional distinction between basic and applied research: physics versus engineering, biology versus medicine, etc. However, the basic-applied difference is smallest in the social sciences.

As Simon [47] has persuasively argued, because the phenomena of the social sciences are generated by agents

---

10This criticism is outdated at least with respect to Wright's laboratory. He is now tape recording subjects' cognitive responses [58].

adapting to man-made environments, these phenomena are "artificial." He contrasts these with the "natural" behavior of objects obeying physical laws. The most important implication of the artificiality of economic and social phenomena is their impermanence. A ball on an inclined plane will behave today just as it did for Galileo, but the behavior of agents in the marketplace reflects the profound economic and social changes of four centuries.

This continual change in the environment, and therefore in behavior, complicates the work of the social scientist. Consider, for example, the role of nutrition in shoppers' evaluation of food products. This is a complex concept and tracing its role in the purchase decision is quite difficult. But this task becomes even more complex when we recognize the recent changes in the composition of foods (vitamin fortification and other chemical additives), in knowledge about nutrition (the value of fiber and the danger of refined sugar), and even in food advertising (the promotion of "natural" brands). The continual change in the phenomena of social science undercuts the concept of a scientific fact. What is true today of the role of vitamins, fiber or sugar in food purchase decisions may not be true in a few years.

The transitoriness of economic and social behavior presents both a problem and an opportunity. The problem is ecological validity. The opportunity is to create novel environments. This paper concludes with a consideration of each of these issues.

Ecological Validity

The admission that (social) scientific phenomena reflect transient environments prompts the question: how do we know that we are studying the right environment? This question is more than rhetorical. Economists have sometimes been accused of building models of an economic system that has not existed for 10 or even 50 years. Similarly, psychoanalysts are sometimes accused of relying on a theory of personality that might have been true in Freud's time but is not in ours (e.g., with respect to sex).

The issue is one of ecological validity. Does the environment we are modelling, or simulating in the laboratory, correspond to the real-world environment to which we expect our results to generalize? The problem is not only the study of anachronistic environments like the examples given above. It is also a matter of focusing on the most important aspects of the environment. For example, social psychologists who study the criminal justice system have tended to focus on the behavior of juries. However, in a recent analysis of felony arrests, Konecni [24] found that fewer than 2% eventually get to a jury trial. The remainder are decided by the police (released without charging with a felony), by the district attorney (refusal to file a complaint or reduction to a misdemeanor), and by the judge (dismissal of the case or having the judge, not a jury, serve as trier).

Creating New Environments

The existence of "artificial" transitory environments presents an opportunity. To solve an applied problem, we can consider changing the environment as well as changing people. It may be more effective to provide product information in a way that adapts to people than to educate consumers to adapt to existing information environments. That is, changing the environment to adapt to people may be more (cost) effective than changing people to adapt to the environment.

Consider the following problem facing researchers attempting to help consumers improve their purchase decisions. There is some (tentative) evidence that consumers prefer attribute-based decision strategies. These are strategies that compare two or more brands attribute by attribute. Similarly, some recent data suggest that product information is remembered better when it is organized by attribute [19]. Unfortunately, the typical point-of-purchase information display is organized by brand, not by attribute. Similarly, most of the product information that people acquire elsewhere and must remember at the point of purchase is brand-based rather than attribute-based. This is true, for example, of advertisements and of use experience. If shoppers really perform better in an attribute-organized information environment, what course of action should the applied researcher take? Will it be more (cost) effective to alter the environment into a more attribute-based structure or to educate people to use brand-based strategies for decision and memory?

Both pure and applied researchers might consider the following schema.

	Environment	
	Present	Optimal
Strategy Present		
Optimal		

Most of our research is conducted in the present-present cell. We observe the strategies that consumers presently use to adapt to existing environments. Occasionally we address the question of the optimal strategy in the present environment. Rarely, however, do we consider constructing the optimal environment for the present strategy. One is hard pressed in all of the research presented or surveyed by Bettman, Olson and Wright to find any studies that explicitly seek to develop the optimal consumer environment given present strategies, knowledge, etc. Finally, I know of no research directed to the jointly optimal cell of the matrix: the simultaneous education of consumers and improvement in the environment that will lead to a global maximum for consumer performance.

The goal of finding the joint optimum blurs the distinction between basic and applied research. It takes full advantage of the mutability of economic and social environments. It is an exciting scientific challenge for both economists and behavioral scientists studying market behavior.

REFERENCES

1. Abelson, R. P. "Social Psychology's Rational Man," in S. I. Benn and G. W. Mortimore, eds., Rationality and the Social Sciences. Boston: Routledge and Kegan Paul, 1976, 58-89.

2. Allais, M. "Le Comportement de l'Homme Rationnel devant le Risque, Critique des Postulats et Axiomes de l' Ecole Americaine," Econometrica, 21 (1953), 503-46.

3. Amihud, Yakov. "Critical Examination of the New Foundation of Utility," Discussion Paper Series No. 74-16, Center for Applied Economics, New York University, August 1974.

4. Barnes, Ralph M. Motion and Time Study: Design and Measurement of Work, 5th ed. New York: Wiley, 1963.

5. Benn, S. I. and G. W. Mortimore, eds. Rationality and the Social Sciences. Boston: Routledge and Kegan Paul, 1976.

6. Bettman, James R. and Pradeep Kakkar. "Effects of Information Presentation Format on Consumer Information Acquisition Strategies," Journal of Consumer Research, 3 (March 1977), 233-40.

7. Blattberg, Robert and Abel Jeuland. "A Micro Modelling Approach to Determine the Advertising-Sales Relationship," Journal of Marketing Research, 1978, in press.

8. Chase, William G. "Elementary Information Processes," in W. K. Estes, ed., Handbook of Learning and Cognitive Processes, Vol. 5. Hillsdale, New Jersey: Lawrence Erlbaum, 1978, in press.

9. Clarke, Darral G. "Econometric Measurement of the Duration of Advertising Effect on Sales," Journal of Marketing Research, 13 (November 1976), 345-57.

10. Coombs, Clyde H. "Portfolio Theory and the Measurement of Risk," in M. F. Kaplan and S. Schwartz, eds., Human Judgment and Decision Processes. New York: Academic Press, 1975, 63-85.

11. Davidson, Donald, Patrick Suppes, and Sidney Siegel. Decision-Making: An Experimental Approach. Stanford: Stanford University Press, 1957.

12. Edwards, Ward. "Optimal Strategies for Seeking Information: Models for Statistics, Choice Reaction Times, and Human Information Processing," Journal of Mathematical Psychology, 2 (1965), 312-29.

13. Edwards, Ward, Marcia Guttentag, and Kurt Snapper. "A Decision-Theoretic Approach to Evaluation Research," in Elmer L. Strueing and Marcia Guttentag, eds., Handbook of Evaluation Research, Vol. 1. Beverly Hills, California: Sage, 1975.

14. Ellsberg, Daniel. "Risk, Ambiguity and the Savage Axioms," Quarterly Journal of Economics, 75 (1961), 643-69.

15. Fischhoff, Baruch. "Cost Benefit Analysis and the Art of Motorcycle Maintenance," Policy Sciences, 8 (1977), 177-202.

16. Gardner, Meryl P., Andrew A. Mitchell, and J. Edward Russo. "Chronometric Analysis: An Introduction and an Application to Low Involvement Perception of Advertisements," in H. Keith Hunt, ed., Advances in Consumer Research, Vol. 5. Chicago: Association for Consumer Research, 1978.

17. Gatewood, Robert D. and Robert Perloff. "An Experimental Investigation of Three Methods of Presenting Weight and Price Information to Consumers," Journal of Applied Psychology, 57 (February 1973), 81-5.

18. Grether, David M. and Charles R. Plott. "Economic Theory and the Preference Reversal Phenomenon," American Economic Review, forthcoming.

19. Johnson, Eric J. and J. Edward Russo. "The Organization of Product Information in Memory Identified by Recall Times," in H. Keith Hunt, ed., Advances in Consumer Research, Vol. 5. Chicago: Association for Consumer Research, 1978.

20. Kahneman, Daniel and Amos Tversky. "Subjective Probability: A Judgment of Representativeness," Cognitive Psychology, 3 (July 1972), 43-54.

21. Kahneman, Daniel and Amos Tversky. "A Prospect Theory: An Analysis of Decision under Risk." Paper presented at the NSF Workshop on Risk Assessment and Evaluation, Eugene, Oregon, January 1977.

22. Katona, George. Psychological Economics. New York: Elsevier, 1975.

23. Kershaw, David N. "A Negative-Income-Tax Experiment," *Scientific American*, 227 (October 1972), 19-25.

24. Konecni, Vladimir J. Personal communication, May 1977.

25. Konner, Melvin. Review of *Evolution, Development and Children's Learning* by Harold D. Fishbein (Pacific Palisades, California: Goodyear, 1976), *Science*, 196 (June 17, 1977), 1310-11.

26. Lichtenstein, Sarah and Paul Slovic. "Reversals of Preference Between Bids and Choices in Gambling Decisions," *Journal of Experimental Psychology*, 89 (1971), 46-55.

27. Lichtenstein, Sarah and Paul Slovic. "Response-Induced Reversals of Preference in Gambling: An Extended Replication in Las Vegas," *Journal of Experimental Psychology*, 101 (1973), 16-20.

28. Miller, Ross M., Charles R. Plott, and Vernon L. Smith. "Intertemporal Competitive Equilibrium: An Empirical Study of Speculation," *Quarterly Journal of Economics*, 91 (November 1977), 599-624.

29. Morgenstern, Oskar. "Some Reflections on Utility," Discussion Paper Series No. 74-16, Center for Applied Economics, New York University, August 1974.

30. Newell, Alan and Herbert A. Simon. *Human Problem Solving*. Englewood Cliffs, New Jersey: Prentice-Hall, 1972.

31. Newman, Joseph W. and Bradley D. Lockeman. "Measuring Prepurchase Information Seeking," *Journal of Consumer Research*, 2 (December 1975), 216-22.

32. Nisbett, Richard E. and Timothy DeCamp Wilson. "Telling More Than We Can Know: Verbal Reports on Mental Processes," *Psychological Review*, 84 (May 1977), 231-59.

33. Norman, Donald A. *Memory and Attention: An Introduction to Human Information Processing*, 2nd ed. New York: Wiley, 1976.

34. Pechman, Joseph A. and P. Michael Timpane, eds. *Work Incentives and Income Guarantees: The New Jersey Negative Income Tax Experiment*. Washington, D.C.: The Brookings Institution, 1975.

35. Posner, Michael I., Mary Jo Nissen, and William C. Ogden. "Attended and Unattended Processing Modes: The Role of Set for Spatial Location," in H. J. Pick, ed., *Modes of Perception*. Hillsdale, New Jersey: Lawrence Erlbaum, 1978, in press.

36. Posner, Michael I. and Charles R. R. Snyder. "Attention and Cognitive Control," in Robert L. Solso, ed., *Information Processing and Cognition*. Hillsdale, New Jersey: Lawrence Erlbaum, 1975.

37. Russo, J. Edward. "The Value of Unit Price Information," *Journal of Marketing Research*, 14 (May 1977), 193-201.

38. Russo, J. Edward. "Adaptation of Cognitive Processes to the Eye Movement System," in John W. Senders, Dennis F. Fisher, and Richard A. Monty, eds., *Eye Movements and the Higher Psychological Functions*. Hillsdale, New Jersey: Lawrence Erlbaum, 1978.

39. Russo, J. Edward. "A Proposal to Increase Energy Conservation Through Provision of Consumption and Cost Information to Consumers," in Barnett A. Greenberg and Danny N. Bellenger, eds., *Contemporary Marketing Thought, 1977 Educators' Proceedings*. Chicago: American Marketing Association, 1977, 437-42.

40. Russo, J. Edward. "Eye Fixations Can Save the World: A Critical Evaluation and a Comparison Between Eye Fixations and Other Information Processing Methodologies," in H. Keith Hunt, ed., *Advances in Consumer Research*, Vol. 5. Chicago: Association for Consumer Research, 1978.

41. Russo, J. Edward and Barbara Anne Dosher. "An Information Processing Analysis of Binary Choice," unpublished manuscript, Carnegie-Mellon University, 1976.

42. Russo, J. Edward, Gene Kreiser, and Sally Miyashita. "An Effective Display of Unit Price Information," *Journal of Marketing*, 39 (April 1975), 11-19.

43. Russo, J. Edward and Larry D. Rosen. "An Eye Fixation Analysis of Multialternative Choice," *Memory and Cognition*, 3 (May 1975), 267-76.

44. Russo, J. Edward and Robert A. Wisher. "Reprocessing as a Recognition Cue," *Memory and Cognition*, 4 (November 1976), 683-89.

45. Segal, Erwin M. and Roy Lachman. "Complex Behavior or Higher Mental Processes: Is There a Paradigm Shift?," *American Psychologist*, 27 (January 1972), 46-55.

46. Simon, Herbert A. "Rational Choice and the Structure of the Environment," *Psychological Review*, 63 (1956), 129-38.

47. Simon, Herbert A. *The Sciences of the Artificial*. Cambridge, Massachusetts: The MIT Press, 1969.

48. Slovic, Paul, Baruch Fischhoff, Sarah Lichtenstein, Bernard Corrigan, and Barbara Combs. "Preference for Insuring Against Probable Small Losses: Insurance Implications," *Journal of Risk and Insurance*, 44 (June 1977), 237-58.

49. Slovic, Paul and Sarah Lichtenstein. "Comparison of Bayesian and Regression Approaches to the Study of Information Processing in Judgement," *Organizational Behavior and Human Performance*, 6 (November 1971), 649-744.

50. Slovic, Paul and Amos Tversky. "Who Accepts Savage's Axiom?," *Behavioral Science*, 19 (1974), 368-73.

51. Stigler, George J. "The Economics of Information," *Journal of Political Economy*, 69 (June 1961), 213-25.

52. Tversky, Amos. "Additivity, Utility, and Subjective Probability," *Journal of Mathematical Psychology*, 4 (1967), 175-201.

53. Tversky, Amos. "Intransitivity of Preferences," *Psychological Review*, 76 (January 1969), 31-48.

54. Tversky, Amos. Invited address at Mathematical Psychology Meetings, Los Angeles, August 1977.

55. Tversky, Amos and Daniel Kahneman. "Judgment under Uncertainty: Heuristics and Biases," *Science*, 185 (1974), 1124-31.

56. Wicker, A. "An Examination of the 'Other Variable'
    Explanation for Attitude-Behavior Inconsistency,"
    Journal of Personality and Social Psychology, 19
    (July 1971), 18-30.

57. Wright, Peter. "Decision Times and Processes on
    Complex Decision Problems," Research Paper No. 406,
    Stanford University Graduate School of Business,
    October 1977.

58. Wright, Peter. Personal communication, October 1977.

PART III: INFORMATION AND PUBLIC POLICY

INFORMATIONAL IMPERFECTIONS IN LOCAL CONSUMER MARKETS

E. Scott Maynes, Cornell University

This paper has two objectives: (1) to show how informational imperfections of local consumer markets may be assessed; (2) to present sample results of actual assessments of the informational imperfections of such markets.

THE CONCEPT AND ITS IMPORTANCE

As a first approximation, a local consumer market is _informationally perfect_ when a single price is charged by all sellers for the same quality. A market may be designated as _informationally imperfect_ to the extent that different prices are charged for the same quality.

The emphasis in the definition is with the _results achieved_. It should be noted, however, that a uniform price for a given quality may be obtained when only a fraction of consumers are fully informed. Just how many consumers must be fully informed to discipline a market is unknown. It probably depends upon their visibility or activism, the product class, the number and character of sellers, the type of market (small-town vs. urban, growing vs. stable), etc. By the same token we are indifferent as to whether consumers are behaving "rationally," habitually, or satisficingly. It is the dispersion of prices upon which we are focusing.

The informational imperfections of local consumer markets are important in several contexts. First, there is the _public policy interest_. To the extent that consumers pay more than the lowest price for a given level of quality, their purchasing power is reduced and their economic welfare is decreased. If this phenomenon is widespread, it poses important questions as to new policies and possibly new institutions that might improve the situation.

The informational imperfections of local markets should be of interest to individual consumers and consumer organizations. To the extent that informationally imperfect markets exist and persist, they present _opportunities for consumer payoffs_ to individual consumers and to the consumer organizations that might assist them. Careful documentation of informational imperfections at a particular point in time would provide both individual consumers and consumer organizations with a "map" of potential consumer profits.

For professional students of local markets-consumer economists and marketers-the informational imperfections of markets should be of paramount interest. To the extent that markets are informationally perfect, these groups have done their job well. But to the extent that they are informationally imperfect, a challenge remains. Evidence on informational imperfections should guide the activities of consumer economists, helping to sharpen their theory, their analysis, and their advice. The same information should be useful to marketers and the firms they serve in deciding what markets to enter and what products to push.

Reasons for Informationally Imperfect Markets

It is the author's expectation that many, perhaps most, local consumer markets will be characterized by substantial informational imperfections. The "culprits" behind this expectation are three. First, there is the technical complexity and multi-component nature of products. These factors make it difficult for consumers to assess both quality and price accurately. Second, there is

affluence which has increased both the consumption possibilities and the consumer's information problem. Specifically, affluence has: (1) enlarged the number of average purchases that each family can make; (2) enlarged the set of products, brands, models, retailers from which choices are to be made; and (3) increased the value of individual's time and hence reduced the extent of his shopping/search actions. Finally, agricultural productivity and the automobile together have made urbanization possible and thus increased the set of products, brands, models, and retailers to which a consumer has access. More detailed discussion of these issues is provided in [3, pp. 305-325].

Small wonder - after this recital - that consumers are burdened with the informational overload problem that Jacob Jacoby and other market researchers have so appropriately identified and investigated; an excellent review of this research may be found in [6, pp. 34-36].

THE ASSESSMENT OF INFORMATIONAL IMPERFECTIONS: THE PERFECT INFORMATION FRONTIER

Our basic instrument for assessment of informational imperfections will be the perfect information frontier. The concept embodies the notion that, quality constant, the fully informed consumer will opt for the lowest price. Why should he pay more? The logic, it will be recognized, is at least as old as Adam Smith.

The _perfect information frontier_ is defined, on a chart depicting price and quality, as "the positively sloped line segments connecting those points, representing price and quality, for which a given quality may be purchased for the lowest price." For a product of uniform quality, the frontier will consist of a single point. For a product of variable quality, it will consist of line segments. As an example--to be fully explained later--look at Figure 3A.

In the sample results that follow the quality data will consist of the numerical quality scores published by Consumers Union in _Consumer Reports_.

The concepts of quality, market (needed to delineate the set of sellers whose offers will be depicted on a price-quality chart for a particular market), and product (needed to determine which product variants are appropriately compared with one another) are proposed and discussed exhaustively in earlier work by the author [3, 4].

Quality, briefly, consists of "a subjectively weighted average of service characteristics." A service characteristic is defined as "the basic factor giving rise to utility." Examples might include durability, beauty, safety. These _service_ characteristics differ from the "characteristics" found in Kelvin Lancaster's work or in the hedonic price index literature. My service characteristics may be viewed as the _output_ of a production system embodied in a good. Lancaster and the hedonists often identify _inputs_ to this productive process as their "characteristics." By way of example, the durability of a hot water heater would be a _service_ characteristic while Lancaster and the hedonists might identify as characteristics the copper pipes and glass liner that, plausibly, help produce durability.

For marketers, it may be useful to identify the concept of quality proposed here as the mathematical equivalent of the Rosenberg-Fishbein multi-attribute model [2]. However, my use of the model differs. In marketing the multi-attribute model has been employed to ascertain what consumers want, given their existing state of ignorance. By contrast, for this analysis it is assumed that quality represents what the _fully informed_ consumer would achieve, accepting that Consumers Union's assessments are correct and are followed by the fully informed consumer.

The distinction between _varieties_ and _specimens_ of product is essential for an understanding of the charts that follow. A _variety_ of a product is a product-brand/model combination, e.g., a 1971 Buick Sportswagon. A _specimen_ is a product-brand/model-retailer combination, e.g., a 1971 Buick Sportswagon _purchased at Seaside Buick_. On the charts, quality pertains to varieties of products while prices, necessarily, pertain to specimens.

Assumptions for this Analysis

For the perfect information frontier framework to serve as a valid standard of assessment, several assumptions must be made. The first is that the identification of varieties of products and retail outlets is complete and accurate for some representative consumer in a particular market. A second is that the prices quoted are accurate. In this investigation the "actual" price represents the lowest price a seller was willing to quote when told that the information he provided would be widely distributed. For some products competent bargaining could secure a lower price. Third, fully informed consumers would accept Consumers Union's assessments of quality for different varieties of products.

Interpretation of Price Quality Relationships

The discovery of extensive price dispersion above the perfect information frontier need not signal an informationally imperfect market. A number of factors other than consumer ignorance might account for such dispersion. From an interpretive viewpoint the basic question is this: to what extent could the observed dispersion of prices above the frontier be reasonably attributed to such "other factors"? To the extent that the dispersion is _not_ reasonably attributable to other factors, we will conclude that the market in question is informationally imperfect. We turn now to a discussion of the "other" factors that might produce such dispersion.

Intrinsically Subjective Characteristics

The quality data on which we will rely, based as it is on the work of Consumers Union, takes no account of the intrinsically subjective characteristics of products. An example might be the "style of an automobile." An estimate that took no account of style would tend to underestimate the quality of a variety of automobiles that rated high in style; the price, on the other hand, should reflect what the average consumer is willing to pay for style (as combined with other characteristics in a particular variety of car).

Different Product Sets and Different Product Uses

A _product_ is defined as "the set of goods which, for some maximum outlay, will serve the same general purpose in the judgment of the purchasing consumer." Consider single-lens cameras as an example. A professional photographer may include in his product set only cameras with a broad family of accessories while an amateur may include cameras offering a lesser assortment of accessories. Thus, the set of cameras defined as "single-lens reflex cameras" by the professional may differ from that of the amateur.

By the same token the professional photographer, in assessing the quality of the identical single-lens camera, may arrive at a different quality score because he has assigned different weights and different ratings to (say) the family of accessories, as compared with the amateur.

Thus, together different product sets and different uses of the same varieties may produce different perfect information frontiers or differences in the price-to-frontier ratios that are not attributable to informational imperfections.

Non-Uniform Market Sets

A similar reasoning pertains to the delineation of "market" sets. Plausibly poor vs. rich consumers might differ in the search (shopping) costs they incur. If search costs are less for the poor, as compared with the rich, then the set of retail outlets in the poor man's market would be greater, _ceteris paribus_, than that of the rich consumer. Again, the depiction of a different set of retailers on a price-quality chart might give rise to differences in frontiers or in price-to-frontier ratios that are not attributable to informational imperfections.

Non-Uniform Quality Assessments

For products of variable quality there is no gainsaying the possibility that different quality assessments may be made by different consumers even for products whose characteristics are predominantly "objective." It is reassuring to learn that in 1970, among _Consumer Reports_ purchasers-subscribers, 48 percent to 81 percent reported the purchase of models that were "top-rated" in _Consumer Reports_.[1] But it is not conclusive. Until convincing research has been undertaken on the matter of uniformity of quality assessments by fully informed consumers, each of us will have to estimate in each case how uniform or variable such quality assessments might be.

Characteristics of Retailers

In the charts, prices but not quality assessments may take account of such characteristics of retailers as their friendliness, convenience, etc. To the extent that fully informed consumers value such services, a finding of informational imperfection may be less justifiable.

Price Discrimination Based on Objective Factors

Often sellers practice price discrimination by charging different prices to consumers of different objective characteristics, e.g., adults vs. children. Obviously, differences in prices arising from this source are not chargeable to informational imperfections.

By contrast, some price discrimination is made possible by consumer ignorance. This would occur when a knowledgeable consumer successfully bargains for a lower price that is not generalized to other, less knowing consumers. Other examples abound. Since the data presented here assign but a single price to a particular retailer, neither kind of price discrimination affects _these_ results. The net effect of this omission is to underestimate the extent of informational imperfection.

Comparing Markets: Other Questions That Might Be Asked

This paper focuses mainly on the problem of informational imperfections. Here the central question is: To what

---

[1] The product set included hair shampoo, color televisions, coffee makers, sewing machines, record changers, TV antennas, and AM-FM radios. Source: [1, Table T 21].

extent does there exist price dispersion above the perfect information frontier that is properly chargeable to informational imperfections in that market?

But there are two other questions that might be appropriately asked and answered by our price-quality diagrams. The first question is: what are the best achievable terms in Market I vs. Market II? The answer to this question calls for a comparison of the perfect information frontier in alternative markets—its height and its slope.

A second important question pertains to the richness of choice offered by particular markets. The answer to this question calls for a comparison of: (1) the number of varieties that are purchasable in Market I vs. Market II; (2) the number of retail outlets from which a particular variety may be purchased in each market; and (3) the number of products that may be purchased "locally."[2]

SAMPLE RESULTS AND THEIR INTERPRETATION

The author, in collaboration with Greg J. Duncan of the University of Michigan and Loren V. Geistfeld of Purdue University, is engaged in a pilot study designed to document the informational imperfections of local consumer markets over several dimensions: for different types of products, for markets of different sizes (Minneapolis vs. Ann Arbor vs. Ithaca), and over time. Unfortunately only one result is available thus far from this study. However, two sample results from an earlier investigation are available. These are presented below along with one sample result from the new investigation

Products of Uniform Quality: Life Insurance, Film

These sample results pertain to two products of approximately uniform quality—life insurance and Kodachrome 126 color film—and one product of variable quality—pocket cameras. For the first two products the market is Ann Arbor, Michigan which in 1974 had a population (for our purposes) of about 150,000; for pocket cameras data are available for Minneapolis and Ithaca as well as Ann Arbor.

Life insurance, our first sample product, should be of great interest to both consumers and students of markets. For purchasers, it accounts for three and one-half percent of their disposable income. What is more, consumers purchase it in large amounts and tend to stay with the same company for a long time. Term life insurance, the type with which our example deals, is a product of uniform quality because it embodies a single characteristic: protection. Die and the payment of the policy's face value provides income replacement, or "protection", for your beneficiary.[3]

Figure 1 tells the story for two variants of term life insurance, non-participating and participating. The results in both cases are emphatic. There is a high degree of price dispersion. And, what is equally undesirable from the viewpoint of a consumer in this market, the very

lowest priced policies are not "readily accessible" to would-be purchasers in Ann Arbor. Tick off the factors other than imperfect information that might account for such a degree of price dispersion: intrinsically subjective characteristics, different product sets and uses, non-uniform market sets, non-uniform quality assessments, characteristics of retailers, price discrimination. All are irrelevant to this case. The judgment that this is an informationally imperfect market cannot be avoided.

Our second product of (approximately) uniform quality is Kodachrome 126 film. Figure 2 shows that the highest price exceeds the lowest price by about 60 to 70 percent and that the dispersion of prices was roughly constant over a one-month interval. It is worth noting that in each month the highest price was charged by a large chain drug store located in a large shopping center. An informationally imperfect market? Our answer is "yes." Undoubtedly, such retailer characteristics as locational convenience and friendliness do account for some quality differences not recorded here. But how much of this price range would informed consumers be willing to pay for such characteristics? If the answer is "only a small part" then we can conclude that this market is informationally imperfect. (This assumes that the other factors cited above are of negligible importance in this case.)

A Variable Quality Product: Pocket Cameras

Our third example confronts us with a product of variable quality, pocket cameras. Here, for the first time, we can compare three markets—Ithaca, Ann Arbor, and Minneapolis—representing "small", "medium," and "large" markets.

First, we must understand Figures 3A, 3B, and 3C. The set of pocket cameras includes the 36 varieties for which ratings were published in the June, 1976 issue of Consumer Reports. Each variety of camera is denoted by a letter or double letter (A, B, C,...AA, BB, etc.) Missing letters represent cameras available in the national, but not the local market. The numerical quality scores are those published in Consumer Reports. Differences of less than 10 points were judged "not very significant" by Consumer Reports. Each + on the chart represents a price quoted by an Ann Arbor retailer. The sample of retailers is exhaustive, including all outlets selling the varieties listed in Consumer Reports.

For purposes of assessment, we should reiterate the limitations of Consumer Reports' quality scores: (1) they take no account of characteristics for which valid, reproducible tests cannot be devised, e.g., durability; (2) they take no account of intrinsically subjective characteristics such as the reputation of the manufacturer; (3) they do not reflect characteristics of retailers.

Now we can compare the three markets. First, the perfect information frontier (the site of the best opportunities) is substantially higher in Ithaca (a small town with a population of 30,000), less high in Minneapolis (a relevant population of about 500,000), and lowest for Ann Arbor (a market of 150,000). Second, the range of choice in terms of numbers of varieties available is Ithaca-11, Ann Arbor-22, and Minneapolis-24. These two findings conform well to a priori expectations. A third does not. Both the dispersion of prices above the perfect information frontier and the price dispersion per camera variant (i.e., model) are much greater in the largest market—Minneapolis—and least in the smallest market.

We turn back to the central question of this paper: to what extent are these markets informationally imperfect? Again our method is to tick off the list of factors other than informational imperfections that might account for the extent of price dispersion above the perfect information frontier in each market. Clearly for this product

---

[2] Depending upon "my" search costs, "my" local market may or may not include mail-order or telephone-order retailers.

[3] Some may note that life insurance agents provide other services or "characteristics", e.g., advice on estate planning. Hence, it might be argued that quality varies among agents. The argument is irrelevant here since prices are companywide and it is the dispersion among the prices of different companies (not agents) that we seek to explain.

FIGURE 1

Term Life Insurance: Prices and Access
in Ann Arbor, February, 1975[a]

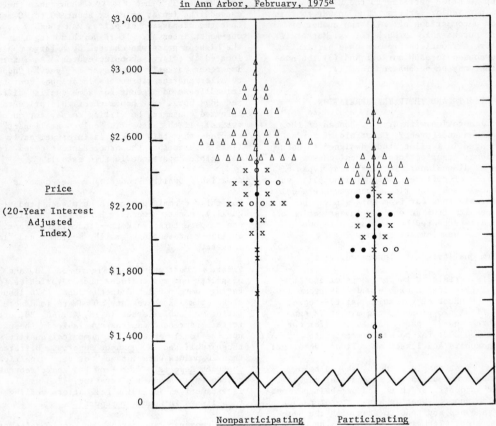

Nonparticipating   Participating

5-Year Renewable and Convertible[b]
Term Policies

Symbols: ● Readily accessible (company listed in Yellow Pages)

x Accessible with difficulty (sales by mail, or company has
agent in Michigan; not listed in Yellow Pages)

s Special clientele: available only to special class of buyers,
e.g., teachers

o No access from Ann Arbor (not licensed in Michigan, no agents
in Michigan)

Δ Accessibility not investigated.

[a]Source: Price data from Consumer Reports, January, 1974, pp. 43-45, accessibility
data from Survey Research Center, University of Michigan.

[b]Price estimates pertain to 25-year-old male in good health assumed to have purchased
face amount of $25,000. The price charted represents the 20-year cumulative cost.

FIGURE 2

Kodachrome Film: Prices in Ann Arbor,
May and June, 1975[a]

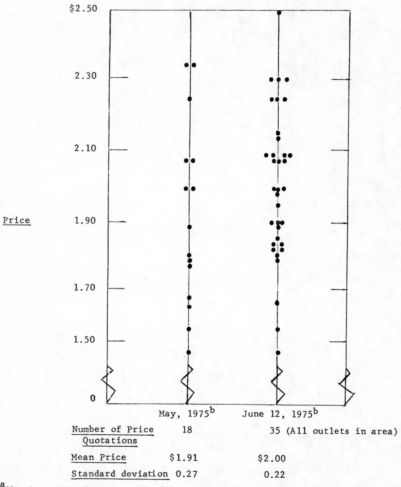

	May, 1975[b]	June 12, 1975[b]
Number of Price Quotations	18	35 (All outlets in area)
Mean Price	$1.91	$2.00
Standard deviation	0.27	0.22

[a]The item priced was a roll of 20-exposure Kodak Kodachrome 126 color film.

[b]May prices were obtained over a two-week period by James A. McIntosh; June prices were obtained on June 12, 1975 by Judy Hanna. The June sample covered <u>all</u> outlets in the Ann Arbor area which sell this type of film; the May sample covered about half of the total with a special effort being made to contact outlets whose prices were expected to be different.

81

PERFECT INFORMATION FRONTIER, ITHACA

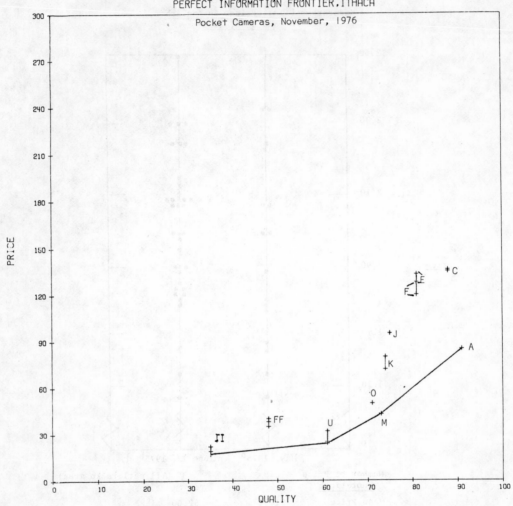

Pocket Cameras, November, 1976

Source: Quality scores--Consumer Reports, June, 1976.
         Prices--Collected by Anthcny Schiano in July 29, 1976.
         Letters denote varieties of pocket cameras. Each + represents
            an actual price quotaticn.

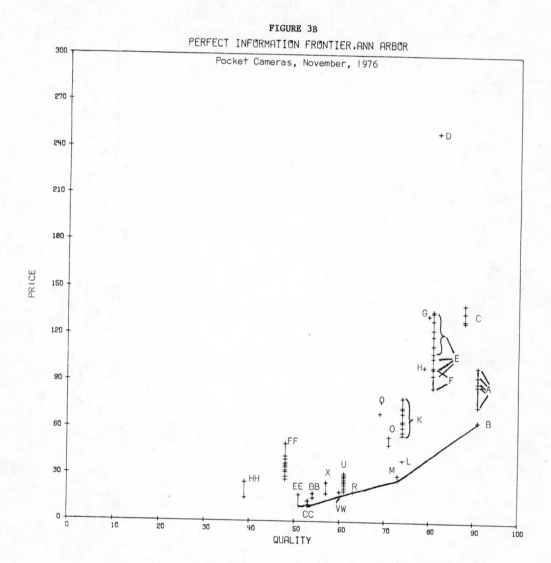

FIGURE 3B

PERFECT INFORMATION FRONTIER.ANN ARBOR

Pocket Cameras, November, 1976

Source: Quality scores--Consumer Reports, June, 1976.
Prices--Collected by Patience Nelson from July 22 - August 2, 1976.
Letters denote varieties of pocket cameras. Each + represents an
actual price quotation.

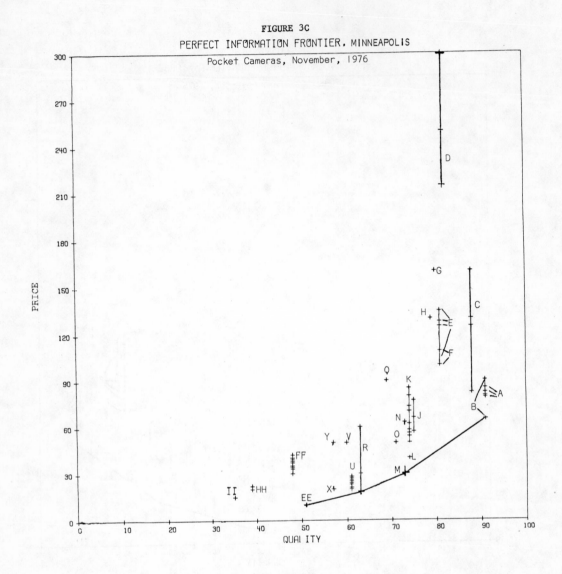

FIGURE 3C

PERFECT INFORMATION FRONTIER, MINNEAPOLIS

Pocket Cameras, November, 1976

Source: Quality scores--<u>Consumer Reports</u>, June, 1976.
Prices--Collected by Karen A. Vogl from September 23-24, 1976.
Letters denote varieties of pocket cameras. Each + represents
an actual price quotation.

most of the factors on our list might account for some of the price dispersion observed: intrinsically subjective characteristics, different product sets and uses, non-uniform market sets, non-uniform quality assessments. But two should be ruled out. First, since retailers were asked to supply a single price for each model, price discrimination may be ruled out by definition (price discrimination being defined as charging different prices to different customers with no associated differences in selling costs). Second, we ask whether the omitted characteristic of retailers could account for the difference. This is a tempting hypothesis. Could it be that the stores quoting the lower price for a particular variant have poor reputations for service, reliability, and amenities? It turns out that none of the retailers tend to be consistently low or high in price. Instead, what may be happening is behavior conforming to a hypothesis of Salop [5]. Salop hypothesizes that many retailers sort our consumers by their apparent knowledgeability and practice price discrimination among product variants. Thus, a particular retailer will charge a very low price for a particular variety of (say) camera, expecting to attract knowledgeable, price-conscious consumers. At the same time he will charge a high price for another variety, expecting to sell this variety to less knowledgeability, less price-conscious customers.

Each of you will have to form a judgment as to which (if any) of these markets is informationally imperfect. It would be the author's judgment that each exhibits informational imperfections, the degree becoming greater (contrary to the intuition of many) as one goes from the small market (Ithaca) to the largest market (Minneapolis).

The varying level of the perfect information frontier is chargeable to monopoly elements in a small market (Ithaca) and not to informational factors.

A STRATEGY FOR INTERPRETATION

These results are illustrative. In a large-scale investigation of the informational imperfections of local consumer markets, it would be my judgment that the greatest weight should be placed upon results relating to products of approximately uniform quality. As the examples above underline, an inference of informational imperfection is more certain in such cases. A finding that a particular local market is informationally imperfect for a number of products of uniform quality would suggest that it is also informationally imperfect with respect to products of variable quality.

But products of variable quality cannot and should not be avoided in such an investigation for two reasons. First, many products--perhaps even most--are variable in quality. Second, difficulties in assessing quality are likely to contribute to informational imperfections in markets. If a consumer finds it difficult to judge quality, how is he to know when he is achieving more quality per dollar of outlay? And if he cannot make this judgment readily and accurately, how is the market to be disciplined?

A major difficulty in assessing the informational imperfections of markets for products of variable quality is the necessary assumption (to this task) that fully informed consumers would make uniform assessments of quality. For some intrinsically subjective products, e.g., the aesthetic properties of a painting, uniformity is extremely unlikely. For other goods the question of uniform assessments is a matter of empirical determination. This is a research task in which the author is presently engaged.

SUMMARY

This paper has argued that the local market for many consumer goods is informationally imperfect. The paper has proposed and illustrated a conceptual and operational framework for assessing such informational imperfections. From the data presented it appears that the markets for term life insurance, Kodachrome 126 film (products of roughly uniform quality) and for pocket cameras (a product of variable quality) are informationally imperfect in differing degrees. These sample results are seen as a prelude to a systematic investigation of informational imperfections of markets over many product classes, markets of differing sizes, and over time.

REFERENCES

1. Benson and Benson. "Survey of Present and Former Subscribers to Consumer Reports," unpublished report. Mt. Vernon, N.Y.: Consumers Union, 1970.

2. Green, Paul E. and Yoram Wind, Multi-Attribute Decisions in Marketing. New York: Holt, Rinehart and Winston, 1973.

3. Maynes, E. Scott. Decision Making for Consumers, An Introduction to Consumer Economics. New York: Macmillan, 1976a.

4. Maynes, E. Scott. "The Concept and Measurement of Product Quality," in Nester E. Terleckyj (ed.), Household Production and Consumption, Studies in Income and Wealth, Volume Forty. New York: National Bureau of Economic Research, 1976b, 529-560.

5. Salop, Steve. "The Noisy Monopolist: Imperfect Information, Price Dispersion, and Price Discrimination," in Review of Economic Studies. Forthcoming.

6. Wilkie, William L. How Consumers Use Product Information. Washington: Government Printing Office, Stock No. 038-000-0002376, 1975.

CONSUMER RESEARCH AND THE POLICY
PLANNING OF ADVERTISING REGULATION

John Eighmey
Medill School of Journalism
Northwestern University

Six years ago Mary Gardiner Jones, then a member of the Federal Trade Commission, spoke to a meeting of academic consumer researchers about the Commission's need for consumer research to better inform its decisions with respect to case selection, formulation of remedies, and activities related to providing information to consumers [1]. Although the use of consumer research by the Commission has increased since that time, it is not yet an organization that uses this kind of research as well as it could or should. However, given the usual managerial problems encountered in large-scale organizations, it would seem likely that no organization could seriously make such a claim.

This paper discusses the Commission's use of consumer research as it relates to one of its responsibilities, the regulation of advertising claims.[1] The organization of the paper follows the Commission's policy planning protocol for deceptive and unsubstantiated claims. This protocol consists of approximately thirty questions which were designed to insure that decisions to go forward with investigations will be based on due consideration of every possible reason for proceeding or for not proceeding. The protocol was approved by the Commission in December of 1975 after development by the Commission's Office of Policy Planning and Division of National Advertising.

The questions fall into eight basic areas: first, the nature of the alternative interpretations of the advertising message; second, the magnitudes of the consumer groups likely to adhere to each of the various interpretations of the message; third, the materiality of these interpretations, including the nature and extent of possible consumer injury; fourth, the adequacy of sources of self-correction in the marketplace; fifth, the possible effects on the flow of truthful information to the market if the investigation were pursued; sixth, options for a remedy and their import as deterrence; seventh, the appropriateness of the Commission as a forum for resolving the issues involved in the proposed investigation; and, eighth, several questions about such issues as the vulnerability of the consumers involved and the relationship of the message to current public policy concerns.

These question areas guide the regulator to seek out information on the wisdom of investing resources in a proposed investigation. The value of the protocol, therefore, is that it reduces the likelihood that investigations will be started or stopped on the basis of happenstance or some abstract, deductive view of the way advertising works. The following sections of this paper describe the relationship of consumer research to each of the eight policy planning areas.

---

[1] The author was formerly Deputy Assistant Director for National Advertising at the Federal Trade Commission and program director of the Commission's advertising substantiation program. This paper conveys the author's own views and is not necessarily reflective of the views of the Commission or its staff.

I. CONSUMER INTERPRETATIONS OF ADVERTISING CLAIMS

This section of the protocol asks the regulator to set forth the main interpretations that consumers may place on the advertisement in question. This is not an activity that should focus exclusively on the isolation of a troublesome aspect of an advertisement and, therefore, the protocol calls for a discussion of those interpretations of the ad that may be true or substantiated as well as those that may be false or unsubstantiated.

These determinations about the claims conveyed by ads have usually been made on the basis of a reading of the ad in question and inference about how the elements of the ad -- the headline, illustration, and body copy -- combine to convey the alleged claims. Given the difficulties in obtaining valid and reliable evidence with respect to consumer responses to advertising claims, determinations about the capacities of ads to convey particular claims have been recognized by the courts as a matter calling for pragmatic judgment. In reviewing Commission decisions the courts essentially look for a sufficient rationale or reasonableness in the Commission's decisions about meaning. For example, the Supreme Court, in sustaining the Commission's interpretation of a commercial involving a mock-up demonstration for Palmolive Rapid Shave, held that the meaning of that ad was "a matter of fact resting on an inference that could reasonably be drawn from the commercials themselves"[6].

This claim to administrative expertise is subject to some questioning when the regulator must select between alternative interpretations of an advertising claim or when the interpretation is particularly subtle. However, it is precisely the point at which pragmatic judgment can be challenged that consumer research is also most susceptible to giving erroneous results. It is at this point that copy test questions are most likely to interact with consumer reactions to a claim, and that the particular means of recording consumer responses are most likely to affect the answers actually given by consumers [4].

An excellent demonstration of some potentials for difficulty involved in using consumer research to determine the meaning conveyed by an ad is found in United States v. Firestone, where the Final Judgment called for the use of a well-known procedure for copy testing [13]. This matter involved the compliance by Firestone with an earlier Commission order against the company. Although Firestone disagreed with the Commission, the company consented to a judgment which involved, in part, the preparation and dissemination of an advertisement that would convey the messages that tires are not safe under all conditions of use, and that tire safety depends on proper tire maintenance and vehicle operation. The judgment also included the provision that the results of a copy test would be part of the determinations as to whether the ad met the two communications goals.

The agreed upon copy test procedure was that of Audience Studies, Incorporated, wherein respondents view and evaluate a series of programs and commercials as they are shown in a theater setting. In order to ask a series of specific questions, this particular test included a second showing of the tire safety commercial which followed the completion of the standard series of programs, commercials, and questions. Included in this second questionnaire was a list of ten ideas which the respondents were asked to select as being in the commercial or not being in the commercial.

Three of the ten ideas set forth on the questionnaire were not part of the commercial. Nevertheless, as shown in the table below, certain proportions of the sample of 327 men and women who viewed the commercial selected the response category indicating that these ideas were included in the commercial. The results for item "b" suggest that 17 percent of the respondents either misperceived the ad or misunderstood the question. While the results for items "e" and "g" may demonstrate the possibility that, since ads generally are persuasive messages, a certain proportion of copy test respondents will report that any ad conveys a superiority claim. The percentages of correct responses for the ideas which were actually in the commercial ranged from 39 percent to 92 percent [3].

> Please read through the list and then indicate whether or not you feel these ideas were in the message by marking the box under the appropriate column.

b. Radial tires give you less trouble than other tires.

In the message	17%
Not in the message	65%
Don't know	10%
No answer	8%

e. Firestone tires are better than other brands.

In the message	16%
Not in the message	68%
Don't know	9%
No answer	7%

g. Some brands of tires require more care than others.

In the message	21%
Not in the message	60%
Don't know	12%
No answer	6%

This copy test is, of course, only one example of the difficulties involved in attempts to obtain valid and reliable behavioral evidence about the effects of particular ads. Other testing procedures and other ways of asking questions may produce different kinds and levels of erroneous responses. Nevertheless, these results do indicate that copy research can be used to assist in Commission determinations about the meaning conveyed by ads, and are suggestive of a promising approach to the design of copy research for such use. This approach would involve the preparation of copy tests so that they can establish the level of endorsement for a claim which is not in the ad as well as for each of the alternative interpretations of the ad. This approach would accomplish two important objectives. First, it would lessen the likelihood that the advertiser might be held responsible for consumer responses which are comparable in magnitude to a known error level; and, second, it would assist in making judgements about the relative importance of the alternative interpretations of the ad.

The availability of well designed copy tests should not, however, result in a transition from a standard of proof which is based on pragmatic judgment about the capacity of an advertisement to one which is based on actual behavioral evidence. Pragmatic judgment is, I believe, both valid and reliable in most situations, and research would serve only to introduce delays for its conduct and side issues about its import. Moreover, such a transition might tend to constrain the Commission to boundries determined by the state of the art of research methods. For example, it might be difficult for researchers to demonstrate the effects of a particular advertising practice on young children, but pragmatic judgment might indicate that the Commission should respond to the practice. In such a situation it would be unfortunate if the Commission stayed its hand for too long.

II. SCALE OF DECEPTION

This section of questions asks about the number of consumers likely to be affected by each of the alternative interpretations of the advertisement. The complete answer involves an estimate of the extent to which each of the interpretations might be adhered to by the relevant audience, the amount of the exposure of the advertisement to this audience, and the duration of this exposure.

The issue of likely adherence, as was explained in the previous section of this paper, is largely a matter of pragmatic judgment. When copy research is available, the difference between the error level and the proportion endorsing each claim might be viewed as a rough estimate. An initial estimate of the amount and timing of the dissemination of the advertising for the brand is usually obtained by reference to standard media research services. When an investigation is pursued, the records of the advertiser provide the details about the exposure of the challenged advertising claim.

Although it is not specifically requested by a policy planning question, the issue of the scale of deception should also involve a determination about the possible existence of a residual of consumer beliefs in the marketplace which could have been created or reinforced by the alleged deception. It has been suggested elsewhere that the advertiser should bear the burden of proving that such a residual had not been affected by the challenged advertising claim or that the residual had dissipated before a corrective advertising remedy could be imposed by the Commission [11].

III. MATERIALITY

The section on the materiality of the challenged advertising claim addresses the issues surrounding the "commercial relevance" of the proposed investigation. It would seem reasonable to assume that advertising techniques, in general, have the capacity to affect purchasing behavior and, therefore, the courts have held that, "when the Commission finds deception, it is also authorized, within the bounds of reason, to infer that the deception will constitute a material factor in a purchaser's decision to buy" [6].

The purpose of the questions in this area, then, is to direct the attention of the regulator to the nature of the public interest to be served by the investigation. These questions encourage the gathering of information about the number of purchases which could be affected, or the market size, and the import of the injury which would be likely to result. The questions serve to focus investigations on those practices which would be most likely to involve significant misallocations of consumer resources or the health and safety of the public.

The basic conceptual and methodological tools for measuring consumer economic injury resulting from deceptive advertising are at a rather early stage of development. There are, however, several rather simple ways to examine market prices which do provide some guidance for making choices among proposed investigations. At the first level, the regulator can merely note the selling price for the advertiser's brand and recognize that the advertising claim was a factor in consumer expenditures of that magnitude. Obviously, such information would allow choices to be made between groups of products like deodorants and air conditioners. A second approach involves the determination of whether consumers pay premium prices for the advertised brand. Presumably, the alleged deception led, at least in part, to the choice of that brand as against brands with lower prices. A third approach calls for the determination of the price level for the group of brands which do not possess the advertised attribute or claimed level of performance. If such a group of products exists, their price level could serve as an estimate of the true value to consumers of a deceptively advertised brand. Although clearly rather rudimentary in nature, these methods do encourage the regulator to examine the marketplace and attempt to estimate the magnitude of the consumer interest in a proposed investigation.

Investigations involving the possibility of resitution would, of course, call for more exact measurement of the magnitude of consumer injury. This, I would suggest, is an opportunity for the conduct of consumer research studies using the analytic methods which have become known as conjoint measurement. The attraction of these methods is that they are able to produce estimates of how changes in the characteristics of products relate to consumer reports of perceived utility and dollar value [7]. Perhaps the methods could be applied in a manner which would determine the value to consumers of the actual level of performance of a deceptively advertised product. Although the validity of these procedures has not yet been subjected to intense cross-examination, the methods have apparently come into fairly common use in consumer research conducted for managerial purposes.

IV. ADEQUACY OF CORRECTIVE MARKET FORCES

The issue involved in this area of questions is whether the marketplace is likely to correct the alleged deception or unfairness without Commission action. In order to make this determination the regulator looks for information about such subjects as the expertise of consumers with respect to the product category involved, the potentials for consumers to judge product performance both before and after purchase, the availability of alternative sources of product performance information, and the frequency of repurchasing for the product category.

With respect to the general status of consumer decision making in the United States, the only national survey of which I am aware was an effort by the U.S. Office of Education to assess the ability of adults to apply simple decision skills in five areas of knowledge important to everyday life [1]. This project involved the development of proficiency indices for occupational knowledge, consumer economics, government and the law, health, and community resources. As shown in the table below, the results of this study indicate that consumer economics is the area of greatest difficulty with almost thirty percent of the adult population, or about 35 million individuals, belonging in the lowest of the study's three levels of proficiency. While the study does not speak directly to the abilities of consumers to judge product performance or the quality of consumer activity in seeking out information prior to purchase, it does suggest that many adults are not adequately prepared to act as consumers.

Knowledge Area	Percent of Adults in Lowest (Unsatisfactory) Level
Occupational Knowledge	19.1%
Consumer Economics	29.4%
Government and the Law	25.8%
Health	21.2%
Community Resources	22.6%

Focusing more directly on the aggressiveness of consumer shopping behavior and ability to judge products, a national survey conducted in 1968 by the Survey Research Center of the University of Michigan found that, when asked about the extent of their store-to-store shopping for a recently purchased major household durable, 54 percent of the respondents reported that they shopped at only one retail store before making the purchase [12]. The survey also included an open-ended question, shown below, asking the respondents about their ability to judge the product they had purchased. While such self-reports about competency to evaluate products may not be the most valid approach to assessing consumer knowledge, these results do indicate that only about half of the respondents specifically claimed that they could judge the durable good they purchased without obtaining additional information.

Some people know a lot about (product purchased) and can judge them well; other people have little experience and must put their trust in someone else or in some other source of information; how is it in your case?

a. Knows a lot; can judge them well 31.0%
b. Knows some; has experience; no information needed 15.1%
c. Knows some or a little; information needed; I trust others 27.0%
d. Received information whether needed or not 18.3%
e. Don't know 8.5%

In examining the particular market situation surrounding a proposed investigation, there is a set of concepts which can be used to categorize product attributes in an attempt to deduce the likelihood of consumer detection of the alleged deception. This categorization procedure, developed by economists, involves making a determination as to whether the product attribute involved in the deception is an example of a so-called search quality, experience quality, or credence quality [5 and 9]. Search qualities are those which the consumer can, and is likely to, determine before purchasing the product; experience qualities are those which can only be assessed by the consumer on the basis of actual usage experience with the product; and, credence qualities are those which, even after extensive usage of the product, cannot be assessed reliably by the consumer. With respect to refrigerators, for example, inside space would be a search quality, durability would be an experience quality, and energy consumption would be a credence quality. In the case of energy consumption, the consumer would not normally have individual meters for every household appliance and, therefore, would not be able to assign fluctuations in total monthly energy consumption to individual appliances.

Theoretically, these concepts enable the regulator to decide whether consumers would be able to detect a deceptive advertising claim by themselves and, thereby, to make a determination as to whether the marketplace would be likely to correct the deception. It might seem reasonable to assume that a deception involving a search quality would have little effect on consumers and that, if the product in question is frequently repurchased, consumers would quickly discipline deceptive advertising regarding an experience quality by refusing to repurchase the brand. In the latter situation, if the cost of the product is minor and there are no other kinds of injury involved, then the level of public interest may be insufficient to justify Commission action. Deceptive claims involving credence qualities would be free of the possibility of marketplace discipline and, other policy planning areas excepted, most likely to call for Commission action.

I would hasten to point out, however, that there may be a tendency to apply these concepts in a superficial manner. Therefore, a determination about which category of product quality should apply in a given situation should be based on an intensely realistic consideration of such factors as the conditions under which the particular product is made available for examination in stores, the ability of consumers to judge the product attribute in question, and the likelihood that consumers will actually exercise their judgment. For example, when consumers attempt to examine the performance of competing brands of durable goods the in-store and store-to-store facilities may not be condusive to useful product comparisons. Additionally, many smaller durable products and most non-durables are sold as packaged goods, a practice which results in efficient distribution, but one which also inhibits close pre-purchase examination of competing brands by consumers. These kinds of limitations lead consumers to rely on easily available proxies for pre-purchase examination of the characteristics of products.

V. EFFECTS ON THE FLOW OF TRUTHFUL INFORMATION

The Commission's Pfizer Doctrine requires the advertiser to possess and rely on adequate substantiation for advertising claims, both literal and implied, at the time the claims are first disseminated to the public [10]. It is important to recognize that a determination about the adequacy of an advertiser's substantiating materials does not involve a narrow examination of the abstract quality of the materials relied upon by the advertiser. Rather, the determination focuses on the manner in which the import of the materials was characterized by the advertising claim. In other words, the claim serves as an hypothesis for which the substantiating materials must provide reasonable support.

Product performance tests, studies of consumer preferences and experiences, evaluation by experts, and references to generally recognized scientific findings and principles are examples of sources of information upon which advertising claims might be based. This area of policy questions leads the regulator to consider the kinds of materials which could be capable of producing adequate information bearing on the claim in question, and to determine the appropriate standard for evaluating materials, or level of significance if the substantiating materials include product tests or consumer research.

These considerations call for both close analysis and a certain amount of pragmatism. For example, with respect to the issue of the appropriateness of various sources of information, the most valid data about the comparative repair rates of a durable good would consist of long-term records of actual consumer experience. However, if an advertiser wished to make a repair rate claim for a new product designed for superior durability, it would seem proper to allow the advertiser to rely on another form of substantiating material until consumer repair records became available.[2]

The selection of appropriate standards for evaluating research results, whether by businessmen, academics, or government officials, tends to center on conventions which have evolved for the sake of convenience. For example, when evaluating consumer research results, the most common level of statistical significance used by researchers, the 0.05 level, holds the chances of approving a finding which should, in truth, be disapproved to less than five in one hundred.

A basic problem with such conventions is that they are likely to be followed blindly by individuals who are concentrating on avoiding the acceptance of a statement which is, in fact, false. In doing this, these individuals either overlook or discount the possibility that they may set their standards so high, under the particular circumstances at hand, that they encounter an unreasonable risk of disapproving a statement which is, in fact, true. There is, however, a mathematical formula which can be used to balance the costs of accepting a false statement against the costs of rejecting a true statement in order to determine the optimum level of significance for a given decision-making situation. In the context of the decision to approve a given advertising claim, this formula might be used to balance the costs to consumers of approving the claim when the claim was, in fact, false against the costs to consumers of disapproving the claim when the claim was, in fact, true.

This mathematical formula can be expressed as shown below, where P designates the optimum level of significance, A designates the cost to the consumer of the disapproval of a true claim, and C designates the cost to consumers of the approval of a false claim.[3]

$$P = \frac{1}{1 + \frac{C}{A}}$$

As a demonstration of the operation of this formula, assume that the cost to consumers of a false claim about a product is $10 million and the cost to consumers of the loss of a true claim is also $10 million. In such a case the Commission would be justified in prohibiting the claim if the chances were greater than five in ten that the claim were false. If the ratio of the two types of costs is changed by reducing the costs of the loss of a true claim to $1 million, then the Commission would be justified in prohibiting the claim if the chances were as small as one in ten that the claim were false.

---

[2] For an example of such analysis see the Notice Order in General Electric Company (FTC Docket No. 9049).

[3] For further discussion of the application of this formula see "Decision Theory and the Fact Finding Process," by John Kaplan. Stanford Law Review, Volume 20, p. 1065-1092; and "Research Methodology and Advertising Substantiation," by Robert A. Mittelstaedt and Nils-Erik Aaby. Proceedings of the Association for Consumer Research Sixth Annual Conference (October, 1975).

The major problem in operationalizing such a formula is in obtaining accurate measures of the appropriate costs. For example, if a claim made about a product test were false, these costs would include the costs to consumers of acting on the basis of a deceptive statement and the costs to other firms of any sales lost to the deceptive competitor. If a true claim about a product were wrongly prohibited, these costs would include the cost to the advertiser of not being allowed to make the truthful claim and the costs to consumers of not having access to the claim. Both of these types of costs should be estimated in order to determine the optimum level of significance for a given claim. Obviously, these costs are difficult to assess; and, in some cases the cost of obtaining the information needed to find the proper "scientifically determined" level of significance might exceed the cost of the product test in which the significance level would be used.

As a result of the difficulty of finding good measures of the cost factors involved in a given situation, conventional standards have evolved. These standards, the most common of which seems to be the 0.05 level of significance, place a high premium on avoiding the acceptance of a false statement. Thus, the question for the regulator is whether, in the context of particular advertising claims, there are circumstances for which these conventional standards might be too rigorous.

VI. DETERRENCE

This area of policy planning questions asks the regulator to set forth a proposed remedy for the alleged deception and to evaluate its likely impact in terms of capacity to provide guidance for advertising decision-makers and in terms of capacity to deter the occurrence of related forms of deception or unfairness. Proposed remedies, of course, may involve orders against one or more advertisers (and their advertising agencies) or they may involve industry-wide rules. And, the remedies may set forth proscriptions against certain kinds of deceptive or unfair claims as well as affirmative duties to disclose certain material facts when particular products are advertised or claims used.

Effective decision-making with respect to these matters calls for a rather substantial Commission commitment to the conduct of consumer research. The specific kinds of decisions most in need of a research base are those about the scope of the claims to be covered by proposed orders against advertisers and by the provisions of proposed rules; the content and form of affirmative disclosures of product related information; and, the impact of various remedies and other programs on behavior in the marketplace.

With respect to scope of the order issues, advertising copy research can assist in the determination of the range of advertising claims which would be sufficiently related to the challenged claim and which, therefore, should be covered by a proposed order or rule. For example, an advertiser might be found to have disseminated a deceptive claim regarding the energy efficiency of an appliance. Copy research could assist in the discovery of the kinds of claims, like "saving you money," which would be likely, in the context of appliance advertising, to suggest efficient energy use to consumers.

The need for consumer research is particularly acute with respect to the content and form of affirmative disclosures of product information and user warnings. Such research should both guide the design of the disclosure and demonstrate that the information has the capacity to inform and affect the decision-making of the appropriate consumers. This research should also be capable of detecting unintended negative consequences of disclosure proposals.

For example, an advertising copy research study was conducted to test the performance of a disclosure of two of the antacid contraindications involved in the antacid warning rulemaking [2]. The final five seconds of a 30-second commercial for a well-known antacid were modified to include a warning for individuals taking prescription drugs and a warning for person wishing to avoid sodium. Two versions of the disclosure, video alone and video with audio, were tested with the original ad as a control. The results showed that the unaided recall of the video with audio disclosure was 28 percent, a level which was close to the 35 percent level of aided recall obtained by the sales message.

VII. LAW ENFORCEMENT EFFICIENCY

The questions in this area relate to the issues of whether there are other government agencies which should be concerned with the proposed investigation and their relationship to the Commission's involvement; the capacity of the Commission to resolve the issues involved; and, whether the Commission should proceed by litigation or by rule-making.

The second of these questions, the capacity of the Commission to resolve the issues which would be involved in the proposed investigation, has a particular bearing on the Commission's conduct and use of consumer research. It would, for example, be possible to delay in the examination of some advertising practices by determining that the Commission should await the further development of research techniques or knowledge by academic consumer researchers. However, it could just as easily be argued that, as an agency of experts, the Commission should take a more active role with respect to consumer research.

VIII. ADDITIONAL CONSIDERATIONS

This area contains several questions which ask the regulator to determine whether there are other important factors which bear upon the merits of the proposed investigation. In particular, the regulator is asked to determine whether the alleged deception has the capacity to affect a vulnerable segment of the population or whether the claim has the capacity to deceptively exploit the legitimate concerns of sectors of the population.

Studies documenting the consumer skills of young children or the particular concerns of individuals suffering illnesses would be obvious examples of the Commission's need for research. Another would be the need for periodic surveys which would inform regulators about the day-to-day concerns of the general public. The availability of such information would serve to bring a sense of the country at large to sometimes remote offices.

CONCLUSION

The previous sections of this paper demonstrated how the policy planning questions direct the regulator to thoroughly examine the public interest involved in a proposed investigation. The protocol poses the questions which must be answered. Moreover, as a public document, the protocol enables all of the parties interested in advertising regulation to examine the decision-making process of the regulatory agency and to determine whether the actions of the agency are well chosen and consistent. It is, therefore, the kind of document that can make government more effective.

REFERENCES

1. "Adult Functional Competency: A Summary," Division of
   Extension, University of Texas at Austin, (March,
   1975).

2. ASI Audience Reaction Tests Conducted for the Federal
   Trade Commission, Bureau of Consumer Protection,
   April 17-19, 1975.

3. ASI Audience Reaction Test, "Firestone Tire Safety
   Message Commercial," January 9, 1977, p. 13-16
   (FTC Docket No. 8818).

4. Eighmey, John. "A Perspective on Advertising Copy
   Research and Advertising Law Enforcement," Proceedings
   of the Eighth Annual Attitude Research Conference of
   the American Marketing Association, March, 1977
   (In press).

5. Darby, Michael R., and Edi Karni. "Free Competition
   and the Optimal Amount of Fraud," Journal of Law and
   Economics, Volume 16, (April, 1973).

6. Federal Trade Commission v. Colgate-Palmolive Co. et
   al. 380 U.S. 374 (1965).

7. Green, Paul E., and Yoram Wind. "New Way to Measure
   Consumers' Judgments," Harvard Business Review,
   (july-August, 1975).

8. Jones, Mary Gardiner. "The FTC's Need for Social
   Science Research," Remarks before the Second Annual
   Conference of the Association for Consumer Research,
   September, 1971.

9. Nelson, Philip. "Information and Consumer Behavior,"
   Journal of Political Economy, Volume 78, (March-April,
   1970).

10. Pfizer, Inc., 81 FTC 56 (1972).

11. Pitofsky, Robert. "Beyond Nader: Consumer Protection
    and the Regulation of Advertising," Harvard Law
    Review, Volume 90, (February, 1977).

12. Summer Omnibus Survey for 1968, Survey Research
    Center, Institute for Social Research, University of
    Michigan.

13. United States v. Firestone Tire and Rubber Company,
    (FTC Docket No. 8818), (February 13, 1976).

Local Consumer Information Systems for Services: The Market for Information and Its Effect on the Market*

Michael L. Ray and Donald A. Dunn, Stanford University

There are several worlds that might be investigated when considering the effects of information on consumer and market behavior. There is the pure world of the theoretical economist, the messy world of the advertiser, the political world of the consumerist, and the demanding world of the consumer information processing researcher. In our NSF-supported work on consumer information systems [4] we are trying to consider all of these worlds, but we have ended up with a very specific one of our own.

We are concerned primarily with providing consumers with information about local services. Our feeling was that national consumer information on products was good and getting better. But it was in the area of local service that the consumer seemed to be losing more because of a lack of good information. (To understand this on a personal level, consider your own experiences with automobile repair.) Also, we were preceded into this area by an excellent concept at the University of Michigan [7] utilizing survey data from consumers as a source of information on local businesses.

Our goals are very simple. They are also elusive. First, we want to design a local consumer information system on services. Second, we want to develop a business plan for such a system that could be implemented by local consumer groups. Third, and most important for this conference, we want to assess the impact of such a system.

General Findings

We've learned four things in our research and these are the topic of this paper. First we have learned that a viable local consumer information service of the type we are developing is a rare commodity. Second, our hypothesis to explain this rarity is that consumers don't want the information. Not only will they not pay for it, in some cases it seems they would pay to avoid it. Third, there do seem to be three stages or levels of information need -- such as developing use opportunity, discovering alternatives and choosing -- that correspond quite closely to levels suggested by consumer decision process analysis or consumer behavior models [6]. The trouble is that consumers don't seem to act as if they have information needs. They don't seek, and sometimes avoid, information. Fourth, this lack of consumer response, coupled with the lack of business acumen represented in most consumer groups, usually has led to failure for local consumer information services.

Of 600 local consumer organizations identified by our colleague Richard Zackon, only about 150 were judged, by his contacts in New York and Washington, to be active enough to have some sort of information service. Postcard questionnaires sent to those organizations plus advertisements in consumer newsletters produced about 70 organizations that had some sort of information contact with consumers. A more detailed questionnaire to these latter organizations revealed only about 15 organizations that had local consumer information services of the type we were seeking, and none of them met our standards for information service in our ideal world.

*The project reported in this paper is supported by grant # NSF-APR 75-23685 from the NSF, RANN program. We are grateful for help and guidance from George Brosseau of NSF as well as our research collaborators Gabriel Biehal, Mary Ann Kriewall, Diogo Lucena, Panayotis Stoucas, Richard Urso and Richard Zackon and our outstanding oversight committee.

In some cases we found that these information services had their primary effect directly on the businesses that provided local services. Instead of the information going to consumers and resulting in consumer action which in turn would affect provider behavior, we found that the awareness that information is being made available to consumers can directly affect service providers' behavior.

The Ideal System

Let us look first in greater detail at what we mean by local consumer information systems. Our ideal system would have nine characteristics.

1. Local with potential for network. It is possible that once viable information systems are set up in local areas they might be organized into cooperating networks. One such system, Vector Enterprises of Santa Monica, California, started out by providing food price information in the Los Angeles and San Diego areas. It now does this via cable television systems in those two areas as well as three New York cities, three New Jersey cities, Milwaukee, and Honolulu.

2. Provides information on services, not products. Many services tend to be local while products tend to have a national character already covered by other information sources.

3. Information before and during decisions, not after. Many local information services are simply complaint lines, columns or bureaus. The purpose of the system we are interested in is to avoid complaints. We want to help people make decisions.

4. Important decisions -- community, home, medical, legal, financial, automobile, appliances. Consumer decisions concerning each of these local services has somewhat different information needs, so we are analyzing these markets separately. It is unlikely that one system can cover all of them, but one business or organizational entity could provide different systems for the various service decision areas. We have listed them above in order of increasing consumer power and, perhaps, decreasing importance. Our belief is that consumers have the least power in the assessment of and resulting effect on community services such as the schools, police, fire, water, and sanitary services. The researcher working on that aspect of the project is developing a model of political action in which part of the information service would involve just letting people know their community services have some deficiencies. In selecting an automobile service outlet, on the other hand, the decision is much less important but consumers have more power which comes from the many choices available.

5. Individualized -- detailed and specific. While it is possible to take many of the difficulties out of making service decisions by providing a general guidance newsletter or mass media features, the real difficulties and needs for information are at the individual level. This does not, of course, eliminate price or service characteristics listings and ratings in newsletters, booklets, magazines or in other media, however we feel our system will need interaction and feedback in order to provide adequate information. This would mean telephone, personal contact or computer terminal interaction with the system data bank.

Our belief is that there is a need for a person between the

user and the data bank. Both the user population and the data banks are so large and textured that we have a situation not unlike that of the computer facility, the reference library or KWIC index system. We could use those services without a consultant, but a consultant can cut a tremendous amount of time and effort out of the process. In fact, for the type of information system we are developing, an intermediary may make the difference between the system being used or not. Despite the fact that this is the dawning of the age of the home computer for the masses (it has to be. There was an article on home computers in the April, 1977 issue of United Airlines Mainliner magazine), the terminal-oriented consumer information systems we have discovered don't get used very much. Consultants help.

We have also learned that consumer information systems work best when they are developed by the users. When consumers provide information for the data bank, this commitment gets them to be users. It would seem that paying for the information would also constitute a form of commitment, but few operating systems have tried and/or succeeded in charging for information of this type.

6. Wide range of information -- prices, quality, timing, extras. Pricing information itself is very difficult to get. Consider the complexity of automobile servicing, financial or legal services. How does one establish price comparisons across all the possible service offerings? One thing we know from marketing is that with services the production occurs at the point-of-purchase. This means that our ideal information system must have an extremely large data bank to include the wide range of information beyond prices.

7. Financially self-supporting. We know of no comprehensive local consumer information system that is financially supported by the sale of information to consumers. The only ones that come close are auto and medical diagnostic centers. But they fall far short of selling the type of information we are seeking. The few organizations that have been financially self-supporting usually sell other consumer services or sell the consumer information to businesses as well as consumers. In fact it is frequently true that a substantial proportion of, say, booklets comparing banks, go to the banks themselves. More on this later.

8. Affects haves, have-nots and those in-between. It is frequently true that social programs are used most by those who need them least. In consuming local services it is also often true that the have-nots have less access to good information. The same reasons that put them in this disadvantageous position could lead to their not using the information system. This is particularly true in the financial services area. Low income people make decisions in this area with very little information and even some misinformation. Very high income people can afford financial consulting services.

9. Legally free of problems -- ability to withstand legal attack. There are apparently few legal problems with the sort of information system we are researching. The problem comes when an already weak consumer organization is threatened with legal attack by a business. The consumer group may be on firm legal ground, but they lack the resources to legally defend themselves. And the attack itself can lower the credibility of the information system. Volunteers may become harder to get. Sometimes the organization can fold before any formal charges are filed. If the system is based on a solid business plan with adequate financial support, however, it is likely that such legal challenges will be ineffective.

Three Levels of Information Need

Each of the services mentioned earlier involves a slightly different decision and information process for the consumer. Our review of the literature, however, indicates that there are three levels of information need common to decision making in all of the service areas. These three levels correspond to the problem recognition, search for alternatives and choice stages of most consumer decision process analyses. In fact if we were concerned with complaints in our information system we could include the fourth -- post purchase behavior -- stage.

The problem recognition stage requires general information about the broad needs that can be satisfied by the service. This stage also includes the general procedure one should use in decision-making. In the real estate area, for instance, one wants to know what characteristics are important in a house as well as about the neighborhoods where housing may be purchased.

Once a buyer gets to the stage of searching for alternatives, he or she has an idea of the important characteristics. Now information is needed on the extent to which each of the alternatives contains these characteristics. In the real estate area, the buyer needs information on the houses in the selected neighborhood(s) in terms of the required characteristics.

The problem with consumer information at this level, particularly with regard to services, is that it is usually difficult for consumers to get any information at all. Usually when it is available, it is limited and under strict control of the service providers, and normally there is not enough information that relates to the characteristics consumers desire.

In the real estate area, the information of multiple listing services is quite complete in terms of physical characteristics of the house and some neighborhood characteristics, but many other characteristics meaningful to individual consumers are not covered. What's more, the multiple listing book is under the control of the real estate agent who is biased. There typically are few summary listings by attribute (which information processing research tells us would be more helpful to the consumer). In general, although the multiple listing service is one of the better information systems at the local level, it has serious shortcomings.

Other local services are almost hopeless in terms of information at the stage of searching for alternatives. For medical services the yellow pages listings at least provide information on doctors' specialties. This is not true for lawyers. Beyond the yellow pages the consumer is left to recommendations from friends, the local medical or law school, some guidebooks, and referral services in the legal area. The situation is so bad that even Consumer Reports in its May 1977 issue hailed as "a major victory for consumers" that advertising for lawyers was allowed in Maine. When Consumer Reports supports advertising as an outstanding information source, you know there is a need for better information.

The third stage of information need is at choice itself -- this is when the consumer needs information on how to purchase the service, what to look for in terms and credit and what hidden problems might be connected with the choice. In home buying, the consumer would like to have an expert analysis of the chosen house in terms of any problems it might have. The home buyer would also like to know what the standard real estate settlement procedures are, and how costs and effort may be eliminated. There is also a need for backup on bidding procedures.

Our findings have been that it is usually at the choice stage that the greatest anxiety or potential anxiety occurs in the decision process. This usually means that information processing is avoided or incomplete. People buying automobile repair service often don't have control over actual costs. Estimates are not clear. For medical and legal services the time of choice and setting terms is often so traumatic that the purchaser is not clear as to what is happening. Terms aren't really set until later when it might be too late.

For all the service areas we have examined and for all three stages of decision making leading to purchase, information has been inadequate in relation to consumer needs. Partially this is due to the services' reluctance to provide full information. Partially this is due to the scant amount of information being presented on a service-by-service basis (usually through advertising) rather than on the more efficient attribute-by-attribute basis. But the most important barrier to good information seems to be consumers' reluctance to process and use it. We must examine that tendency before looking at the possible effect of the information on consumer and market behavior related to local consumer services.

The Information Avoidance Pattern

From other research done by the first author it has been possible to identify three major information processing strategies used by consumers [10]. Both experimental and correlational research as well as theoretical speculation indicate the situational variables that would tend to lead to three "hierarchies of response" -- the learning hierarchy (cognition change first, then affect and finally behavioral tendencies), the dissonance-attribution hierarchy (some behavior first, then affective rationalization and cognitive shift to bolster) and the low-involvement hierarchy (gross and superficial cognitive shifts first, then behavior and finally affective change primarily on the basis of product experience). One aspect of this analysis was that most consumer information processing research was seen as forcing consumers into a high involvement learning hierarchy situation, which was unrealistic for many product decisions and which missed the important attention and rote learning phenomena of low involvement processing [11].

But all this analysis was for product purchasing. As we explored individual service markets and looked at the common failure of local consumer information systems, we began to see that there was a fourth hierarchy or information processing strategy that was being utilized for services and some very important product purchasing. Unfortunately, we do not have direct experimental evidence on this information processing strategy. What follows here, then, is somewhat speculation. We will be testing this notion of a fourth hierarchy or information processing strategy in the research described in the final section of this paper.

We call this fourth hierarchy the information avoidance strategy. For most of the services we have studied it appears that the most significant segment of consumers waits until the last minute to decide. They seem to be highly anxious, have been unable in the past to obtain sufficient information to make a rational choice, have been disappointed in their service purchase decisions, know that there are big differences between services but they can't determine what they are, and feel that there are big stakes in the decision that they just can't protect. So they avoid information. It hasn't helped them in the past, and they believe it probably won't help them now. They make a choice because it is a necessity. Their car won't run. They have a pain in their side. Their husband wants a divorce. So with no prior search or information processing, they look in the telephone directory or ask the first friend they meet or get referred by a professional in the field or visit the service station, doctor or lawyer that is physically most convenient to their home or office.

What this means is that no substantive information pro-

cessing takes place. The three levels of information need are not really satisfied. There is almost no problem recognition information processing since there really isn't time to develop an awareness of specific needs and of how the decision should be made. There is no search for information on alternatives because of the belief that there is no adequate information on alternatives or that even if it were available it would be too technical to understand anyway. At the point of choice there may actually be some learning over a number of choices in the past, but these service decisions are made so infrequently and are often so painful to consumers that this kind of learning is probably rare.

What probably happens is that these consumers repeatedly go through the dissonance-attribution hierarchy. They make a choice, try to rationalize it and then try to learn something about it. What we are guessing here, however, is that, with services, consumers often don't even bother to make a rationalization or seek information to support their choice. Being obviously wrong or in such a poor information gathering situation, they probably avoid information or even thinking about the issue. What little learning occurs could qualify these consumers for what our ex-colleague Edward C. Strong [16], now with Tulane University called the Budweiser hierarchy. The consumers are, of course, sadder Budweiser.

What evidence do we have for the existence of this information avoidance strategy? The evidence comes from many sources, although none of it is experimental. In fact we doubt whether the typical consumer information processing experiment could tap this process, simply because consumers in those studies are forced to process information. Our evidence, then, includes the following:

--All of the 15 outstanding information systems we have discovered in our research offer complaint services and about half are primarily complaint services. This indicates that consumers wait until after purchase to redress wrongs rather than obtaining information beforehand.

--To our knowledge, based on extensive search, there has never been an information system on local services that has existed on the basis of charging consumers for information. In fact there are some strong examples indicating that consumers refuse to pay for information systems that can save the equivalent of the annual charge each week! Clearly these consumers are avoiding information.

--In several European countries consumer advisory services were set up on a commercial basis. Usually these become government-run after a short period of time. Part of this was due to legal difficulties, but this was also due to consumer apathy when a charge is involved.

--The median number of houses actually seen by a home buyer ranges around two to three, depending on the study [1,5]. Apparently there is a large segment of home buyers who buy the first house they see [8]. This is information avoidance of the highest order.

--Extensive research on the effects of the Truth in Lending requirements indicated a general lack of effect, primarily because consumers apparently didn't search for information. As Day and Brandt [3, p. 31] put it "Indeed the credit-related decisions are often decided by default once the dealer or retailer is chosen."

--One consumer group representative after another has told us that they cannot charge for information or complaint services. Telephone complaintants often ask if there is a charge for service. Conferences with a charge are under-attended.

--Certain services, for example medical and legal, are so difficult to choose, so devoid of good information and so anxiety-provoking that the information search process is avoided completely. For instance, the New Orleans Mayor's Office of Consumer Affairs received 5053 inquiry and complaint calls in 1976. Of these only four related to legal services and eight related to medical ones.

--In most of the service areas we have investigated (community, real estate, medical, financial, automobile) there is a paucity of research on consumer information processing. Perhaps this is due to a lack of actual processing. This interpretation is bolstered by the few studies which have been done [e.g., 9, 12] which show rather trivial characteristics (such as drive time as a motive for selecting a medical provider) importantly affecting decisions.

If this information avoidance strategy actually exists to any important degree, it has important implications for developing viable local information services and for their effect. A viable service must somehow reduce anxiety and convince consumers that it provides valuable information. The devices of creating consumer commitment and using intermediate persons as well as standard marketing techniques provide some hope for reducing information avoidance. If this can be done and consumers get and use good information on services, the effect on market behavior should be substantial. In effect, consumers would change the very basis on which choices are made. But developing a viable system will be quite difficult.

Analytical Studies Now in Progress

Five analytical studies of the role of information in markets are now in progress.

1. <u>Homogeneous goods</u> - When the only variables concerning a good are price and quantity, price dispersion can occur as a result of consumer ignorance [15]. Where consumer search is costly, an information system might be able to provide information to consumers on the results of previous searches at a price less than the average search cost. This project is concerned with models similar to that of Butters [2] that allow us to analyze the effects of an information service in a market of this type.

2. <u>Real estate</u> - Unique goods like houses can be modeled by considering the market to consist of many segments, each of which includes a number of homogeneous goods such as apartments that are very similar to each other [17]. A consumer information service for such a market will probably look very much like a real estate broker, although the fee structure might be different. A model of a market in which goods can be sold either by direct advertisement or through a broker (or information service) is being developed. Various fee structures and broker objective functions can be modeled.

3. <u>Public services</u> - Goods provided by a monopolist, whether public or private, may still be viewed as being offered in a market in which the competitors are potentially capable of entry, or in which the market is for the management of the firm or public agency. In either case the monopoly provider or its management will be sensitive to public (consumer) opinion concerning the service offered. Therefore, a consumer information service can have a significant effect in this situation, often by way of an implicit threat to allow entry or to change management through political action. Such systems have been found to be effective in real situations [13, 14]. This project consists of a study of models of the political system in which the probability of re-election or of keeping out new entrants is a function of perceived cost and performance by the monopoly service provider. Information can be supplied by consumer groups that can alter these probabilities. In a real situation, for example, the information might be a cost and performance comparison between the local provider and other provi-

ders in similar cities throughout the U.S.

4. <u>Automobile repair</u> - A logical flow model of automobile repair service purchasing has been developed, taking into account the possibility of information avoidance. This service area is one for which diagnosis can be "unbundled" from the actual servicing or cure. In fact diagnostic centers are quite common. The problem is so complex, in terms of large numbers of types of service problems, types of consumers and service outlets, that a variant of a system developed by the Ontario Motor League (Canada) is being proposed. This diagnostic center suggests two or three service providers to fix each particular automobile problem. Then, for an extra charge, the automobile may be brought back to the diagnostic center to determine if the car has been repaired properly. If a questionnaire on the pricing and other crucial aspects of the service is filled out by consumers as they wait for the check-up diagnosis, the system would develop a data bank on providers which would feed back to better recommendations after diagnosis.

5. <u>Medical services</u> - These have many of the characteristics of auto repair with the important exceptions that treatment usually takes longer and is less subject to effectiveness checking. Diagnostic centers are available in the medical area, but their use is probably far below potential. A side project under our grant has concentrated on the nutrition aspect of medical care. An interactive information system to be used by nutritionists has been proposed.

Conclusions and Next Steps

The potential of local consumer information systems on services is great. Because this potential has not been realized, however, it is difficult to determine precisely what the effects on consumers and markets might be. We are currently extending our research in at least five areas.

1. <u>Business plans</u>. A special seminar at Stanford entitled "Providing Consumer Information as a Business Venture" is leading to a series of business plans which can be utilized by consumer groups to set up viable local information systems.

2. <u>Test marketing</u>. We are making arrangements to test various system configurations with some active consumer groups. The objective will be to determine the effectiveness of various methods for getting over the invormation avoidance barrier. Also we will be able to determine, at least in the short run, consumer and market effects.

3. <u>Cable TV delivery test</u>. In cooperation with one of the most active and effective Public Interest Research Groups and a very large cable TV system, we will be adding features and consumer information advertisements to a special consumer channel. Results will be monitored.

4. <u>TV commercial test</u>. One consumer affairs office has developed a series of short public service announcements of consumer information. These will be tested in a realistic laboratory experimental environment to determine their actual or potential effects.

5. <u>Computer terminal delivery</u>. A few systems with computer terminal delivery of local consumer information have been developed. An excellent one has been developed for deaf consumers. This special population will allow very clean research designs. Combined with our other work with computer oriented systems, this research should provide a reasonable assessment of this configuration of information provision.

6. <u>Auto diagnostic center development</u>. At present local diagnostic services do not have the service provider recommendation or check-up and questionnaire after repair. We will work in the AAA centers to add these features and assess their impact.

Summary

An NSF-supported program of research on consumer information systems for local services has discovered a dearth of such systems. The reason for this dearth seems to be consumers' pattern of <u>information avoidance</u> in connection with making decisions on services. The only hope for developing information systems that are used for service decision-making seems to be in appealing to those segments of the population actually seeking information. Several studies are underway in this direction.

References

1. Johan Arndt, <u>Consumer Search Behavior: An Exploratory Study of Decision Processes Among Newly-Married Home Buyers</u> (Oslo: Universitelsforlaget, 1972).

2. Gerald Butt ers, "Equilibrium Distributions of Sales and Advertising Prices," <u>Review of Economic Studies</u>, 1977.

3. George S. Day and William K. Brandt, "Consumer Research and Evaluation of Information Disclosure: The Case of Truth in Lending," <u>Journal of Consumer Research</u>, Vol. 1 (June 1974).

4. Donald A. Dunn and Michael L. Ray, "Consumer Information Systems: An Assessment of a New Social Technology," Proposal to the National Science Foundation, June 1975.

5. Donald J. Hempel, "Search Behavior and Information Utilization in the Home Buying Process," in Philip R. McDonald (ed.), <u>Marketing Involvement in Society and the Economy</u>, Proceedings of the 1969 Fall Conference of the American Marketing Association (Chicago: American Marketing Association, 1969), pp. 241-49 .

6. G. David Hughes and Michael L. Ray (ed.), <u>Buyer/Consumer Information Processing</u>, (Chapel Hill, N.C.: University of North Carolina Press, 1974).

7. E. Scott Maynes, James N. Morgan, Weston Vivian, and Greg J. Duncan, "The Local Consumer Information System: An Institution - To Be?" <u>Journal of Consumer Affairs</u>, (Summer, 1977).

8. William Mindak, Personal Communication, 1977.

9. Barnett R. Parker and Venkataraman Srinivasan, "A Consumer Preference Approach to the Planning of Rural Primary Health-Care Facilities," <u>Operations Research</u>, Vol. 24, No. 5 (September-October 1976), pp. 991-1025.

10. Michael L. Ray, "Attitude as Communication Response," N. Deborah Johnson and William D. Wells, (eds.), <u>Attitude Research at Bay</u> (Chicago: American Marketing Association, 1976), pp. 87-112.

11. Michael L. Ray, "When Does Consumer Information Processing Research Actually Have Anything To Do With Consumer Information Processing?" in William D. Perrault, (ed.), <u>Advances in Consumer Research</u>, Vol. 4 (Atlanta: Association for Consumer Research, 1977), pp. 372-5.

12. Stanford Research Institute, <u>The Automotive After Market</u>, Long Range Planning Report Series 1969.

13. C.H. Stevens, "Citizen Feedback: The Need and the Response," <u>Technology Reviews</u>, Vol. 73, No. 3, (January 1971).

14. C.H. Stevens, John D.C. Little and P. Tropp, "Citizen Feedback System: The Puerto Rico Model," <u>National Civic Review</u>, Vol. 60, No. 4 (April 1971).

15. George Stigler, "The Economics of Information," <u>Journal of Political Economy</u>, Vol. 69 (June 1961), pp. 213-25.

16. Edward C. Strong, "How the Other Half Looks," Unpublished memo, Tulane University, 1973.

17. J.L. Sweeney, "Quality Commodity Hierarchies, and Housing Markets," <u>Econometrica</u>, Vol. 42 (January 1974), pp. 147-67.

COMMENTS ON PUBLIC POLICY AND INFORMATION*

William L. Wilkie, University of Florida

INTRODUCTION

In preface to my discussion of the papers delivered in the "Public Policy and Information" session, it is appropriate to indicate that these are excellent representatives of some frontier issues and emerging activities within this topic area. I found the papers to be well done, informative and interesting, and do not wish to take major issue with them in this discussion.

In terms of the "field" of consumer information -- and potential increased interaction between economist and consumer behaviorist -- however, some discussion of related context and issues may be useful. I will therefore raise some brief points on each paper in the order of their presentation, then turn to another emerging area for public policy information -- government mandated provision of product information via "Trade Regulation Rules."

Consumer Research and Public Policy for Advertising Regulation

Professor John Eighmey's paper reports on and discusses the FTC's recently developed "policy planning protocol" for deceptive and unsubstantiated advertising claims. It does so in a realistic manner, reflecting the need for consumer researchers to straddle the world of public policy and research.

This is a descriptive -- not normative -- paper. It tells us where matters stand at present, not that this is an ideal system for allocating efforts and resources. One message which comes through clearly, however, is that this is seen to be a major step forward for the FTC's Division of National Advertising, and that consumer research can clearly be productively applied within this system.

In further evaluating these dimensions, it is helpful to consider some aspects of the utilization of such a policy planning protocol. In particular, the organizational climate of FTC provides a significant context for this structured approach; an historical overview can help us understand why a real need for the protocol was seen and why there are some costs associated with it.

Following the Nader's Raiders and ABA Committee reports in the late 1960's -- both of which were critical of FTC's alleged lack of activity in general, and lack of innovative programs and remedies in particular -- the commission undertook major organizational changes to hike productivity. One crucial change involved a shift toward "decentralized" management, wherein lower levels of the professional staff (i.e., attorneys) were now encouraged to bring new cases, advance new legal theor-

*Support of the author's research reported herein, by the National Science Foundation (grant APR76-00638), the Marketing Science Institute, and the Public Policy Research Center of the University of Florida, is gratefully acknowledged. Also, the author's perspectives on the regulatory climate at FTC have been much influenced by the informed insights of Professor Neil Beckwith (Wharton) and Professor H. Keith Hunt (Brigham Young).

propose new remedies. It would then be the job of the Division Directors, then the Bureau Director and finally the five Commissioners, to ensure that imprudent, impolitic, or otherwise poorly chosen cases or programs would be nipped in the bud.

In addition, a fledgling "Office of Policy Planning and Evaluation" (OPPE) was established to provide rational and considered analyses and recommendations to the Commission as to the proper directions and program activities for FTC. As might have been predicted, the classic line/staff struggle was underway, with the line (Bureau Divisions) pretty much holding sway over OPPE for the first few years.

This is not surprising given the external successes enjoyed by the newly "activist" Commission during this time (roughly 1971-73). A number of new legal rationales were applied in an array of new program areas, together with new forms of regulatory requirements and remedies. In essence, the newly activist FTC was attempting to probe the boundaries of its mandate, which if you look back into the original FTC Act of 1914, you will see is quite vague but potentially quite broad.

Probing one's mandate is in effect setting legal precedent, which I understand is an exciting activity for attorneys. It is, I might add, a key process in the evolution of public policy. At any rate, the excitment of probing the boundaries of FTC's mandate was accompanied by substantial support where it counts most for a quasi-independent agency such as FTC. Congressional appropriations for FTC's budgeted activities more than doubled within a few years. Law review types -- the top graduates of the top law schools -- were anxious to join the growing Commission staff. Consumer advocates, representing one possible constituency for FTC, were issuing positive statements on the value of the programs, particularly those attacking deceptive advertising at the national level.

During this time, the internal allocation of resources shifted clearly away from economics and competition matters (e.g., monopoly, merger, concentration, etc.) and toward the Bureau of Consumer Protection. Within the BCP, moreover, national advertising was receiving particular attention. In addition to being highly visible, national advertising has the desirable regulatory characteristic of being relatively easy to identify and work with at the national level, as relatively few agencies and advertisers account for the bulk of this activity. Also, compliance is reasonably straightforward to monitor and, presumably, obtain. (For the converse of these reasons, I would point out that we have not seen such stress on areas such as in-store sales practices or local retail advertising.)

In an historical sense this period of time might be viewed as a phase of "idea generation" and intial action. Cases and programs were being created in large number, remedies were being proposed, and initial evidence being gathered. To gain some further perspective on the degree and intensity of this burst of activity, we need only consider the fact that within a three-year period programs in the following areas were advanced or in process:

-- comparative advertising
-- corrective advertising
-- counter-advertising extended to all products
-- advertising substantiation
-- unfairness as a rationale
-- restitution
-- holder-in-due-course
-- consumer research as legal evidence
-- cooling-off
-- FTC power to issue industry-wide required marketing behaviors.

As we are aware, these activities were not received with universal favor, particularly by affected parties in the business and advertising community. In addition to major efforts in self-regulation of advertising claims, legal challenges to FTC's programs were instituted and political pressures applied. New appointments at the top levels of FTC reflected some differences in approach to the mandate and to regulation generally; the areas of economics and competition became relatively more salient, with some significant initiatives undertaken there. OPPE came under the direction of conservative economists, and began to push hard for cost-benefit assessments of existing and proposed programs. Accompanying this stress was the more favorable reception to arguments of market self-correction and the relative advantages to be gained from deregulation across a range of government activities. The new makeup of the Commission itself was favorably disposed to this view also.

These changes coincided with the natural progress of a number of the initiatives undertaken several years earlier by the more activist consumer protection staff. Some of the more significant cases had been decided, some important court decisions had come in, and some very significant legislation -- for example, the Magnuson-Moss Act and the 1975 Energy Act -- had been passed. The net result, while composed of victories and defeats for the consumer protection activist, was one of dramatically increased boundaries of responsibility for FTC.

The past year or two may be viewed as a period in which the Commission and its staff have endeavored to develop and streamline programs to meet its expanded responsibilities and authorizations. The key requirements thus became those of strong program management, planning, and control more so than legal theorizing and advocacy skills. It is within this background that I would place the role and potential impact of the advertising planning protocol described and, I believe, substantially developed by Professor Eighmey.

Given this background context, the protocol may be seen to serve several significant functions in the management of advertising regulation. As a planning tool, it forces the staff attorney to consider most or all of the relevant aspects of a potential case, something which normally might not occur. Also, it provides a summary source for information germane to a potential case, this to be used by higher management in its planning. Note also that these attributes can be used at later points as a control function.

Also, it in effect provides for greater centralization of the regulatory activity, which may be a desirable characteristic given the current needs for managing the increased boundaries of the agency. Perhaps most significantly, as noted in the paper, the protocol makes the relevant data available for purusal and consideration by others, thus opening the doors for external evaluation and inputs into the advertising regulation process. Finally, it attempts to employ objective analyses and measures in order to allow for rational decisions. This may tend to reduce the degree

of disagreements based upon differences in philosophies or values. (Note, however, that the eighth sector of the protocol could allow for considerable sensitivity to the prevailing political climate.)

As a rational planning guide, then, the protocol is designed to serve an important management function. The key issue regarding its pragmatic value, however, depends on the way it is used. I see four dimensions relevant to this issue. First, the presence of this protocol and its stress upon analysis and rationality suggests that the line organization -- particularly at lower levels -- may not be receptive to it, and may employ it in an advocacy role rather than as an analytical aid. In the longer run, extensive reliance upon strict use of the protocol could reduce the incentive for innovation at this level of the line performance.

Second, and somewhat related to the first point, is the impact that the reliance upon rationality has in terms of the kinds of actions brought under the planning protocol. The stress is necessarily on objective (measurable) factors where possible; this may tend to reduce the impact of subjective or "value-laden" factors. At any rate, it is interesting to note that "misleading" or deceptive rationales are prominent throughout the protocol, while "unfairness" seems not to crop up at all, even though the 1973 Supreme Court decision in the S & H case decreed that an unfairness rationale was to be developed by FTC.

Third, the potential role of consumer research is in part a function of how potentially illegal activities are defined (i.e., whether unfairness or deception is used as the rationale). Given the strong stress on deception in this protocol, the potential uses of consumer research appear to be rather bright. However, Professor Eighmey's assessment is better taken as indicative than definitive, as there are still many unresolved issues in the topic areas discussed. Also, it should be noted that there is a potential timing difficulty likely to be encountered for using consumer research in many of the early stages when the protocol is employed. Unless directly relevant data can be subpoenaed or a "quick and dirty" study can be inexpensively mounted, it is likely that consumer research in an evidenciary sense is not going to be available on the key issues of whether or not a given ad is deceptive or unfair. As consumer research is becoming more recognized, however, there will likely be increasing willingness to invest in obtaining this information at earlier stages of the process.

The political climate is, of course, the really key dimension in determining the pragmatic impact of this protocol. By this I intend to refer to politics both outside and within the agency. As I meant to suggest in my historical discussion above, the climate and needs of the agency in recent times were such that this document appears to be entirely appropriate and useful for its intended purposes.

Within the past few months, however, there have been major new appointments of top level personnel at FTC, including the arrival of Michael Pertschuk as Chairman of the Commission. His key appointees have activist backgrounds in the area of advertising, and it appears likely that we will see a resurgence of activism in advertising regulation. Also, it appears that OPPE will be repopulated and positioned to take a more active, as opposed to reactive, role in setting directions for Commission involvement. In summary, it appears that the FTC setting is about to undergo some major revisions. Apart from the substantive directions to be undertaken, it will be interesting to observe the effect of such changes on the management system which has been developed, including such protocols as this one for advertising planning.

In closing my remarks in this section, I would like to raise one different but equally important dimension with respect to the paper's meaning for us. This involves its contribution to the development of a field of consumer research and public policy. Unlike economics, our field does not have a history of interaction, insight, and influence on public policy. Professor Eighmey's presence at FTC, for example, was a part of an in-house consultant program begun only in 1971, and typically involving only one academic in residence at a time.

Description and informed assessment of policy areas and activities is thus an extremely valuable contribution to the growth of our field. By providing a structure with which to look at the area of advertising regulation, and a realistic assessment of the current status of its various components, Professor Eighmey provides our field with a needed basis for stimulating further thinking and research on this topic.

Information Imperfection in Local Consumer Markets

Professor E. Scott Maynes' paper differs in topic and orientation from that discussed above. Its main purposes are to develop and explain an integrated system for assessing the extent of "informational imperfection" in local market areas, to present some initial results indicative of the level of such imperfection in existing markets, and to suggest some policy programs to improve this state of affairs.

For the purposes of this volume, there are additional dimensions embodied in this paper which deserve attention. Although Professor Maynes is an economist, his treatment of this topic has brought him close to the work of academics in marketing and consumer behavior; he has read our literature and integrated some of it into his work. In fact, it may well be that Dr. Maynes holds the signal distinction of being the first economist in history to do so!

Beyond this, as I am sure he would agree, the area is open for further exploration and is amenable to evolving approaches and methods in consumer behavior research.

Along with these positive indicators, however, there are at least two significant caveats that should be raised early. First, this is an area which embodies value judgments in moving from science or research to policy implications. Many persons in our field -- especially those associated with marketing -- are not likely to react favorably to taxing consumption or advertising in order to finance information provisions by consumer controlled organizations. However, I would hope that this would not deter us from pursuing the important and challenging issues raised by Professor Maynes concerning consumer behavior and informational imperfections in markets, nor from attempting to employ our theory and findings as we individually see them to impact on policy determination.

The second potential constraint may be more significant in the short-run. There is, to me at least, a healthy dose of economic nomenclature and orientation to this paper, both of which come hard to the typical consumer behavior researcher. In the remainder of my discussion of Professor Maynes' paper, I will (head unbowed) highlight my points of ignorance and difficulty.

First, this paper is normative rather than descriptive. This is not a criticism, but the appearance of a normative paper in consumer behavior stimulated a reaction of how rare this is in our field. One real advantage of this normative orientation is that it can provide overt criteria for our evaluation of the goodness or quality of a consumption decision and the process leading up to it. A long-standing difficulty in marketing is that the most appropriate "criterion" for a marketer to use -- brand purchase -- happens to change as a function of for which brand the observer is working.

Related to the advantages brought by a normative approach are some questions involving the definitions and criteria discussed in this paper. First, the definition of the "perfect information frontier" was not quite clear to me; given the requirement of a positively sloped line, it appears that the further requirement "for which a given quality may be purchased" is not quite accurate. Many brands in the examples possessed a unique quality grade, yet their prices were above the frontier; the quality represented by that brand could not be purchased without an imperfection being judged. This places an amazing burden on the accuracy and validity of the "quality" measure.

In the abstract, it appears that "quality" should be viewed to include the sum of all benefits, while "price" might be viewed as including the sum of all costs. Thus such additional dimensions as convenience of location, parking, service and repair facilities, assortment available, seller's expertise, and status might be placed on either side of the equation as a function of positive or negative scores for the manufacturer or retail outlet. Professor Maynes does a good job in recognizing and discussing the possible factors which hinder estimation of the degree of imperfection, primarily by rendering measures of "quality" to be difficult. He then provides an interesting example of testing alternative rival hypotheses to come down to the interpretation of informational imperfection. I am left, however, with the question -- given the severe, and as yet insurmountable difficulties in handling the quality assessments -- how should we deal with the process of examining alternative hypotheses?

One useful step may be to explicitly differentiate between findings of different prices across retail outlets for the same brand from the situation of comparing different brands and different outlets. In this sense, we are holding quality constant and are able to focus on price differences across retailers. This problem may be reasonably handlable, perhaps by using a consumer survey to ascertain the level of consumer awareness of alternative sources and alternative low-cost retailers. Also, the literature in retail store image and distance models may be helpful in distinguishing variance attributable to non-informational influences.

My second concern -- even assuming that some high level of imperfection is isolated and accepted -- is whether and how we are legitimately able to label this imperfection as "informational", and what the term "informational" really means here. For example, I wonder whether the existence of different retail prices for the identical product is an imperfection in a market sense rather than a consumer sense; prices are -- for many products at least -- relatively easy to obtain by phone as well as personal visits. The fact that a large percentage of consumers may never check, and thus not be aware of alternative prices is not necessarily an indictment against the informational characteristic of the marketplace per se. I realize that this is not particularly germane to the theoretical conception of an imperfection, but it appears to be quite significant in terms of what would seem to be appropriate policy kinds of programs.

Turning from the economic question, there are some notions in consumer behavior research that have potential to assist in the further development of this topic. The concepts of individual differences and market segmentation appear to be relevant for both advancing measurement and, more importantly, advancing estimation in this setting. In terms of Professor Mayne's model for quality laid out in the paper, it could be that an adaptation of the ideal point version of the multi-attribute model -- in which a difference score is calculated between each consumer's perception (belief) of the degree of service chacteristics offered by an alternative and the ideal level of that characteristic for that consumer -- would assist in operationalization. This would allow improved diagnostic ability in assessing whether consumers tend to differ in their perceptions or their desires, or both. Informational remedies would presumably be more appropriate for variations in perceptions, especially of objective attributes. If we find variations in desires (values) or ideal points, we must confront the issue of whether consumers already know what they want, versus automatically moving to assume a need for consumer education.

In conclusion, I find Professor Maynes' work interesting and suggestive of new areas for consumer researchers to investigate. In order to do, however, we consumer researchers must guard against simply reacting with negative points or problems, and attempt to bring insights from our field to the evolving state of the art. This is an excellent bridge between the fields.

Local Consumer Information Systems for Services

In this paper Professors Michael L. Ray and Donald Dunn provide an overview and progress report on an NSF-sponsored research grant to investigate local information systems for services. Their initial findings do not sound encouraging for the potential of these systems, apparently due to consumers' lack of willingness to seek out and process relatively complex information on these purchases.

With respect to the details of the paper, I have little with which to quarrel. Overall, I found it to be interesting and wide-ranging in scope and coverage. Given its "engineering" or applied orientation, this project fits nicely with the more abstract, theoretical orientation of Professor Maynes' work.

There are several points within the paper that I would make. First, with respect to the consumers' needs in the "Problem Recognition" and "Choice" stages, I would suggest that it may be more useful to cast these as requiring consumer education rather than consumer information, in that these essentially refer to setting up processing dimensions and rules for the generic product or service decision. My view of consumer information, conversely, is that it provides essentially pieces of data on particular alternatives which are to be processed via the dimensions and rules set up during education. At a practical level, the adoption of this view may assist in suggesting means by which to overcome consumer anxiety, which Professor Ray points out as being a major stumbling block to increase utilization of these information systems.

In terms of consumer research, the conceptualization of a fourth hierarchy -- the "Information Avoidance Strategy" -- suggests a useful increase in the external validity of the hierarchy framework. I am not sure that this process merits the term "strategy" in its title, however, and it will be instructive to learn how further research will indicate that the other hierarchical components are ordered or, if rejected, the nature of the process or cause of such rejection.

If the Information Avoidance hypothesis is borne out in continued research of the project, it would seem to raise a further difficulty for interpretation of existing market imperfections as being "informational," at least in

terms of the causal agent and appropriate policy alternatives. In this sense, however, the efforts of the Stanford project may well have complementary benefits for Professor Maynes' work; by not assuming that there will be a natural response to the availability of new information, this project has been able to design part of its task to be an investigation of means by which such consumer response can be stimulated. The orientation of its consumer research portions is also slightly more activist than most academic research; it appears to be searching for hints by which to change behavior, rather than simply waiting to explain why that behavior hasn't occurred. In keeping with these orientation, it appears that the authors have chosen services with especially high pay-offs for informational utilization, and with some history of success. The notion of imparting business techniques for successful program implementation by consumer groups, should these work, is potentially a major benefit of the project to the real world of consumer information provision. I look forward to further reports of findings and conclusions from it.

Trade Regulation Rules (TRR's)

I have run on at greater length than I had planned, but in order to round out the session's coverage of significant new developments, I believe it is necessary to briefly mention that there is an emerging program, concentrated at FTC, which merits the careful attention of economists and consumer researchers alike if we are to truly address the issues raised by the term "consumer information." This new program -- termed Trade Regulation Rule-Making -- in essence allows the Federal Trade Commission to legislate certain behaviors for marketing practices which all marketers in a given product of service category must perform. The FTC's power to issue such TRR's was suggested in court rulings during the activist period noted earlier, and was legislatively granted by the Magnuson-Moss Act. One of the major routes taken by FTC to implement these rule-making procedures has been to stress potential rules involving the required provision of product information. This information would normally be of a standardized nature, amenable to objective measurement and reporting, and provided in forms intended to be easily available, timely, and allowing if not encouraging comparisons between alternative brands.

A number of these rules are underway, with extensive public hearings required in order to build a record of pro and con arguments and evidence. Substantial research funds -- not historically a common occurrence -- have been made available for consumer research relevant to these rules. A partial listing of the rules in progress includes: nutritional information restrictions and requirements in food advertising, status and repair record of used automobiles, restrictions on efficacy claims for FTC drugs, energy consumption labeling for appliances, standardized dollar cost comparisons for life insurance, and standardized cleaning performance labeling for laundry detergent. As might be expected, the need for theory and evidence regarding the introduction of such information TRR's is substantial. I am hopeful that the kind of effort we have seen in this conference will also be employed in this very new, but very significant area.

PART IV: EPILOGUE

Andrew A. Mitchell, Carengie-Mellon University

The purpose of this conference was to bring together leading researchers from the areas of economics, consumer psychology and public policy who are concerned with understanding the effect of information on consumer and market behavior. Its goals were to give the participants a better understanding of major issues, to make them aware of major developments in other areas and to identify important new research directions.

During the conference three major themes were apparent. The first theme concerned differences in the methodological approaches used by economists and behaviorists. The second involved a presentation and discussion of the basic findings and concepts from the relevant economic and behavioral literature. The third theme centered on two substantive areas where the merging of economic and behavioral research would appear to be useful. These areas were advertising and the development of procedures for identifying and correcting information imperfections in markets.

In this summary, I would like to review and elaborate on these major themes in the order mentioned above. This discussion of the themes reflects, to some extent, my admitted bias toward the behavioral view.

METHODOLOGICAL DIFFERENCES

The discussion focusing on the alternative methodological approaches of economists and behaviorists was triggered by the discussion paper of George Haines (chapter 4) which presented empirical evidence that individuals may exhibit intransitive preferences. The problem, however, seemed to be more fundamental.

To put this discussion in proper perspective, we first should recognize that it is inevitable that there will be some conflict between economists and behaviorists. Even though they may study the same phenomena, they are concerned with different levels of analysis. Behaviorists are generally interested in understanding the behavior of individuals or small groups while economists are ultimately interested in understanding the behavior of aggregates of individuals. The end goal of any science is the development of general theories which provide an understanding and prediction of the phenomena being investigated. The most powerful theories are generally the most parsimonious theories--theories which explain the phenomena of interest with a small number of variables or constructs. Since economists are interested in explaining the behavior of aggregates of individuals, their models by necessity must exclude variables that behaviorists find useful in understanding and predicting the behavior of individuals and small groups. Consequently, behaviorists will generally be upset with economic models since, by necessity, they must leave out explanatory variables that behaviorists consider important.

The conflict between behaviorists and economists, however, seemed to go beyond this. First, behaviorists questioned the exclusive reliance of economists working in the area of the economics of information on the deductive method. Under

this approach, axioms or assumptions are explicitly stated and their implications are derived. Following Friedman [5], model testing relys primarily upon face and predictive validity as opposed to a testing of the assumptions or axioms of the model. One of the dangers of testing only the predictions and not the assumptions is that, in many cases, models derived from alternative sets of assumptions or axioms may fit the data equally well and may imply different policy decisions.

Second, the assumptions and axioms of most economic models center on the rational behavior of buyers and sellers. Although exactly what constitutes rational behavior is not clearly defined, it seems to involve, for instance, the use of the marginal principle in decision making and Baysian analysis in information updating. To justify this assumption for firms, economists frequently argue that firms must behave rationally or they will go out of business in the long run. Although, there is some question as to the validity of this argument with respect to firms, it certainly does not appear to be applicable to households (Simon and Stedry [10]).

Behavioral research has indicated that, in general, humans do not appear to behave according to the tenets of the economic rational man. In his paper, Russo (chapter 8) discusses reasons why they do not. These include the failure of economic models to capture human complexity, to account for personal knowledge limitations, and to consider information processing costs. This suggests that human behavior might be more realistically modeled as constrained maximization. Given the environmental constraints and limited knowledge and cognitive abilities, individuals are simply trying to make the best decisions possible (i.e. they are rational if their decision making constraints and costs are taken into account).

Behaviorists were also concerned that economists take buyers' evaluations (e.g. assessment of utility) of products and services as given and that these evaluations are independent of the price charged by the firm and its advertising. Behaviorists are concerned with understanding how buyers form evaluations and recognize that evaluations are subject to change over time. In forming evaluations of products, individuals integrate information from different environmental cues. These cues may include the price of the product, the color of the package, the advertising copy and usage experience. Previous research has indicated that not only is it important to understand which cues are used to form evaluations, but also the order in which they are experienced.

Given these problems, a very fundamental question needs to be answered. Even though the assumptions made by economists are not realistic at the individual level are they reasonable enough to provide good predictions of the effect of changing the policy variables in the model? It is probably safe to say that they will provide reasonable predictions in some situations, but not in others. An examination of the conditions under which these models will yield reasonable predictions would provide a very interesting area of research.

In contrast to economic research, behavioral research relys heavily on the inductive method. Here a particular phenomena is examined and generalized constructs are developed and tested to determine how well they explain the phenomena. However, much of behavioral research, especially in

*Appreciation is expressed to Robert Avery and Richard Staelin for their comments on an earlier draft of this paper.

information processing remains at a very descriptive level. Current research on consumer behavior using an information processing approach indicates that individuals exhibit very heterogeneous behavior with respect to acquiring and processing information. Consequently, there is a definite need to develop generalizable constructs which will explain this heterogeneity. In addition, much of the behavioral research seems to be overly concerned with internal as opposed to external validity. For instance, behaviorists have a good understanding of how individuals process nonsense syllables, but little understanding of how they process information from advertisements which are much richer in terms of meaning.

ECONOMIC AND BEHAVIORAL CONCEPTS

Economic Concepts

The current research on the economics of information, as reviewed by Salop (chapter 1) has demonstrated quite clearly that information imperfections can result in inefficient markets. If all buyers or a large subset of buyers are able to correctly assess the value of alternative products in the market, then the prices of these products will reflect their value and the markets will operate efficiently. If buyers are unable to assess the value of alternative products then market failure may occur as demonstrated by the classic "lemon" example (Akerloff [1]).

Salop also discusses the basic economic approach to examining the effect of information on the behavior of markets. Under this approach information about a product is treated as a commodity and markets are examined for inefficiencies. Although information is similar to commodities in many ways (e.g. there is always a "cost" associated with acquiring information), there are also important differences. First, information is infinitely divisible. Once information is acquired, it may be passed on to a large number of individuals. Second, the value of information is affected by its source. The same information will be more valuable if it comes from a reliable as opposed to an unreliable source. Third, information has no intrinsic value itself. It is valuable only if it has meaning to an individual and allows him to make "better" decisions. Finally, most information in the market place is provided for a purpose and, therefore, may be biased. For instance, sellers of products have the "best" information about their products, however, they will only provide buyers information that will enhance the value of their product vis-a-vis other products.

In examining the effects of information imperfections in markets, economists have developed a number of interesting concepts that researchers in marketing and consumer psychology may find useful. These include market signalling; search, experience and credence goods; and models of search. Market signalling occurs when buyers cannot evaluate the quality of a good and rely upon related signals from sellers in making their evaluations. In his paper, Salop (chapter 1) uses an example where patients use the number of hours a doctor works as an indication of their quality. Other examples of market signalling that have appeared in the literature include education as an indication of the value of a prospective employee (Spence [10]) and the quantity of advertising for a particular product as an indication of its quality (Nelson [17]). In the latter case, buyers may assume that a large number of buyers must be satisfied with the product and continue to repurchase it in order for the firm to be able to afford large advertising expenditures.

As Salop demonstrates in his paper (chapter 1), sellers may discover that buyers use a particular signal or screening device in evaluating a product or service and by emphasizing this signal (e.g. working longer hours) may increase demand and possibly profits in the short run.

Competitors, however, will soon discover that buyers use this signal and they will also begin to emphasize it. The end result of these dynamics may be an equilibrium where each competitor produces more of the signal than would normally be desired or a situation where the signal becomes a very imperfect indicator of quality.

Search, experience and credence goods represent a classification of different product classes based on a buyer's ability to evaluate the quality of the product. Search goods may be evaluated prior to purchase, experience goods may be evaluated only with usage and credence goods can never be evaluated. It has been suggested that clothing is a search good, tuna fish is an experience good and some automobile repairs may be a credence good (Nelson [6], Darby and Karni [2]). Bettman (chapter 5) suggests that few goods are pure examples of each type and that it may be more useful to use this typology to classify product attributes. For instance, the roominess of an automobile can be determined by inspection, however, its repair rate cannot.

Economists have developed models for predicting the search strategy that a buyer will use in a given purchase situation. In these models, the buyer is assumed to tradeoff the costs and benefits of search in determining the optimal search strategy. For instance, in searching for the retail outlet that has the lowest price for a particular product, it is assumed that the buyer has a prior as to the distribution of prices for the product and a constant cost for each search (e.g. visit to a retail outlet). Under these conditions, Rothschild [8] has shown that the prior and search costs determine a price called the reservation price, and that the optimal search strategy is to continue searching until a price is found that is less than or equal to the reservation price.

Behaviorists may find some of these economic concepts useful in their research. Future research, for instance, might be directed at testing whether the economic models of search provide good predictions of actual behavior when the costs and benefits of search can be quantified into monetary terms. The cost benefit approach might also be used as a general framework for examining consumer information search behavior. Here behaviorists would need to conceptualize factors which may determine the psychological costs and benefits of search and develop measures of these factors.

Behavioral Concepts

One of the main points made by the behaviorists was that humans have definite cognitive limitations. These limitations are primarily due to the limited capacity of short term memory which places a constraint on the amount of information that an individual can process at any given time and the limited ability of humans to retrieve previously stored information. Consequently, motivation is not the only determinant of performance in a particular task situation. The cognitive limitations of an individual may determine the strategy that is used in the task which may, in turn, affect performance.

A second point made by the behaviorists concerned a definition of information and the difference between information and data. The study of human behavior has indicated that an individual's behavior is a function of his perception of reality--not reality itself. Consequently, when George Haines (chapter 4) suggested that we should define precisely what we mean by information, the behaviorists immediately suggested that we should define it as an individual's symbolic representation of reality. In other words, it is an individual's set of beliefs, perceptions or organized knowledge about his environment.

This definition has a number of important research implications. First, it means that product information is an individual not a market characteristic. Second, it implies that there will be no direct method of quantifying the "amount" of information a buyer has about alternative products in a market. Finally, it suggests that we need to direct our attention at understanding the content of consumers' stored information, how individuals transform data from the environment into stored information (e.g. encoding processes) and how this stored information influences behavior. In his paper, Olson (chapter 6) reviews the relevant literature from cognitive psychology on encoding processes and memory structures.

These relationships are shown in Figure 1, where there is a function mapping raw data from the environment into stored information and a second function mapping stored information into behavior.

FIGURE 1
RELATIONSHIP BETWEEN DATA, INFORMATION AND BEHAVIOR

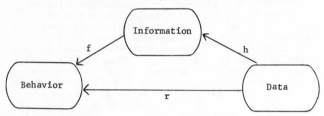

As discussed by Olson (chapter 6) and Haines (chapter 4), much of the previous behavioral and economic research has been directed at estimating the relationship between raw data from the environment (e.g. price) and behavior or behavioral intentions. Olson points out, however, that the use of this approach assumes that the consumer's encoding of raw information preserves the interval scale properties of the original information. For instance, in encoding price information the relative difference between prices is maintained. This assumption would seem to be particularly critical in measuring demand functions with time series data. In this case the implicit assumption is that buyers store the exact price of each product that they purchase so that they may react to any price changes. Previous research, however, has indicated that consumers have limited knowledge of the absolute prices of many grocery products (Monroe [6]).

This definition of information also has implications for the regulation of advertising. It means that the Federal Trade Commission should not just monitor advertisements for false copy claims but should also be concerned with advertisements that may cause consumers to form false impressions about the advertised product. Regulating this latter type of advertising is a more difficult task since it requires research to determine what beliefs consumers form about products from specific advertisements. In his paper, John Eighmey (chapter 10) discusses procedures that the Federal Trade Commission has developed to determine if specific advertisements have caused consumers to form erroneous beliefs about products.

Recently economists have begun to recognize the importance of modeling aspects of buyer behavior (e.g. information search strategies) in gaining a better understanding of market behavior. In developing these models, economists should become familiar with the relevant behavioral literature or work with behaviorists. Bettman (chapter 5), for instance, provides an excellent review of the literature on consumer information acquisition strategies.

In addition, if economists are to develop models which will provide "good" predictions of consumers' evaluations of alternative products, they will need to start measuring consumers' perceptions of the products as opposed to their

physical characteristics. This of course, will get economists into the sticky areas of measurement and scaling and questions as to the reliability and validity of the measures. These are areas that behaviorists have been concerned with for years.

SUBSTANTIVE AREAS

Advertising

The paper by Butters (chapter 2) presents an excellent review of alternative economic views of advertising and the fundamental dilemma that it presents to economists. This dilemma occurs because the primary purpose of advertising appears to be the changing of buyers' "tastes" (e.g. switching buyers from one brand to another), however, if advertising changes tastes then economic models which assume fixed tastes are inappropriate and the analysis of the welfare implications of advertising becomes difficult if not impossible.

Economists have traditionally gotten around this dilemma by simply measuring the effect of advertising on firm sales or rates of return. This direct approach has been used to determine if firms are behaving optimally (i.e. [12]). or if firms in markets with large advertising expenditures also tend to have large rates of return (i.e. [2]). As Butters (chapter 2) points out, little has been resolved from this analysis for a number of reasons. First, the data that is typically used in this type of analysis is too highly aggregated. Second, directions of causality are difficult to separate; and third, since economists have little theoretical understanding of how advertising affects purchase behavior, any structural model that is estimated is highly arbitrary.

Recently economists have begun to treat advertising as information. Under this approach it is assumed that a buyer's evaluation of a product is a function of his knowledge about the product and that advertising may change this knowledge by adding new information or changing previous information. Changing the knowledge set will change the buyer's evaluations of the product which may, in turn, result in a change in behavior. Avery and Mitchell (chapter 3) use this approach to examine how the behavior of firms may change depending on the type of information that is communicated in their advertising. They examine situations where firms transmit the same information that may be obtained from inspection and use of the product and situations where information that can not be obtained from purchase and use is transmitted. The results of their analysis indicate that in the former situation, firms will charge lower prices and have lower advertising expenditures over time than firms in the latter situation.

In their analysis, Avery and Mitchell use a relatively simple model of how advertising may affect buyer behavior and, consequently, their paper should be viewed as a first step in this direction. Future research should attempt to integrate the findings of behavioral research into the models.

In his paper, Peter Wright (chapter 7) discusses alternative approaches used by behaviorists to examine advertising effects. Two of these approaches are the cognitive structure approach which examines the effect of advertisements on the beliefs of individuals and the cognitive response approach which examines the thoughts generated during exposure to advertisements. Although these two approaches have proven useful in examining advertising effects, Wright suggests that we still have little real understanding of these effects. Most of the previous research has emphasized internal rather than external validity and has examined only the effect of advertising on product related beliefs or thoughts as opposed to more general problem framing activities.

Clearly, more research needs to be directed at understanding advertising effects. Initially much of this effort should be directed at understanding these effects at the individual level. The central question, of course, is how does advertising affect consumer behavior? Does it simply provide information about alternative products in the marketplace of does it also change the way consumers evaluate information (i.e. change consumers' utility functions)? Does a consumer's evaluation of a product depend on whether or not the consumer is exposed to advertising for the product? What is the effect of advertising repetition? Once an understanding of these effects at the individual level is obtained, we should be able to build better structural models for understanding and evaluating advertising effects at the market level.

Information Imperfections in Markets

Economists have demonstrated that information imperfections in markets may lead to inefficiencies. The question then is, how to identify markets with information imperfections and once they are identified to develop procedures to remedy these conditions. In his paper, Scott Maynes (chapter 9) discusses a procedure directed at identifying markets with information imperfections. The procedure is based on plotting the price and quality of alternative brands in a market. If markets are operating efficiently, all observations should lie on a line where price is a montonically increasing function of quality. If information imperfections exist, alternative products with the same quality but different prices will exist in the market.

The critical aspect of this procedure is the determination of the quality of the alternatives. With some products, such as ten speed bicycles, the determination of quality may be very objective--almost all consumers would make the same evaluation. However, in other product categories the determination of quality may not be so straight forward. When alternative brands differ along a number of attributes, different segments of the market may evaluate the quality of the same product differently. This may occur because the different market segments evaluate the attributes differently. Automobiles, for instance, vary along a number of attributes. One group of consumers may place a high value on size and comfort and a low value on economy of operation. Consequently, these two groups will tend to evaluate the same automobile differently.

The above points out that the determination of information imperfections in markets is not a straightforward task. Even if one can identify these situations, however, other problems exist in attempting to correct information imperfections. One approach to this problem is to develop a consumer information system. In their paper Ray and Dunn (chapter 11) discuss a set of qualities that an "ideal" consumer information system should contain and the results of a survey of existing consumer information systems. This survey indicated that there are very few consumer information systems currently operating and none of these systems contain all the qualities of their "ideal" system. However, perhaps more disturbing, Ray and Dunn provide some evidence that segments of consumers may actually avoid information even when it is provided.

In examining problems of markets with information imperfections, a number of different questions should be asked. Are there markets with information imperfections that may be "corrected" with the provision of information? Do consumers really demand more information or are they suffering from an "information overload"? If consumers demand more information, then why haven't agents appeared to provide that information? The current lack of consumer information systems may provide evidence that consumers are not willing to pay for more information.

There are a number of possible answers to these questions. First, consumers may desire more information, but may feel that the cost of this information exceeds its benefits. Some consumers may actually view information as a "free" or public good that should be provided to consumers by either the market or government. Second, as Ray and Dunn (chapter 11) suggest, some consumers may be suffering from an "information overload" and deliberately avoid additional information. Third, the information that is provided by consumer information systems may be of little value to consumers because they do not know how to use it. The most valuable information to a consumer would be an overall evaluation of products (e.g. which product provides the "best" value for a given price level), however, legal and practical constraints may not allow this type of information to be provided. For instance, since most products differ with respect to the amount of a particular attribute that is provided, a determination of the "best" product implicitly assumes a weighting of the different attributes and usually any weighting system that is selected is somewhat arbitrary. Finally, some consumers may receive utility from the search process itself. They would prefer to search for information as opposed to simply having it provided to them. Clearly, additional research is needed to determine which of these explanations or combination or explanations is the reason for the lack of agents or consumer information systems.

SUMMARY

This conference has suggested a number of interesting future research directions for each area. For instance, it would seem that economists need to develop more realistic models of markets that include advertising so that the welfare implications of advertising may be determined. Consumer psychologists need to develop a better understanding of how consumers encode and store information from the environment and use this information to form evaluations of products. Public policy decision makers need to obtain a better understanding of the causes of information imperfections in markets.

During the conference the interdependencies of these different areas became evident. Economists will have to rely on the results of behavioral research in constructing models that include human behavior. Behaviorists should look to economists to determine which aspects of human behavior need to be examined. Public policy decision makers need to rely on research from both economics and the behavioral sciences in attacking their problems.

One of the goals of this conference was to expose researchers from the different areas to recent developments in other areas. I think this goal was largely achieved during the conference. To what extent this cross fertilization will generate new and interesting research is still unknown. The potential is certainly there. In addition, I had hoped that economists and behaviorists might see the value of working together to examine important research questions. I think the conference indicated that this might be exceedingly beneficial. Unfortunately, I strongly suspect that this will not occur.

REFERENCES

1. Akerlof, G. "The Market for Lemons: Qualitative Uncertainty and the Market Mechanism" Quarterly Journal of Economics, 84 (August, 1970), 488-500.

2. Comanor, W.S. and T.A. Wilson, Advertising and Market Power, Cambridge, Mass.: Harvard University Press, 1974.

3. Darby, M. and E. Karni. "Free Competition and the Optimal Amount of Fraud," Journal of Law and Economics, 16 (April, 1973), 67-88.

4. Day, G.S. and W.K. Brandt. "Consumer Research and the Evaluation of Information Disclosure Requirements: The Case of Truth in Lending," Journal of Consumer Research, 1 (June, 1974), 71-80.

5. Friedman, M. "The Methodology of Positive Economics," in Essays in Positive Economics, The University of Chicago Press, 1935.

6. Monroe, K. "Buyers Subjective Perception of Price," Journal of Marketing Research, 10 (February, 1973), 70-80.

7. Nelson, P. "Information and Consumer Behavior," Journal of Political Economy, 78 (March-April, 1970), 311-329.

8. Nelson, P. "Advertising as Information," Journal of Political Economy, 81 (July-August, 1974), 729-754.

9. Rothschild, M. "Searching for the Lowest Price When the Distribution of Prices is Unknown," Journal of Political Economy, 82 (July, 1974), 689-712.

10. Simon, H.A. and A.C. Stedry. "Psychology and Economics," The Handbook of Social Psychology, Second Edition, Vol. 5, Reading, Mass.: Addison-Wesley Publishing Company, 1969.

11. Spence, M. "Job Market Signaling," Quarterly Journal of Economics, 87 (August, 1973), 355-374.

12. Wildt, A.R., "Multifirm Analysis of Competitive Decision Variables," Journal of Marketing Research, 11 (February, 1974), 50-62.

APPENDIX

Robert Avery
Graduate School of Industrial Administration
Carnegie-Mellon University

Neil Beckwith
The Wharton School
University of Pennsylvania

James Bettman
Graduate School of Management
University of California, Los Angeles

Paul N. Bloom
College of Business and Management
University of Maryland

C.A. Brooks
Health and Welfare Canada

John Prather Brown
Federal Trade Commission

George Brosseau
National Science Foundation

Gerald Butters
Department of Economics
Princeton University

John Cady
Graduate School of Business Administration
Harvard University

John Eighmey
Medill School of Journalism
Northwestern University

John Farley
Graduate School of Business
Columbia University

Frances Ferguson
Market Facts, Washington, D.C.

John Fitts
Graduate School of Industrial Administration
Carnegie-Mellon University

Steven Garber
Federal Trade Commission

George Haines, Jr.
Faculty of Management Studies
University of Toronto

Milton Harris
Graduate School of Industrial Administration
Carnegie-Mellon University

Tatsuro Ichiishi
Graduate School of Industrial Administration
Carnegie-Mellon University

I. Curtis Jernigan
Office of Consumer Affairs
Department of Health, Education & Welfare

Charles Kriebel
Graduate School of Industrial Administration
Carneigie-Mellon University

William F. Long
Federal Trade Commission

E. Scott Maynes
College of Human Ecology
Cornall University

Timothy McGuire
Graduate School of Industrial Administration
Carnegie-Mellon University

Andrew Mitchell
Graduate School of Industrial Administration
Carnegie-Mellon University

Joseph W. Newman
College of Business Administration
University of Arizona

Richard W. Olshavsky
School of Business
Indiana University

Jerry C. Olson
College of Business Administration
Pennsylvania State University

Steven E. Permut
School of Organization and Management
Yale University

Larry Percy
Gardner Advertising

Edward Prescott
Graduate School of Industrial Administration
Carnegie-Mellon University

Brian Ratchford
School of Management
State University of New York

Artur Raviv
Graduate School of Industrial Administration
Carnegie-Mellon University

Michael Ray
Graduate School of Business
Stanford University

Thomas Romer
Graduate School of Industrial Administration
Carnegie-Mellon University

John Rossiter
The Wharton School
University of Pennsylvania

Michael Rothschild
Department of Economics
Princeton University

J. Edward Russo
Graduate School of Business
University of Chicago

Steven Salop
Federal Trade Commission

Allan Shocker
Graduate School of Business
University of Pittsburgh

Richard Staelin
Graduate School of Industrial Administration
Carnegie-Mellon University

W. Fred van Raaij
Department of Economic Psychology
Tilburg University

William Wilkie
College of Business Administration
University of Florida

Peter Wright
Graduate School of Business
Stanford University